THE
EVERYDAY
HERO
MANIFESTO

THE
EVERYDAY
HERO
MANIFESTO

ROBIN
SHARMA

Thorsons

Thorsons
An imprint of HarperCollins*Publishers*
1 London Bridge Street
London SE1 9GF

www.harpercollins.co.uk

HarperCollins*Publishers*
1st Floor, Watermarque Building, Ringsend Road
Dublin 4, Ireland

First published by HarperCollins*Publishers* 2021

1 3 5 7 9 10 8 6 4 2

Text and illustrations © Robin Sharma 2021
All photographs are courtesy of Robin Sharma, except for the following:

The photograph of Cora Greenaway on page 9 © 2021 by N.G. Versteeg.
Reprinted with permission. All rights reserved.

The photograph of Jean-Dominique Bauby on page 216 © Estate of
Jeanloup Sieff. Reprinted with permission. All rights reserved.

The painting of Gordon Downie on page 267, *Grace too* © 2021 by
Jim Middleton Art. Reproduced with permission. All rights reserved.

Robin Sharma asserts the moral right to be identified as the author of this work

A catalogue record of this book is available from the British Library

ISBN 978-0-00-831287-9

Printed and bound in the UK using 100% renewable electricity at CPI Group (UK) Ltd

MIX
Paper from
responsible sources
FSC™ C007454

This book is produced from independently certified FSC™ paper
to ensure responsible forest management.

For more information visit: www.harpercollins.co.uk/green

A Personal Message from Robin Sharma

This is a book about the vast genius, decency and heroism that live within every beating heart on our planet today.

Creating this work for you has been exhilarating, frightening, inspiring and exhausting.

Writing *The Everyday Hero Manifesto* caused me to go to places within my craft, character and duty to serve well beyond what I'd previously known. On finishing it, I was a different man than when I started the process.

On the pages ahead, you'll discover a calibrated philosophy to materialize your finest talents, a revolutionary methodology to produce masterwork and a steady stream of insights to lead a life of breathtaking beauty, enduring joy and spiritual freedom.

I've shared more of myself here than I have in any of my earlier books. Revealing this vulnerability has been a scary yet ultimately satisfying process. Taking an honest look at our failings helps us turn them into wisdom, right? And embracing our hurt allows us to remake it into strength.

As you read of all I've gone through, my sincere hope is that you will learn what dangers to avoid, how to turn troubles into triumphs and of the wonderful way that life always unfolds in your favor, even when it doesn't seem like it.

The Everyday Hero Manifesto has been handcrafted for you as if it were my last book. I hope and pray I get to write many more. Yet a human life is a fragile ride and none of us know what tomorrow brings. And so I've given you the best I have to give in this manual for supreme productivity, elite performance, sustained happiness and unusual service to society.

My genuine and heartfelt wish is that the knowledge you are about to acquire illuminates the gifts slumbering within you, electrifies the fire you have to create your magnum opus and helps you realize your personal magic so you lead the life you most desire. While making our world a better place.

With love + respect,

P.S. To access all of the learning models, implementation templates and tactical worksheets mentioned in this book, along with teaching videos to deepen your growth, go to TheEverydayHeroManifesto.com

Thousands of geniuses live and die undiscovered—either by themselves or by others.
—MARK TWAIN

Only those who devote themselves to a cause with their whole strength and soul can be true masters. For this reason, mastery demands all of a person.
—ALBERT EINSTEIN

People always say that I didn't give up my seat because I was tired, but that isn't true. No, the only tired I was, was tired of giving in.
—ROSA PARKS

It is easy to break down and destroy. The heroes are those who make peace and build.
—NELSON MANDELA

CONTENTS

THE
EVERYDAY
HERO
MANIFESTO

1.

A Manifesto for the
Everyday Hero within You

"If you have not discovered something you would die for," said Martin Luther King, Jr., "you are not fit to live."

I would easily die fighting for the idea that you are great.

I would take a bullet for the concept that you are meant to make marvelous works, experience majestic events and know of the secret universe of mastery that was populated by the advanced souls who walked before us.

As a citizen of the earth, you have been called to harness your primal power to do amazing things, to make astonishing progress and to uplift the lives of your brothers and sisters with whom you caretake the planet.

I believe all of this to be truth. No matter where the hands of nature have now placed you, your past need not prescribe your future. Tomorrow can always be made into something better than today. You are human. And this is what humans are able to do.

Yes, we show up in different colors, sizes, genders, religions, nationalities and ways of being. Nelson Mandela, Harriet Tubman, Mahatma Gandhi, Florence Nightingale and Oskar Schindler are heroes of the highest order. Yet those who lead quieter lives—the ones who teach in schools or work in restaurants, write their poetry or launch their startups, pursue their trade in bakeries or parent their children at home; those who help within communities as first responders, firefighters and aid workers—may also be worthy of being called heroes. Many of these good souls do hard jobs, with a noble resolve to do them well. They work with smiles on their faces. And grace in their hearts.

I am humbled when my life intersects with such human beings. Truly. I learn from them, am uplifted by them and am somehow transformed upon meeting them.

These are everyday heroes. So-called "ordinary people" conducting themselves in virtuous and honorable ways.

And so, with sincere respect for all the possibility within you longing to express itself, as we begin our journey together, these words flow as my encouragement to you:

> Starting today, declare your devotion to remembering the sublime soul, brave warrior and undefeatable creator that your natural wisdom is calling on you to be.
>
> The trials of your past have skillfully served to reinvent you into one who is tougher, more aware of the powers that make you special and more grateful for the basic blessings of a life beautifully lived— splendid health, a happy family, a job that fulfils and a hopeful heart. These apparent difficulties have actually been the stepping stones for your current and future victories.
>
> The former limits that have shackled you and the "failures" that have hurt you have been necessary for the realization of your mastery. All is unfolding for your benefit. You truly are favored.
>
> Oh yes, whether you accept this or not, you are a lion, not a sheep. A leader, never a victim. A person worthy of exceptional accomplishment, uplifting adventure, flawless contentment and the

self-respect that, over time, rises steeply into a reservoir of self-love that no one and no thing can ever conquer.

You are a mighty force of nature and a dynamic producer, not a slumbering casualty caught flat-footed in a world of degrading mediocrity, dehumanizing complaint, compliance and entitlement.

And with steadfast commitment and regular effort, you will evolve into an idealist, an unusual artist and a potent exceptionalist. A genuine world-changer, in your own most honest and excellent way.

So be not a cynic, critic and naysayer. For doubters are degenerated dreamers. And average is absolutely unworthy of you.

Today, and for each day that follows of your uniquely glorious, brilliantly luminous and most-helpful-to-many life, stand fiercely in the limitless freedom to shape your future, materialize your ambitions and magnify your contributions in high esteem of your dreams, enthusiasms and dedications.

Insulate your cheerfulness, polish your prowess and inspire all witnesses fortunate enough to watch your good example of how a great human being can behave.

We will watch your growth, applaud your gifts, appreciate your valor and admire your eventual immortality.

As you remain within the hearts of many.

2.

Being Faithful to Your Ideals Is a Force-Multiplier

When no one believes in you is when you most need to believe in you.

Those committed to the fullest expression of their native genius know that self-faith and staying true to yourself and your mighty mission—especially in the face of ridicule and uncertainty, attack and adversity—is the gateway into legendary. And truly a pathway to immortality. Because your noble example will live on long after you're gone.

The journey to your most heroic life will be colorful, inspirational, messy, marvelous, tumultuous and most definitely glorious. Dedicating yourself to inhabiting your greatness, generating a vast barrage of beautiful results and doing your part to build a brighter world will be the wisest and best ride you'll ever take. This, I promise you. And stepping into the immense splendor of your most creative, powerful and compassionate self will energize everyone around you to awaken to their gifts, making our planet a friendlier place.

If I may, I'd like to take a moment to share a little about my origin story, so you get to know me better. Because we're about to spend a fair amount of time together on these pages.

I'm no one special. No guru. Not cut from some special cloth that you can't wear.

I have my talents, as you have yours, possess very human flaws (don't we all?) and can feel insecure, unworthy and afraid, as well as brave, useful and hopeful.

I grew up in a blue-collar town of about five thousand people. Near the ocean. In a small house. A child of immigrant parents, with very good hearts. I had no silver spoon in my mouth, that's for sure.

Full of enthusiasm at age four   Playing in the snow in front of my house

Yes, that's me at a school play. And in our front yard during a very cold winter. See, no Ferrari in the driveway. No lavish adornments or unnecessary things. All very basic. The best way to be.

In school, I never fit in with the hip crowd. Always loved being in my own head, dreaming up fascinating dreams, marching to my own drumbeat. Doing my own thing, if you know what I mean.

A principal once told my beloved mother that I showed no promise and that it was unlikely I'd graduate from high school. Other teachers quietly warned my parents that I had minimal potential. A few predicted I'd end up as a drifter or a vagrant. Most people simply made fun of me.

Except for one.

Cora Greenaway. My grade five history teacher.

She believed in me. Which helped *me* believe in me.

Mrs. Greenaway taught me that *every* human being is born into some form of giftedness. She explained that each of us can be astonishingly good at something, and are born with special strengths, remarkable capacities and dignified virtues. She told me that if I remembered this, worked really hard and stayed true to myself, good things would happen and great blessings would follow.

This kind teacher saw the best in me, encouraged me and showed a form of decency that is very much needed in a society that all too often demeans our abilities and degrades our mastery. Sometimes, all it takes is one conversation with an extraordinary person to reroute the rest of your life in an entirely new direction, right?

A few years ago, I searched for Cora Greenaway online. What I discovered genuinely moved me.

As a young woman, she was part of the Dutch resistance, going behind enemy lines in World War II to rescue children facing extermination in Nazi death camps. She risked her life and honored her convictions to save young kids. Just like she saved me.

Mrs. Greenaway has since passed on. She died the same year I found out about her past. I thank the gentleman in Amsterdam who so generously cared for her to the end, and who kept me updated about this mentor who meant so much to me.

Cora Greenaway was what I call an "everyday hero." Quiet and humble, mighty and vulnerable, ethical and influential, wise and loving. Improving our civilization—one good deed at a time.

She inspired me to transcend the limited expectations that many had placed on my life and finish high school. And then complete university, with a major in biology and a minor in English. Then secure a seat in law school. Then earn a master of laws, on a full scholarship.

Cora Greenaway at age 101

Trust not your detractors. Pay no attention to your diminishers. Ignore your discouragers. *They do not know of the wonders within you.*

In time, I became a successful litigation lawyer. Well-paid but empty, driven yet creatively unfulfilled, disciplined yet disconnected from who I really was. I'd wake up every morning, look at myself in the bathroom mirror and dislike the man looking back at me. I didn't have much hope. And I had no intimacy with the natural heroism that I've since learned is one of the core benefits to being human.

Success without self-respect is an empty victory, isn't it?

And so, I decided to remake myself. To get to know a truer, happier, more peaceful and better version of the person I was. By starting a campaign of massive personal growth, profound emotional healing and deep spiritual progress.

You absolutely have this power to make tectonic changes, too. Evolution, elevation and even outright transformation are part of the factory-installed hardware that makes you *you*. And the more you exercise this inherent force within you, the stronger it will grow.

Regenerating a more creative, productive, inventive and unconquerable version of your self—one filled with more joy, bravery and serenity—isn't some unreachable gift reserved for The Gods of Sublime Genius and The Angels of Unusual Excellence.

No. *Genius has far less to do with your genetics and much more to*

9

do with your habits. Stepping into the person you've always imagined you could be is a trained result—available to anyone willing to open themselves up, do the work and run the practices that make magic real.

At this period of my life, I set out to rebuild, rewire and re-create the person I was into a human being who drew his power from an inner system of navigation rather than from outer attractions like position, material goods and prestige. One who did not hold back on speaking truthfully (even when faced with unpopularity), one who stood steadfast to his ideals, one whose job never felt like a job but more like a calling, one who did not need to purchase things to experience rich pleasure and one who used his days to make the lives of others happier.

It's far too easy to spend an entire existence climbing a series of mountains only to realize at the end that we scaled the wrong ones.

… By being busy being busy.

… By being addicted to distractions and seduced by diversions that give us a false sense of progress, yet in reality steal the most valuable hours of our most precious days.

… By the hypnotic allure of filling our lives with items and activities that our culture sells as the authentic measures of success when—in truth—they are as spiritually satisfying as a quick trip to the nearest shopping mall.

My devotion to reforming myself by living more to the point just as I was entering my early thirties makes me think of the words of poet Charles Bukowski:

> We are all going to die, all of us, what a circus! That alone should make us love each other but it doesn't. We are terrorized and flattened by trivialities, we are eaten up by nothing.

For a period of three long years, I'd rise early, while my family slept, and experiment with practices that would reduce my weaknesses, purify my powers and more fully align me with my personal destiny.

I'd study books on the great men and women of history—the artistic geniuses, the fearless warriors, the prodigious scientists, the business titans and the tireless humanitarians, learning of the central beliefs, dominant emotions, daily routines and ironclad rituals that generated their luminous lives. I'll share everything I discovered on the pages that follow.

I attended personal growth conferences and invested in self-development courses.

I learned to meditate and visualize, journal and contemplate, fast and pray.

I enlisted peak performance coaches, worked with acupuncturists, hypnotherapists, emotional healers and spiritual counselors, took cold showers, sweated in hot saunas and invested in weekly massage therapy.

Looking back on it now, as a much older man, I see that it was a lot.

I must say that at times the process was confusing, uncomfortable and terrifying. It was also electrifying, fascinating, rewarding and often breathtakingly beautiful. Fundamental personal change is often painful *because* it is so very transformational. And we cannot become everything we are meant to be without leaving behind who we once were. The weaker you must experience a death of sorts before the strongest you can know a rebirth. If improvement doesn't feel difficult, it's not real improvement, is it?

As I steadily did my own inner work each morning, while the world around me was still sleeping, the way I saw myself, how I behaved and the very operating system of my life were completely restructured. As I spent time with my dream team of instructors, many of my major fears vanished; so many of my daily worries and sabotaging behaviors simply fell away. Much of my need to please, to be liked and to follow the herd—while betraying myself—just dissolved.

I grew more loyal to my deepest values, far more healthy, creative, cheerful and peaceful. And I spent less time living in my head and a lot more intimately connected with my heart. This caused my inspiration to soar, my productivity to accelerate and my confidence to escalate. I began to know of a magic that is available to any human being seriously interested in befriending it.

Near the end of those three years of almost never-ending healing and consistent growth, I knew I was ready to begin a new phase of the adventure toward personal mastery and leadership that I still find myself on today. Instinct whispered that I should write a book about my experience—and the lessons I'd learned. So others could make their rise as well.

I called it *The Monk Who Sold His Ferrari*.

Some snickered at the title and suggested that no one would read a self-help book written by a lawyer. Others muttered that the life of an author was hard, so I should give up before I started. I refused to participate in their limitation and very enthusiastically wrote a fable about the path away from a half-lived existence and toward one weighted with wonder, bravery and pure possibility. The process of writing this book was enchanting.

I knew little about publishing and didn't come from an entrepreneurial family (Mom was a teacher and Dad was a family doctor). But I did know that self-education is the highway to making vividly imagined fantasies into readily observed reality. What I didn't know, I could learn. The skills I lacked, I could build. And the results anyone else created, I, too, could forge—with focus, strong effort, superb information and good teachers. So I signed up for a one-night course at an organization called The Learning Annex.

There, I learned about manuscripts and editors, publishers and printers, distributors and booksellers. The course was amazing, leaving me full of fire to fulfill my dream. After the class finished, I walked home in the cold winter night, as snow fell, feeling profoundly hopeful.

12

And extraordinarily committed to getting my book out into the world.

I decided to publish the book myself. My wonderful mother edited the manuscript, poring over each line late into the evenings. A few good friends were my very first readers. I had it printed at a twenty-four-hour copy shop. I still recall my father driving me there at four in the morning so I could advance my mission before heading to my job as a litigation lawyer by eight. Bless him for his unconditional helpfulness and support when I most needed it.

Due to my inexperience, I didn't realize that making a book from letter-sized manuscript pages would shrink the text. So the first edition was hard to read. No matter—I did my best and began sharing the message of *The Monk Who Sold His Ferrari* at service clubs in my community. My first seminar (coincidentally run by The Learning Annex) had twenty-three participants. Twenty-one of them were family members. I kid you not.

Lao-tzu was right about that whole "the thousand-mile journey begins with a single step" thing. I pretty much started as an author from scratch. (If you wait for conditions to be perfect before you launch your highest dream, you'll never begin.)

A famous author agreed to meet with me, as I felt I needed further guidance and wished to learn how to reach a larger audience to positively impact more people. Finding a wise mentor truly is priceless as you begin to lead your most heroic life. I wore a suit, brought him a copy of my self-published book and sat on a well-worn leather chair in front of his enormous oak desk as he held court. "Robin," he said, "this is a hard business. Very few ever make it." He added, "You have a good job as a lawyer. You should stay with that and not take a chance on something so uncertain."

His words deflated me. Discouraged me. Disappointed me. I thought that perhaps my ambition to get *The Monk Who Sold His Ferrari* into the hands of readers who would benefit from it was silly. Maybe I'd miscalculated my ability. I'd never written a book. I was unknown. It was a tough field to break into. Maybe the big-shot author had a point: I should play it safe and stick with my career in law.

Then a blinding glimpse of the obvious appeared. His opinion was merely his opinion. Why give it any more value? The gentleman's assessment wasn't any of my business, really. Someone was going to write the next bestseller; why not me? And every professional starts off as an amateur. It seemed to me that I shouldn't let his counsel smother my passion. And deny my aspiration. Each day, as I sat in my office as a litigator, I thought to myself, "Every hour I'm here is an hour away from what I really wish to do. And what I know I'm meant to do."

I guess my faith was larger than my fears. And my daring was stronger than my doubts.

I pray you always trust your intuition over the cool and practical reasoning of your intellect. Your possibility, mastery and genius do not live there. People now say I was brave to persevere in the face of dissent and challenge. It wasn't bravery at all. To be honest—as I always want to be and absolutely will be during our time together—I felt I had no choice but to follow where my enthusiasm was leading me.

"People living deeply have no fear of dying," wrote Anaïs Nin. Norman Cousins observed that "the great tragedy of life is not death but what we allow to die inside of us while we live." I share these quotes to remind you of the shortness and frailty of life. Too many of us postpone doing those things that make our soul come alive until some imaginary ideal time arrives. It never comes. There's no better time to become the human being you know you can be and handcraft the life of your most exuberant desires than now. The world could completely change tomorrow. History has shown this to be true. Don't live your finest hours in the waiting room of life. Please.

It's wiser to take a chance and risk looking foolish (yet know that you did it) than miss the opportunity and end up empty and heart-broken, on your last day.

So I took *The Monk Who Sold His Ferrari* to a respected editor with the intent of making it better. I was excited to get the feedback of an expert and pretty sure he'd tell me I'd produced something truly special.

Instead, the letter I received from the editor was a litany of criticisms. It began, "There are major problems with *The Monk Who Sold His Ferrari*, Robin. There's no use mincing words."

His take on my characters?

"Your characters don't emerge as much more than stereotypes. For example, Mantle is successful, wealthy, brilliant, charismatic, tough, remarkably funny, etc., but the more you pile on, the more of a cliché he becomes …"

He ended the letter by saying, "I'm sure my reaction to your work has disappointed you, but I hope my suggestions will be helpful. Good writing takes hard, hard work. Unfortunately, good writing looks easy. It isn't." On reading the editor's note, I sat in my car, hardly moving, heart pounding, palms sweating, in front of his red-brick house with neatly trimmed hedges. My manuscript sat on the seat next to me with elastic bands around it. I still remember the scene in detail. And I recall how I felt.

Embarrassed. Rejected. Dejected. He sort of broke my heart, on that sunny day.

And yet instinct really is wiser than intellect. And all real progress has come from daydreamers who were told by so-called "experts" that their consuming idea was foolish and their creative work was unworthy. Please protect your respect for yourself and for your most honest artistry above the fear-fueled, impossibility-filled pronouncements of people who are masters of theory yet creators of nothing.

Some voice or strength or wisdom within me, coming from a place far higher than logic, instructed me: "Do not listen to him. Just like the famous author who didn't encourage you, this letter is just this editor's view. Keep going. Your honor—and self-love—depends on your determination and loyalty to your mission."

And so I continued. As I really, really, really hope you will do when you get knocked down and a little—or a lot—beaten up, bruised and bloodied. Setbacks are simply life's way of testing how much you desire your dreams, aren't they?

As Theodore Roosevelt said in a speech entitled "Citizenship in a Republic," delivered at the Sorbonne in Paris on April 23, 1910:

> It is not the critic who counts; not the man who points out how the strong man stumbles, or where the doer of deeds could have done them better. The credit belongs to the man who is actually in the arena, whose face is marred by dust and sweat and blood; who strives valiantly; who errs, who comes short again and again, because there is no effort without error and shortcoming; but who does actually strive to do the deeds; who knows great enthusiasms, the great devotions; who spends himself in a worthy cause; who at the best knows in the end the triumph of high achievement, and who at the worst, if he fails, at least fails while daring greatly, so that his place shall never be with those cold and timid souls who neither know victory nor defeat.

Life really does favor the obsessed. Great fortune truly does shine on those mesmerized by their gorgeous ambitions. And the universe most definitely supports the human being unwilling to surrender to the forces of fear, rejection and self-doubt.

A few months after publishing the book, I was in a local bookstore with my son, who was four years old at the time. Much credit is due to him, because it was his love of hammers, tape measures and other carpentry tools (he'd wear his checkered work shirt, yellow plastic hard hat and fake leather tool belt to nearly every meal at our dinner table) that led us to the hardware store next to the bookshop. It was a rainy night, with a luxurious full moon that forecast a good omen. I do remember it well.

Once inside the bookstore, we headed directly to the section where my book was displayed. I'd given the owner six copies—on consignment (which means if he couldn't sell them, he could return them). Another self-published author had shared a key piece of advice: once a book has been signed by the author, the retailer must keep it. So I had a practice of visiting every place that carried *The Monk Who Sold His Ferrari* and personally autographing every single copy.

I collected the six copies from the shelf and headed to the front area, where I politely asked permission to sign my book. The cashier approved and with my young son perched on the wooden counter before me, I used one arm to steady him and the other to sign my utterly unknown book.

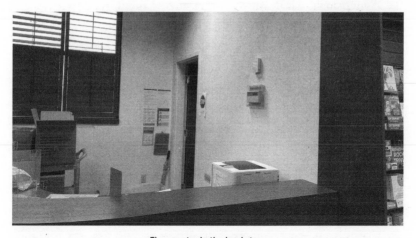

The counter in the bookstore

As I signed my name, I noticed an observer, wearing a green trench coat still wet from the rain, standing off to the side. He watched every move I made.

After a few minutes, the man approached me and said, speaking very precisely: "*The Monk Who Sold His Ferrari.* That's a great title. Tell me about yourself."

17

I explained that I was a lawyer. That I'd been frustrated and unhappy a number of years earlier because I was living someone else's life. I shared that I'd discovered valuable ways to live more happily, more confidently, more productively and access far more aliveness. I said that I had a deep drive to get my book to as many human beings as possible. And to serve society as best as I could. I added that I'd published the book in an all-night copy shop. And that I'd been ridiculed and criticized and minimized as I pursued my project.

He looked at me. He studied me. He waited for what seemed a long time.

Then he pulled out his wallet and handed me his business card. On it were these words: *Edward Carson. President. HarperCollins Publishers.*

Synchronicity is destiny's way of staying silent, right?

Three weeks later, HarperCollins bought the world rights to *The Monk Who Sold His Ferrari.*

For $7,500.

The book has gone on to become one of the bestselling books of all time, serving many millions of good human beings across our precious world in the process.

And so, as I round out this chapter, I encourage you to consider the ethical ambitions that sit silently in your heart, waiting to be made real. I ask you to wonder how you can be the Cora Greenaway of someone's life and the kind of human who makes people braver when they stand in your presence. I invite you to go to the threshold of the fears that chain you, explore the boundaries that bind you and notice all the past hurts that now stop you—and rise above it all.

For this day presents your new dawn. And our world awaits your everyday heroism.

3.

The Final Hours of
Your Defeatable Self

Drinking coffee. Trip hop music's playing. A harsh winter has finally
made way for a more welcoming spring.

I sit in my writing room, a place that I go to when I'm set to work.
I'll share the scene, to make this more intimate:

One of my favorite spaces for creativity at home

I'm in a reflective mood today. As I often am, as an introvert.

I think of the individuals I've met over the nearly three decades I've been in the leadership and personal mastery field. At private speaking events for *Fortune* 100 companies or on the streets of far-away cities or in sprawling arenas in fascinating countries across our completely-worth-saving planet.

Decent people. Superb intentions. Yet so many sharing so clearly with me during our conversations that they long for so much more.

... To know what it means to candidly express their creative genius, enjoy life's treasures and contribute to the construction of a culture where encouragement not criticism, leadership not victimhood, ideas not gossip, and love not hate win the day.

... To feel more optimism, be more daring and know greater purpose while understanding what it truly means to feel supremely inspired, living in the moment instead of scarred from the past or frightened for the future.

... To reclaim a relationship with their truest virtues, grandest potential and most vivid ambitions.

... And to pass through each day with enough wakefulness to savor life's simplest pleasures, without the burden of worry.

You're wise (perhaps even more than you know, at this instant we share).

... You understand that potential unexpressed turns to pain.

... You know that the measures of success that society sells you are empty promises that only serve to distract you from the crusade toward your bravest life.

... You appreciate that the closer you get to your fortune, the louder your fears will scream.

... You are aware that the project that your counterfeit self is most avoiding is precisely the venture your noblest self seeks to be advancing.

… You get that world-class really is less about your genetics and more about your habits. And that all heavyweight producers work really, really hard.

… You know that the clock is ticking and that mastery postponed is genius denied.

… You know that you just can't afford to wait another day to step into the hero you've always imagined yourself being.

And so, I respectfully suggest that you …

… Make your start *today*.

… Develop the guts to play out on the edges of your powers. Because as you visit your limits, those limits will expand.

… Activate the childlike part of you that was once wildly curious and constantly learning before you were schooled to play small and trained to think like everyone else, so that you continually outgrow the person you currently are.

… Gauge your winning by the extent of your progress, and never by the objects in your closets.

… Lead without a title, influence without a position and create the masterwork that exemplifies the promise that nature has invested in you.

… And remember that the easiest path is generally the poorest route.

And that action delayed is greatness betrayed.

4.

It's Okay Not to Be Okay

Our civilization sells us the idea that if we're not smiley and happy and if puppies aren't dancing and rainbows do not stream into the windowpanes of perfect days, something's wrong with us.

Here's what I've learned: an intensely lived life requires getting into the arena, taking multiple risks, pursuing numerous paths, getting knocked around a fair amount and dealing with the stormy gales of treacherous seas more than makes rational sense. These words by Irish playwright George Bernard Shaw offer me inspiration on difficult days: "The reasonable man adapts himself to the world; the unreasonable one persists in trying to adapt the world to himself. Therefore, all progress depends on the unreasonable man."

I've also realized that it's *because* of the tough and tumultuous times we all endure that we are actually able to fully experience the pleasures of the good times, when they show up. And they *always* will—even when it seems that they won't.

"We could never learn to be brave and patient if there were only joy in the world," Helen Keller taught us.

I must admit that when things don't go my way, it can be unpleasant. I don't laugh as much and I worry more. I'm not as energetic or as creative. I don't have the same productive exuberance and can't access the same fire in the belly.

Yet I've learned that not feeling absolutely okay is absolutely okay. That when we are not experiencing the kind of worldly productivity valued by the majority, we are very likely advancing our spiritual productivity. A difficult day for the ego is a splendid day for the soul. And setback, struggle and being stuck in confusion are part of being a human—never to be judged as "bad" and "wrong." It's just a necessary pit stop on the journey that we're meant to experience. During this ride we call a lifetime.

I've discovered that all that I'm living during an uncomfortable season is serving the acceleration of my wisdom, forging priceless strength and unmasking human powers in the hot coals of crisis. Pain has served to make me more humble and definitely more loving, by degrading my ego and fortifying my private heroism. It's simply a scheduled class in the curriculum of earthschool. A chapter in the life of a man reaching for the heavens and doing all he can to raise others with him.

I'd rather get confused, bruised a bit (or a lot) and know that I'm living fully than spend my greatest years watching television in a subdivision or buying things I don't need to impress people I don't know in a store I don't really want to be in. That's just not me. Not what I wish to represent.

So my sincere and truthful encouragement to you—a very real person dedicated (and destined) to lead a gorgeous, productive and high-impact life—is to wear your wounds with pride. Defend the scars that have deepened, developed and refined you. And see the cuts that have hurt you as medals of valor awarded for your courage, as you've pursued your deep goals and lofty ideals.

And definitely remember: *It's okay not to be okay.*

5.

The Gold Miner's Paradox

Old yet true story. Thousands of years ago, in Thailand, a towering statue of the Buddha was made of gold. The monks would pray before it, people would behold its beauty. And all passersby would revere the remarkable masterpiece. Then, word spread of a coming great invasion from foreign attackers and it became clear the idol could be stolen.

So, the monks hatched a plan to hide it, placing layer after layer of soil over the Golden Buddha. Until it became unrecognizable.

The invaders marched right by it, to the relief of the monks.

Centuries later, a visitor caught a glimmer of gold emerging from a small mountain of earth. As more people dug away at the covering, more gold appeared. Eventually, they found that it was the Buddha, made completely of the precious metal.

You are like this.

The more you advance—layer by layer—into the treasures of your inner gifts, the more you will be rewarded with unexpected bounty in your external reality. It's quite a paradox, isn't it? To know that the gateway into success and significance in your public life requires you to take an inner voyage into the depths of your private world. So that you own all that you truly are.

With more of the interior work that delivers self-knowledge, more of the gold you have covered to insulate yourself against life's hardships and troubles will reappear. With more daily practice to mine your gifts, refine your talents and reveal your eminence, all you are built to be will show itself when you are out in the world.

While in Bangkok for a leadership presentation for a quickly growing company, I went to see the astonishing landmark of the Golden Buddha. Here's the photo from my personal archive:

In Bangkok, with the Golden Buddha

25

The insight I'm really attempting to offer you is that—just maybe—the pursuit of anyone seeking to materialize their magnificence, live fearlessly (and beautifully) and achieve feats that upgrade our global family isn't to become someone other than who you now are.

What if the real endeavor is simply to *remember* what you once were, before a cold culture encouraged you to cover your light with the armor of doubt, disbelief and false reasons about why you cannot express your primal genius. And make your life a monument. To mastery, productivity and sincere service to humanity.

6.

The Victim-to-Hero Leap

One of the main messages that I hope this work will integrate within you—at a cellular level—is this: every day, each one of us is presented with an enormous opportunity to shift from any form of victimhood into everyday heroism. So that nearly every move you make as the hours unfold is a vote for the fullest realization of personal greatness.

To materialize your mastery and to lead your finest life, I invite you to make the following five leaps.

Please allow me to walk you through each one:

Leap #1: The Shift from a Mindset of Can't to the Mentality of Can

Victims are prisoners of *can't*. They relentlessly tell you why an ideal *can't* succeed, why an enterprise *can't* work and why an ambition *can't* happen. Beneath *can't* lives fear. Fear of failing, fear of not being good enough, fear of not deserving victory, fear of being criticized, fear of getting hurt and fear of the imagined responsibilities of success. All world-builders and change-leaders are experts at using the language of hope, the vocabulary of execution and the dialect of freedom. *They avoid being infected with can't.*

They understand that the words you deploy are your thoughts made verbal. And that creating a masterwork, initiating a movement or engineering a gorgeous life require the positive energy of *can*. Doubters and defeated thinkers never become history-makers.

THE VICTIM-TO-HERO LEAP

THE VICTIM	THE HERO
1. THE MINDSET OF CAN'T	THE MENTALITY OF CAN
2. MAKES EXCUSES	DELIVERS RESULTS
3. LIVES IN THE PAST	MAKES THEIR FUTURE BRIGHTER
4. IS BUSY BEING BUSY	IS PRODUCTIVE
5. TAKES FROM THE WORLD	GIVES TO THE WORLD

One of my favorite movies is *Darkest Hour,* a film about Winston Churchill's ascent into becoming a legendary wartime leader. In the final scene, he delivers a spirited speech that enchants those on both sides of the political aisle of Parliament.

Lord Halifax, Churchill's nemesis, was stunned by the delivery of Churchill's vocal magic and asked the colleague sitting next to him, "What just happened?" The reply? "He mobilized the English language. And sent it into battle."

Yes, the words you use are seeds for the harvest you reap. Words are powerful. They have been used to inspire—and free—entire nations. And when spoken with evil motives, they have influenced masses of humans to become soldiers of hate.

When you listen to someone with a philosophy of mediocrity, they demonstrate "victimspeak," speaking negatively, arguing for why they cannot represent heroism in the primary areas of their life. They'll explain why they *can't* be graceful in trying times, optimize their performance regardless of the conditions, be a great example to others, get ultra-fit, build their fortune and make their mark. *Can't* is a tower that victims lock themselves into, in the prayer that this will protect them from the danger or risk. Yet in so doing, they avoid all the abundant rewards that inevitably flow from thoughtful (versus ill-considered) risk-taking.

The other day I watched a man on television complain that the government wasn't doing enough to support him to ensure his small business would flourish and to make his life easier. "I *can't* see any solution to this situation, and I *can't* survive in this turbulent environment," he grumbled.

Hmmm.

Not judging (at all), yet it seems to me that this good soul expected a power outside of his own to make his aspirations come true. And as far as I can tell, this isn't how the universe works. It doesn't reward those who blame their circumstances when things aren't working and passively wait for outside help.

Nope. It celebrates those who demonstrate agency over difficulty and remake problems into winning.

Life loves those everyday heroes who understand that they possess abilities, capabilities and the force to shape all events that destiny carefully places on their path.

The words you use have major force fields around them, attracting outcomes that resonate with them the way magnets draw iron filings to them. Also know that the words we use each day reveal our most entrenched beliefs to everyone around us, even if those beliefs don't serve us (they may even be pure lies that someone we trusted early in our lives taught us). In my own life, I regularly use the technique of autosuggestion to re-order my vocabulary toward greater positivity and creativity. Very early in the morning, while my subconscious mind is most available to receiving instructions, I'll recite mantras such as "Today I am showing up with enthusiasm, excellence and kindness" or "I am so very grateful for the day ahead and all its beauty, joys and excitements." During the day, should my mind and heart drift to a hurt of the past or some negative self-talk that dishonors my best, I'll quietly whisper, "We don't do this anymore" or "Let's not go there." I get this may seem strange, but because I really want to serve you, I'm sharing this personal practice that has worked so well for me.

So make the leap to bring greater awareness to the language you use along with the thoughts you think. And then, with that heightened consciousness, begin the process of cleaning out all *can't*. And reprogramming in the power of *can*. Re-ordering your vocabulary toward leadership and exceptionalism is one of the simplest yet most potent ways to escalate your confidence, performance and impact in the world.

Leap #2: The Shift from Making Excuses to Delivering Results

You can make excuses or you can change our world. You don't get to do both. You can spot a victim by watching how they have a near-instant reason to explain why their life is not working (which never has anything to do with them).

Such people have recited these excuses so many times they have actually brainwashed themselves into believing they are true. They have practiced their rationalizations so extremely well they've risen to pro athlete level at offering up their explanations for their mediocrity. Your experience shifts the single moment when you fully appreciate that blaming conditions, events and other human beings for any poverty in your reality gives your power to the condition, event or person that you are portraying as the cause of your discontent. We grow up the instant we assume *absolute personal responsibility* for the way our results look. And, in so doing, we take back our sovereignty to make the improvements we seek. Every time you restrain yourself from descending into an excuse and instead view yourself as the creator of your life, you'll receive a corresponding increase in strength. Do this daily and you'll become an individual of outstanding character, self-discipline, productivity and spiritual liberty.

Leap #3: The Shift from Living in the Past to Making a Brighter Future

Victims are fabulous at living in the past. Yet you cannot embrace your fantastic future with one foot stuck in a bygone era. *See your history as an academy you can learn from versus a jail to stay chained in.* Employ selective amnesia to remember only the good you've been blessed to enjoy. Let go of simmering resentments and languishing disappointments, while exploiting the exquisite growth that hard events have brought to make you a bolder producer and a better person.

In all my mentoring work with industry titans, sports icons and genuine world-builders, every single one of them developed the skill of using all that happened to them *as fuel* to rise even higher. Each one of these superstars made the mission-critical leap from ruminating about the past to optimizing the kind of world-class present that precedes a mastery-grade future.

Leap #4: The Shift from Being Busy Being Busy to Becoming Productive

Please don't confuse being busy with being productive. And definitely don't assume movement equals progress. A packed schedule doesn't mean you're getting marvelous things done. Too many good and potentially legendary performers fall into the trap of doing fake work instead of real work. These things are not the same.

To a victim, busyness becomes a drug of choice, an escape that fills their hours with superficiality and triviality in an unconscious effort to avoid the discomfort that comes with creating towering work that respects human genius. It's so much easier to deceive yourself into thinking you have too much to do—and then blame your lack of artistic victory and productive triumph on a hard and cruel world demanding your attention—than to own your game by blocking out all digital distractions and unnecessary interruptions and honoring your native brilliance by doing work that mesmerizes all who witness it.

Leap #5: The Shift from Taking from the World to Giving to the World

Listen not to the wisdom of the status quo, which says that success means "winner takes all." Rather than taking from the world, make it your consistent enthusiasm to give to the world. And to behave in a way that serves all citizens.

Members of the majority mostly live in scarcity (the fear that there is not enough for *everyone* to be happy). They are survivalists, stuck in limbic hijack, driven by their ancient brain rather than by the greater wisdom of their higher thinking. To experience the rewards that possibility has in store for you, keep reinforcing the mantra that "the one who enriches the most people wins." And let generosity, along with the virtue of ongoing service to many, guide the remainder of your life.

Stateswoman Golda Meir once wrote: "Trust yourself. Create the kind of self you will be happy to live with all your life. Make the most of yourself by fanning the tiny, inner sparks of possibility into flames of higher achievement."

In applying the five elements of The Victim-to-Hero Leap, the trust you have in yourself will grow, your intimacy with your special talents and finest merits will be amplified and you will restore the relationship with that side of you that is sure of your capacity to translate your current wishes into colossal success—personally, professionally, financially and spiritually.

Yes, I agree that the process will not always be easy. (Why does our society celebrate that which is easy?)

Yet do remember that pursuits that don't push you will never improve you.

And those activities that are hardest to do are generally the most valuable to do.

And that fear always screams loudest when your magic is closest.

So press ahead with the mighty wisdom that good things happen to people who do good things. While sharing your treasures with us all.

7.

That Time My Private Journals Were Taken

Without getting into the gory details, and making sure to protect the dignity of those involved (who were operating as best they knew about how to behave), I would like to tell you about the time nine years' worth of my private journals were "borrowed" from me.

All my dream charts and learning sheets that recorded the knowledge I'd gathered were in them. All the deep emotional processing and the substantial healing from heartbreak, hard times and other disappointments were documented within these daily diaries. All the collages of my ideal life, my most vulnerable personal introspections and the steady contemplations on my most needed growth— all taken. And all my general creative observations, insights from my world travels, the notes from my mastermind conversations and tens of thousands of micro-lessons gained from days lived as well as I could—simply vanished.

In one day. In a single morning, to be precise. The universe has a hilarious sense of humor, doesn't it?

So, when people ask me, "Robin, I love your methodologies around journaling to boost optimism, authenticity, gratefulness, expertise and spiritual freedom, but what if someone sees what I write?" I answer from a place of *extreme* experience.

I reply, "Why does it matter? They'll see a human being, leading a life. Both hopeful and scared. Fantastic and flawed. Certain as well as confused. Working on themselves. To become a closer version of their highest vision. How brave. And how glorious."

This splendid loss taught me to let go—one of the most prized skills one can ever learn during this earthwalk you and I are on. This betrayal increased my ability to accept what is and make peace with *whatever* happens. It helped me to know how to detach and release control over *whatever* unfolds. To disidentify with what others might think of me if they read about my fears and failings, as well as of my prayers, aspirations and assets.

At best, any reader of my personal reflections will see a man on the path. Someone who works harder on himself than anyone in any room I'm in. A human being who fiercely wishes to evolve, so as to become more honorable, decent, helpful and compassionate. And perhaps, one day, even noble.

At worst, an onlooker will learn of my errors, read of my frustrations, spy on my bruises and judge me as broken.

And guess what? To my philosophy, this just makes me real. Awake. And alive.

I know of so many celebrities, renowned leaders and so-called "gurus" who, when the stage lights dim, are not at all who they've branded themselves to be. It was all illusion, sharp marketing and a terrific sales job.

Writing intimately in a journal nearly daily has helped me ascend, refined my self-understanding, magnified my creativity considerably, upgraded my emotional fluency, hardwired a near-constant sense of gratitude and removed many of the stains that had been set on my soul.

Candidly, the practice has pretty much saved my life.

What I've written on those pages, between those black leather covers, details my private purification process. My training to forge a more muscular character and become a true servant leader. My attempts to release rather than suppress any negativity and toxicity trapped within me. All my journals provide an archive of the adventure of my greatest self quietly and incrementally triumphing over my insecure and fearful side.

If a brother or sister of our big family that inhabits this tiny planet seeks to condemn me or mock me or downgrade their impression of me on learning of my frailties and faults, then, well, that's just fine with me. Actually, their behavior is on them. It really has zero to do with me. None of my business.

My favorite line from the film *Shoot the Messenger*: "Look inside anyone's life and you'll see a three-ring circus."

A three-ring circus. On looking inside *anyone's* life.

Full of color and comedy, surprises and acrobatics, a little tight-rope walking in the dangerous seasons, as well as a ton of wonder and awe during the days in the sun.

8.

Instruction from Heavyweight Mentors

I pray this message, which I'm writing to you on a flight across the Atlantic, finds you in pristine focus around your craft, in single-minded pursuit of your summits of excellence and in steadfast readiness to make your mark on the world, while you sculpt a life of happiness, sophistication, serenity and usefulness that you'll feel proud of at the end.

I've been fortunate to have had many superb mentors in my life.

As a lawyer in my early twenties, I worked for a leading judge of immense integrity, rare discipline and unforgettable humility. He was revered in the field, Harvard-trained, brilliant and a genuine model of mastery. Yet his life was quite austere. The car he drove, for example, was simple, unremarkable and many years old. This gentleman chose not to be invested in trivial things. Because he was a heavyweight.

After he retired, we kept in touch. He'd send me thoughtful handwritten letters in the mail, thanking me for the various books I'd send him. Unfailingly, he would appreciate my progress and congratulate me on my advances as an author and leadership adviser. His graciousness always made me feel bigger than I was and better than I am. His decency inevitably left me even more hopeful. Such was the greatness of this man.

I'd look forward to those notes, with my name and address carefully etched on the outside of the envelope, in the ink of his ancient fountain pen.

My final visit with one of my greatest mentors, Chief Justice Lorne O. Clarke

When he was nearing his mid-eighties—during a period of my life that was overscheduled with international speaking tours, book deadlines and family commitments—I decided to put everything on hold and hop onto a plane to visit this human being who had influenced me so much. I didn't want to lose the chance to see him again.

Over cups of strong tea, we recalled our time together, laughed hearty laughs and chatted about a wide range of topics that were of interest to both of us.

Before I left, I asked my elderly mentor, "What's the most important piece of advice you have for me as I go forward, Chief Justice Clarke?"

He paused for a few moments. And then he replied softly, "Always be kind, Robin. Oh, that's so important. *Always be kind.*"

Then he did something he'd never done in all the years we'd known each other: he leaned over and gave me a hug, adding, "I love you, Robin."

Two months later, this legal giant and truly great public servant passed away.

Steve Wozniak, the cofounder of Apple, has also been a terrifically influential mentor to me. I met him in Zurich when he was a member of my faculty at *The Titan Summit*, a live event for global leaders and elite entrepreneurs that I ran for many years.

Although he was an icon, Woz arrived at the summit alone, was impeccably polite and was as approachable as a dear friend. During our interview on stage, he revealed his winning formula as a visionary and a technologist, shared little-known insights about the real source of Steve Jobs's mastery and invited all of us not only to commit to becoming the best in the world at what we do, but also to treat each person we meet with exceptional courtesy and extraordinary respect.

We kept in touch for many years and I grew to consider him not only a guide but a much-valued friend.

Backstage at *The Titan Summit* in Zurich, with Apple cofounder Steve Wozniak

Although I've been honored to be a mentor to many well-known billionaires, NBA, NFL and MLB sports legends and the leadership teams of organizations such as Nike, FedEx, Oracle, Starbucks, Unilever and Microsoft, if you asked me who has been the number one influence on my life, I'd say, "That's easy ... My father."

Dad was born to a simple family in Jammu, Kashmir, with a priest for a father and a saint as his mother. A gifted student, according to my uncle (his brother), my father had to eclipse roughly ten thousand competitors to secure a place at medical school in Agra, India, the home of the Taj Mahal.

When it came time to travel there to begin his medical studies, he and his elder brother walked a full day and then traveled by train for three days to arrive at the college, only to be informed by the authorities that his spot had been given to someone else.

Dejected but not defeated, they pleaded with the head of the university for an admission, given my father's superb academic record. (Dad would *never* tell you this, given his humility to a fault, yet my uncle once confirmed he was "completely brilliant.")

After much discussion, Dad was finally granted entry. Which led him to ...

... finish his medical degree and move to Africa, where he met my mother (and I was made).

... work for the Ugandan government as a field doctor. (One day he crossed paths in the jungle with the dictator Idi Amin. My mom says she saved my father's life that day. But that's another story, perhaps for a future book.)

... raise a healthy family (my brother is a widely respected eye surgeon).

My father (and my very wise mother) mean the world to me.

For fifty-four years, Dad contributed to the community as a family doctor.

For decade after decade, he helped those in need, even paying for medicine himself where a patient could not afford it.

And year after year, he'd offer me weighty philosophy that shaped me deeply.

Me and my parents in the garden

In the spirit of helpfulness, I wanted to share the *single best* lesson I've learned from my father. It's a simply profound one and a profoundly simple one (like all great truths).

"Serve others."

... Too many in our uncertain age behave in selfish, entitled and undignified ways that harm our society and degrade our planet.

... Too many have forgotten that we really do belong to just one family—on a very insignificant sphere, in a universe with two hundred billion galaxies and two trillion stars.

... Too many measure winning by accumulating, do not know the meaning of enough and maneuver through their lives as if apprenticed to Machiavelli.

... Too many have been brainwashed into believing that the one who takes the most receives the best.

Really?

What of the riches that flow as you increase the value you lavish on others, rise in your commitment to helpfulness and dramatically elevate your contribution to anyone in need, whether that's a relative or a friend, a customer or a supplier, a neighbor or a total stranger? Generous rewards—such as flawless happiness, enduring serenity and increasing self-love—come from knowing you are living your life for a mission much larger than yourself.

"Serve others," my father would say to me and my brother. Often. And sometimes, with his medical texts stacked next to him as he sat on his favorite chair in our living room, he would add: "This is the secret to a good life, boys."

To reinforce the point, Dad wrote the following poem of Rabindranath Tagore onto the cardboard backing of his prescription pad and taped it to the door of the refrigerator in our kitchen so we would see it before we went off to school each morning:

Spring has passed.
Summer has gone.
And Winter is here.
And the song that I meant to sing remains unsung.
For I have spent my days stringing and unstringing my instrument.

To me, this verse reminds us that life's too short not to go all in. That each of us has music that must not be stifled within us. And that becoming busy just being busy and allowing your hours to be consumed by unimportant pursuits is violently disrespectful to your natural genius.

The words also make me think of the duty each of us carries within us to be of service. They speak of an obligation to lift up others

in a civilization that too often tears people down. They note our collective responsibility to deploy our days in a style that reduces the
injustice, mistreatment and hatred in our current culture and replaces
it with goodwill to all. And a lot more honor.

My father—my greatest mentor—wrote a letter to me while I was
a young lawyer. I have engraved some of the words that I read onto my
heart. And I need to share them with you:

> When you were born, you cried while the world rejoiced. Live your
> life in such a way that when you die, the world cries while you rejoice.

9.

The Joy of Being Laughed At

This is a short chapter, meant for visionaries, dreamers and misfits.

As you execute on your ambitions and materialize your farsighted aspirations, the trolls will come out to play.

As you live your truth and fully reveal your giftedness, critics will mumble and cynics will grumble.

As you bring your previously dormant empires of productivity, prosperity and impact into full waking reality, the naysayers will laugh at you. And try to stop you.

And yet all history-makers were initially ridiculed before they were revered.

The very nature of a brave ideal and the fiery hope to make it happen means you'll stand out from the crowd, be called weird and cause the majority of society to feel threatened by your creative power. This will manifest as jealousy, mockery and sometimes even vicious attack.

Remember (please) that those who try to stunt your dreams are revealing *their* limitations—not yours. So continue at all costs. You must not surrender in the face of their insecurities and "stuckedness."

For the failure to perform right action means the triumph of the mean-spirited, the ungenerous and those who would rather view everyone in darkness than to see all shine brightly.

10.

The Orson Welles Memo

Orson Welles is widely regarded as one of the most advanced film-makers of all time.

... He made *Citizen Kane*.

... He directed and narrated the extraordinary radio adaptation of the H. G. Wells novel *The War of the Worlds*, which generated wide-spread hysteria as listeners, believing that the earth was truly under attack by extraterrestrials, ran for cover.

... He reinvented the way movies were made through the use of his unusual camera angles, eclectic sound techniques and the long takes that became his trademark.

Yet what I most admire about Orson Welles is his artistic integrity. And his dedication to flawlessness as a creative leader.

After three months in the cutting room, ensuring that his film *Touch of Evil* would be a tour de force, Welles was barred by the studio from working any further on the project. (He was always seen as an outsider by the Hollywood establishment and frequently had a hard time getting movies made.)

Welles understood the frustration people had around his perfectionism, saying, "I could work forever on the editing of a film. I don't know why it takes me so much time but that has the effect of arousing the ire of the producers, who then take the film out of my hands."

A few months after he was removed, Welles saw the cut of *Touch of Evil* done by the studio. He grew so distressed that the quality of the movie did not reflect his standards of excellence that—even though he was no longer involved (or being paid)—he wrote a memo to the head of production, detailing—with monumental precision—the edits that were needed.

The document was fifty-eight pages long.

I've read it. And it's breathtaking.

The technical expertise it reveals, the attention to the most seemingly minor points it displays and the respect for the insulation of his good name it shows are *astounding*. And of great inspiration to anyone serious about making work that lasts.

The suggestions were discarded by the producer. And *Touch of Evil* was released as it was.

It remained on the market in that version for eighteen years, until the memo was discovered and published in *Film Quarterly*, where it came to the attention of a director who idolized Orson Welles. He took on a re-edit so the film would be truer to the original vision of the pioneer behind it.

The critics loved it.

Yet, to me, the real victory was not in the rerelease of the movie, but in the writing of that memo.

Which confirms that the making of a masterpiece is much less about the cash to be made and much more about the character of the creator.

11.

Nothing's Perfect

I was in San José, Costa Rica, staying at a stylish boutique hotel situated by a lovely waterway.

On checkout, the young woman at the front desk politely asked, "How was your stay? Perfect, I hope?"

Then, before I could answer, she interrupted herself with, "Of course, *nothing's perfect.*"

Hmmm.

"Nothing's perfect." What a wise insight.

In nature, no sandbank, no garden, no crooked brook, no fragrant flower and no lush forest is perfect.

Same for life, because it's governed by the same natural laws. You won't find anything that is absolutely perfect. Ever.

And once you accept this, you'll find the way things are a whole lot easier to manage. You'll exist with far more cheerfulness, peacefulness and spiritual genius.

Nothing you work on will ever be perfect, even if it's your magnum opus. I'm sure Michelangelo, in hindsight, would have changed a few strokes on the fresco of the ceiling in the Sistine Chapel and that Leo Tolstoy would have structured *War and Peace* slightly differently, given a second chance, and that Marie Curie would have reimagined a number of her scientific innovations, on further reflection.

No business will ever be perfect, even if your merchandise is magnificent and you've selected epic performers for your team.

No dinner at a restaurant will ever be perfect, even if it's the most exquisite meal you've ever had.

No pair of shoes, cake at a bakery, film you watch on TV or sports match between top players will ever be perfect.

And no personal relationship will be perfect. Because I've yet to meet the perfect person.

But here's the wonderful thing …

… the more you embrace this understanding around The Imperfection of All Things, the more you will pretty nearly automatically start to see the magic within the messy.

You'll begin to see the chemistry—and outright alchemy—in objects and experiences and humans that are flawed. You'll learn to trust that it's all perfect *because* of its imperfection.

In Japan, people fix broken pottery pieces by putting them back together with pure gold, a four-hundred-year-old practice called *kintsugi*. It fascinates me tremendously that the once-damaged piece becomes stronger at the broken places. Even more importantly, the method celebrates the truth that something with faults can be reconceived as something even more valuable.

And would this not be a perfect thing?

12.

The Chestnut Seller Doctrine

One night, in a fabled European city, I walked the cobblestone streets alone.

I watched tourists coming out of posh restaurants, studied the carefully arranged mannequins in the windows of luxury shops and marveled at the way the moonbeams illuminated the roofs of the ethereal cathedrals.

In one square sat a lonely figure.

He was hunched over a stove that heated chestnuts. Doing his work like it was the most important job in the world. A gentle smile was radiating from his wrinkled face, though it was nearly midnight.

I stopped. I bought a bag of nuts. I asked him to tell me his story. I then asked a few questions about his family. I wondered about the struggles of his life's journey. And what led him to end up in this square.

"It's late. It's cold. The streets are pretty quiet now. Why are you still here at your chair, selling your chestnuts?" I asked the middle-aged vendor with a blue woolen cap on his head.

He looked at me, silently. "I used to be a very successful business-man in my home country," he replied. "Then I got sick and lost every-thing. My company, my house and my money. But I can still work, thank God. I can still make my life better. I can still make people happy by giving them these chestnuts that I roast with a lot of love. I'm still alive, so I can still dream."

"I'm still alive, so I can still dream," the chestnut seller repeated.

The chestnut seller who made no excuses

"I have had dreams and I've had nightmares. I have conquered my nightmares because of my dreams," said Jonas Salk, the iconic scientist and developer of the polio vaccine.

Every human being with a thumping pulse and throbbing heart has spellbinding power within them. An ability to transform ideals into results, setbacks into successes and promise into prowess. Unfortunately, the majority of people have been taught to disown this force so often they've forgotten they have it.

Here was this man. He'd endured tragedy. Been knocked down badly and beaten up by destiny, pretty seriously. And yet rather than

THE EVERYDAY HERO MANIFESTO

complaining, condemning and doing little with his ability, like an impotent victim licking the hurts of his past and wallowing in self-pity, here he was: smiling, working, helping and doing his part to upgrade his reality. Beautiful. Heroic, actually.

And if he continues with such resolve and passion for his occupation, I have no doubt that he'll soon hire others to help him expand his venture at multiple locations and, should he stay true to the opportunity he has seized, he may in time even purchase a chestnut farm and build a series of chestnut-processing factories, employing many and perhaps finally retiring to pursue philanthropy. Who knows? Sure, Fortune has its script and much of what we live has been written by the guardian of fate. *And yet* as human beings we have been blessed with immense gifts and striking power to shape our future.

My experience with the chestnut seller of robust character makes me think of what I call "The Tale of Two Restaurants."

In a romantic European city favored by lovers sit two restaurants. They are across the street from each other. They serve the same type of food, and from a quick glance they look fairly similar. Yet one always has a long line outside it. Every single evening. The other? Mostly empty tables.

Interesting, right?

I would bet that the owner of the empty place has a thousand seductive justifications and one million attractive excuses for why his restaurant isn't popular. My guess is "They're just lucky" or "They have a better location" or "I can't find a great chef" or "It's hard to find good workers" or "The economy makes it impossible for me to succeed" would be high on his list. Not one of these excuses would be a statement of truth. They just make the owner feel better about the empty tables.

The reality is the acclaimed restaurant *found a way to sparkle*. As could the place across the street. Yet giving away one's power is a whole lot easier. Coasting along with tiny commitment to expertise, a weak work ethic and no fire to create something special is simpler. And blaming the stars for any poverty of mastery and mediocre circumstances just makes a human being feel safer. Because taking absolute personal responsibility over our actions and the consequences that flow from them demands that you wage war against your dragons and do battle with your demons. This requires extreme courage and profound wisdom—which few are willing to develop.

And yet *to have the results very few have, you must do the things very few do.*

We don't really get lucky in life. We *create* lucky. Once we operate in the correct way.

I suggest that—this day—you promise yourself to let virtuosity be your lamplight, diligence be your north star, integrity be your lighthouse and a lifelong pursuit of greatness be your compass.

And when you feel like giving up and are in need of some honest inspiration, please remember my friend the chestnut seller. The one with the blue woolen cap.

13.

The IPOP Principle
for Accelerated Positivity

Your ecosystem shapes your energy. And your surroundings influence your performance. Dramatically.

Everything outside you profoundly affects the way you think, feel, create and execute. Everything.

Your personal ecosystem includes the people you have conversations with, the influencers you follow, the media you consume, the books you read, the food you eat, the tools of the trade you use, the transportation you take, the place you live and the spaces you visit. It all works in concert to either lift you to legendary or reduce you to ordinary.

Which brings me to The IPOP Principle: *Input Positivity and You'll Output Positivity.*

You can't spend hours each day watching the news (which is designed to scare you into watching more rather than showing you the immense good unfolding in the world at this very moment), follow celebrities who are superficial and show-offy, be around people who make you feel bad, and spend your time in toxic physical environments, yet still hope to tap into the wizardry that amplifies your original talents, respects your sterling character and causes you to release your stardust into society.

To increase your inspiration, you need to do the things that increase your inspiration. I know that seems like an obvious insight, yet it is generally observed in the breach. Actively protecting your positivity so you generate elite creativity and peak productivity just isn't common in a culture that encourages medication by digital distraction and escapism by superficial sensationalism. To have the rewards that only 5% of the population experience, you really do have to hardwire the habits and install ways of being that 95% of the population are unwilling to embrace.

My suggestion is that you build a moat around your most hope-filled mindset and a wall around the exuberance of your most exalted aspirations. Allow across the chasm *only* those influences that fuel your enthusiasm, optimize your inherent genius, maximize your performance and glorify your native giftedness. Armor-plate and battleproof those encouraging thoughts that you work so hard for by setting up an invisible fortress that will not allow entry to anyone or anything that threatens your highness. Because you'll never handcraft your visionary venture and fully express your magic if your tank of inspiration is empty. And if you're full of negativity. Oh, and while you're at it, make sure you fill your mind (and heart) with giant ambitions so there is no room for petty worries.

Top artists work in positive and beautiful and quiet surroundings for an essential reason: it activates "flow state," that stream of brilliance that each of us has available to us if we structure our workspace and set up our private life in a way that allows us to play at the height of our powers.

The painter Andrew Wyeth, on becoming one of the most celebrated artists in history, left New York City and spent the rest of his career working in a studio on a farm in Chadds Ford, Pennsylvania, and at a seaside cottage in Cushing, Maine. Staying close to the awesome splendor of nature is a habit of all great masters to remain inspired, focused and joyful in an era of tectonic change and immense upheaval. (They are also alone a lot, because rising to your greatest creative state only occurs in isolation.)

J. D. Salinger, after *The Catcher in the Rye* became one of the biggest-selling books on the planet, retreated from public attention on his thirty-fourth birthday, spending his remaining fifty-seven years writing daily in a small studio that was connected to his main house in rural Cornish, New Hampshire, via an underground tunnel. He could go to his writing room without being seen by the photographers and fans waiting outside.

James Bond creator Ian Fleming purchased a retreat in Jamaica he named *GoldenEye* that was perched over a ravishingly lovely beach to provide him with the epiphanies and artistic fuel that would increase his craft. (I find it fascinating that he instructed his gardeners not to walk past the window of his writing studio as it would break his artistic trance.)

As prime minister of the United Kingdom, Winston Churchill—to get relief from the pressures of being the wartime leader who stood up to the Nazi regime—would spend weekends at Chequers, the official country house of the head of the British government, or at Chartwell, his lakeside residence in southeast England. In these places, he would plan military strategy, carefully write his mesmerizing speeches, paint landscapes and smoke cigars in the verdant gardens.

World-builders, as well as everyday heroes committed to honoring their promise, all understand The IPOP Principle. They appreciate that the fortification of positivity, inspiration and high hopes at a time of general negativity is mission-central to their campaign of producing sublime work and leading a life that surges with happiness, serenity and spiritual freedom.

14.

Stop Calling Your Genius Sh*t

Everywhere you go, you'll hear good people using bad words for great things.

… The way to enlightenment is to not give a f*ck.

… Wear stylish sneakers and you'll be applauded for rocking "sick" kicks.

… Learn to meditate, visualize, journal and pray to release old trauma, banish timidity and boost your confidence and your friends will celebrate you for being "gangster."

… Deliver the most spectacular work performance of your lifetime (yet) and you'll be told you "killed" it.

… Uplift your craft so you grow nearer to your potential and peers will exclaim, "You're doing really cool sh*t."

Really? *Words mean what words say.*

And the words you use send potent messages to your unconscious mind about who you are, what you can achieve and the quality of what you will produce.

I delivered a leadership keynote at an event attended by the senior management of one of the global behemoths of the media sector a while ago.

Two young (and very decent) men drove me and the teammate who travels with me to the airport.

We chatted about fantastic food, interesting music and the importance of following our bliss.

I then asked the driver about his ambitions.

He revealed a secret desire to move to Canada.

He shared that he loved the natural beauty of the nation, the civility of its people and the efficiency of its infrastructure.

"But I know it's *impossible*," he repeated, over and over and over (thereby reinforcing the neural circuit associated with impossibility because, as any good neuroscientist will tell you, brain cells that fire together wire together).

People really do reveal their deepest beliefs by their daily behaviors. And their sabotaging wounds via their spoken words.

The young man's fears had done a con job on his desires. His disloyal doubts had kidnapped his trustworthy dreams.

The false assumptions, fake barriers and untruthful worldview he absorbed from those around him taught him to speak like a powerless victim. To see prison bars that were not there, sort of like when a dog who had an invisible fence around its yard has that fence taken away, yet still won't cross the border.

The young man imagined a blockade where a doorway actually exists. "It isn't what we don't know that gives us trouble, it's what we know that ain't so," said entertainer and humorist Will Rogers astutely.

I pay such attention to the words I speak. I don't even call autumn "fall" because the word "fall" has negative implications in my philosophy. I love autumn. I have no interest in a fall. Those things hurt. Sometimes badly.

I remember reading a message from a reader who said he wished he could attend a live event I was leading but couldn't "because I'd have to cross the ocean."

... Did he think the only way to get there was a month-long sea swim?

... Did he believe crossing oceans can only be done these days in rickety rowboats?

... Did he overestimate that making it to the gathering required him to have the audacity of Sir Edmund Hillary and the lionhearted-ness of Joan of Arc?

The driver's obsession with the word "impossible" (he seriously just kept repeating that swear word) displayed his rigid and unhealthy mentality. And then, sadly, his restricted psychology became a self-fulfilling prophecy. If we don't think something is possible, then we won't do the work, apply the consistency and exercise the patience needed to make the fantasy real. So it doesn't happen. Which then confirms to us that it was all impossible.

And while I'm on the theme of choosing words carefully as a means to maximize your creativity, productivity and prosperity, in a billion years I'd never label the work that fuels my spirit, expresses my talent, provides the oxygen of my life and allows me to serve other human beings "sh*t."

... I'd never compliment anyone by saying they look "sick."

... I'd never demean someone's hard-earned success by saying their high achievement is "crazy."

... And when someone knocked a performance out of the park, I'd never tell them they "murdered" it.

Because sh*t and sickness and craziness and murders are bad. Not good. As I see it.

Splendid language has charisma to it. So exercise yours well.

15.

What J. K. Rowling Taught Me about Relentlessness

The facts:

The author of the *Harry Potter* series has sold more than 500 million books.

This literary titan is the first female novelist to become a billionaire.

The writer who rose from poverty and obscurity to wealth and fame is now a leading philanthropist.

Her father was an aircraft engineer at a Rolls-Royce factory and her mother worked in the chemistry department at the school Rowling studied at.

As a child she "lived for books," describing herself as "your basic common or garden bookworm complete with freckles and National Health spectacles."

This luminary wrote her first book at the age of six and her first novel at the age of eleven (it was about seven cursed diamonds; I only wish I could be so imaginative).

The vision for *Harry Potter* came to J. K. Rowling while she sat on a train that was delayed on its trip from Manchester to King's Cross station in London. Actually, the ideas for all seven books came to

59

her on that single trip, along with the central theme for the first one, *Harry Potter and the Philosopher's Stone*. In a blazing intuitive hit, the concept showed up for her in a single sentence: "Boy who doesn't know he's a wizard goes to wizarding school."

She wrote longhand on scraps of paper that she eventually carried around with her in a suitcase (yes, a suitcase).

Much of the first *Harry Potter* book was written at Nicolson's café and the Elephant House in Edinburgh while Rowling was a single mother on welfare.

During the writing process, the author's much-loved mother died, pushing her into a long-lasting depression. Rowling continued to create, using the emotional darkness as soil to make her characters richer and more memorable. (Difficulty truly can be a trusted companion for creative victory.)

On completing the book, she sent three chapters to a series of prominent literary agents. Only one replied. Rowling said, "It was the best letter I had received in my life."

She received numerous rejections from publishers who said the book would not be commercially successful or interesting to young audiences. Bloomsbury finally agreed to publish *Harry Potter and the Philosopher's Stone*, but asked Joan Rowling (as she was then known) to add a "K" after her first initial, as they believed a clearly female name would turn off the intended audience of young boys. ("K" stands for Kathleen—her grandmother's first name.)

Even after she became one of the bestselling authors of all time, she said that she didn't walk around thinking she's "fab." Her main goal as an artistic laborer is "writing better than yesterday."

She published a series of crime books under the pen name Robert Galbraith. Without revealing who she was, she sent the book to publishers for consideration. One of the many rejection letters she received suggested that "a writer's group or writing course may help."

(Remember what I offered to you earlier? Someone's opinion is just someone's opinion. Do not believe it if it doesn't serve your ascent.)

A Japanese proverb teaches: "Fall down seven times. Rise up eight."

J. K. Rowling lived this wisdom. And this made her great.

16.

Guard Good Health like a Pro Athlete

Okay. A bit of a longer chapter here, yet I promise it'll be worth the trip. So let's get started.

The historian Thomas Fuller once wrote: "Health is not valued until sickness comes."

Hmmm. Deep truth, yes?

An audience member approached me after a presentation I'd just delivered in Qatar to the apex of CEOs in the region and handed me a crinkled note, asking me to read it when I had a quiet moment. That evening in my hotel room, I scanned these words scribbled onto the paper:

> Health is the crown on the well person's head that only the ill person can see.

"Those who don't make time for exercise must eventually make time for illness," Edward Stanley, the British statesman, reminded us.

Few habits will transform your performance and escalate your cheerfulness more than optimizing what I call "Healthset" in the curriculum that I teach to my advanced mentoring clients in my *IconX* program and in my online coaching course *The Circle of Legends*.

So many pundits in the personal development realm speak of

"mindset" and evangelize the "mindset is everything" mantra. With immense respect for all such educators, I take a contrarian approach to the self-mastery equation.

Yes, calibrating your Mindset to install the thinking and mental programming of greatness is essential for domain-dominant performance. Your daily behavior surely does reflect your deepest beliefs. And your income and influence never rise any higher than your self-identity and intellectual story. So Mindset matters. Absolutely. Yet it's *not* everything.

As human beings we are far more than merely our psychology.

We also have a second dimension that I call "Heartset," which speaks to the reality that—along with our psychology—each of us also has an emotionality. We not only possess the ability to think, we also carry a precious capacity to feel. It's simply not possible to step into your highest knowledge, experience intimacy with your hidden powers, accomplish spellbinding results and experience sustained gratitude, awe and wonder if you only live in your head.

Yes, calibrate your Mindset, but—*please*—also make the time to purify your Heartset so it's free of the suppressed toxic emotions of fear, anger, sadness, disappointment, resentment, shame and guilt that every human being accumulates as we advance through a life and endure misfortunes. Fail to deal with and steadily heal this "Field of Hurt" that lurks in your subconscious and you'll find the peak of your energy, creativity and productivity will always be blocked (this is extremely important to understand). In a coming chapter, I'll walk you through some dynamic methods and transformational tactics to clear out this invisible baggage. For now, simply appreciate that doing the work required to release old emotional wounds is essential to upgrading your performance. Otherwise, your excellent intellectual intentions will always be sabotaged by your secret shadows lodged deep within your Healthset.

Working on our Mindset yet neglecting our Heartset is also

the primary reason most learning—whether through books, digital training or live conferences—doesn't last. We get the information at a cognitive level, but don't integrate it as an emotional *knowing* in the body. So it doesn't stick. This means our weaker habits and limiting behaviors stay in place because of our inability to embrace the ideas as a felt truthdue to the blockages within our Heartset.

All right. So as human beings we have the interior empires of Mindset and Heartset. Both need to be attended to and cultivated consistently to enjoy the outer empires of sensational creativity, rare-air productivity, unusual prosperity and heavyweight service to society.

Yet that's not the end of the personal mastery equation. There are two more inner universes in my mentoring curriculum that—when also elevated—complete the algorithm for self-leadership. These are Healthset and Soulset. Let's have a look t the visual framework below.

THE 4 INTERIOR EMPIRES

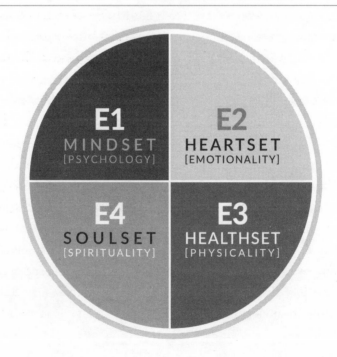

It's only when all four of these human dynasties are awakened and then improved that you will reveal your genius, display your highness, lead your field and experience a life of rare-air positivity, vitality, wonder and spiritual freedom. The primary reason--and this is very important--that most attempts to know your sovereign self fail is because this contrarian approach is not considered. And then applied.

So after Mindset and Heartset is interior empire number three. Healthset is your physicality. You won't change the world if you're sick. Or dead. Optimizing your Healthset—which I'll focus on for most of the rest of this chapter—involves improving your energy, increasing your immunity and reducing inflammation to beat disease and significantly extend your lifespan.

Finally, Soulset speaks to your spirituality, the relationship with that eternal part of you that is flawlessly wise, completely unbreakable, united with every other human on the planet and limitless. Soulset practice is all about reducing the noise of your ego so you can hear the whispers of the primal hero that is who you truly are, underneath the layers of doubt and disbelief that we all collect as we advance through our years.

I need to repeat this because I want to reinforce this: it is only when you do the daily work to grow each of *The 4 Interior Empires* that you will experience *exponential* gains in your exterior empires of creativity, productivity, prosperity and public service to many.

With this extremely important and rarely discussed context covered, let us now zoom in on the key priority of battleproofing your finest health by optimizing your Healthset.

As you raise your physical dimension, you'll build an even better brain, enhance your focus, activate unusual stamina, multiply the amount of willpower at your disposal, uplift your mood, reduce the dangers of chronic inflammation that breeds disease, sleep better and live longer.

One of the learning models that my clients have found valuable when it comes to generating their highest Healthset and getting as fit as a professional athlete is *The Trinity of Radiant Vitality*.

THE TRINITY OF RADIANT VITALITY

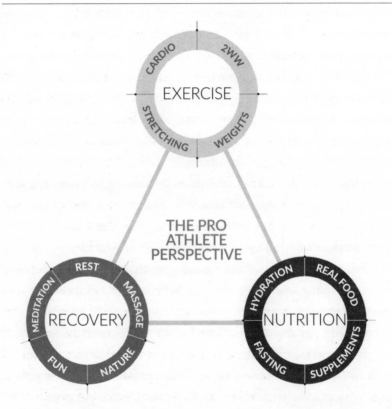

The first element of *The Trinity of Radiant Vitality*, as you can see, encourages you to exercise (ideally, every morning). To play your greatest game you want to be a PMM: a Perpetual Movement Machine (except when it's time to RRR—Renew, Recover and Rest). The exercising habit releases the neurochemical dopamine, which will produce strong gains in the inspiration that you feel for the rest of the day. What is this factor alone worth to you in terms of your influence, income, impact and well-being?

Sweating just after you wake up by running on a treadmill or skipping rope or spinning on a bike (as just a few examples) will also release BDNF (brain-derived neurotropic factor), which promotes neurogenesis (the generation of new brain cells) and repairs brain cells damaged by the previous day's stress. BDNF will also increase the speed at which your brain processes information by increasing the connections among your neural pathways, giving you a massive advantage in the new world we work within.

Morning exercise will further produce norepinephrine, which activates peak concentration in this era of overwhelming digital distraction, as well as serotonin, which regulates anxiety, maximizes your memory and leaves you feeling relaxed. Working out will also raise your metabolic rate, giving you more energy. The simple ritual of moving vigorously in the morning will reshape the excellence of your days. Having a strong sweat before the sun rises is one of the core habits that I live by. I really hope that you wire this one in, as it's so completely revolutionary to every other area of your life.

I also recommend a late afternoon or early evening routine that I call "The Second Wind Workout" (2WW), which ensures that at the end of your workday you schedule a second round of exercise to create even more of the supreme benefits that physical fitness delivers. If you truly agree with me that exercising is a magnificent needle-mover when it comes to establishing peerless productivity, heroic output and automatic optimism, why would you only work out once a day?

After a day of writing, for example, I love heading to the forest near our home and walking in the woods for an hour. The Japanese are masters of *shinrin-yoku*. *Shinrin* means "forest" in Japanese and *yoku* means "bath." Forest bathing via a walk or mountain bike ride in the woods has many advantages, including the reduction of the stress hormone cortisol, a significant increase in natural killer cells—the body's disease-fighting agents—enhanced cognitive function and greater confidence. On my forest walks or rides during my 2WW, I'll often listen to an audiobook or a podcast to get in another hour or two of learning time. Education is inoculation against irrelevance. So I take growing daily very seriously.

To upgrade your Healthset I also encourage you to balance cardio activity with weight training to scale your strength, and daily stretching to increase your mobility. You never want to allow an old stiff person into your body.

As you can see from the main learning model of this chapter, the second element of *The Trinity of Radiant Vitality* is nutrition. "Let food be thy medicine," advised the Greek physician Hippocrates. Your nutritional plan is a primary component of becoming as healthy as a professional athlete and remaining enthusiastic, energetic, jubilant and ultra-effective for a long time.

As much as possible, eat real versus processed foods, as the latter are loaded with chemicals and other toxins that will degrade your performance and diminish your longevity. I do my best to eat organic meals and really try hard to support the local farmers of my community. I'm also committed to polishing my cooking skills so my family and I enjoy healthy and natural food prepared at home, often with wonderful music playing in the background and fascinating conversation flowing between us. (I'm not quite sure how many more books I'll write, as part of me has a romantic dream of opening an eleven-seat restaurant in a difficult-to-find location where I lovingly prepare each plate from the freshest ingredients available, for those intrepid souls who make the trek to come visit me. Maybe we'll have dinner together sometime. I'd love to meet you.)

Another important element of outstanding nutrition is supplementation. Simply said, much of what your body needs to perform at its summit cannot be gained solely from the food we eat. As a matter of fact, the food we now eat is vastly different and far less nutritious than the same food even a decade ago, given the disrespect we as a species have shown the earth. So you really need to add in the supplements required for you to operate at your best.

I also must share that getting my genome analyzed changed my life. My genomicist walked me through which of my genes were suboptimal so that by the power of epigenetics (*epi* means "above," so the study of epigenetics is about rising above your genetics by modifying your lifestyle habits) I could up-regulate genes that would benefit my health most. Taking supplements, installing enhanced daily routines and adopting the new behaviors that will cause dormant genes to turn on and the less-than-ideal genes not to express themselves are all examples of using "biohacking" to actively re-order your genetic destiny. The genes you've inherited from your parents really are *not* your fate. You have *far* more power to shape how your genome expresses itself than you may know.

Okay.

The last two things I wish to mention about nutrition are fasting and hydration. None of what I'm offering you here is medical advice, so kindly discuss any new health regime with your doctor. I will, however, share my personal experience with fasting, because the practice has been so incredibly helpful to my productivity as well as to my good health.

I generally fast on most weekdays when I'm in a work season where I'm writing a new book or doing speaking tours or shooting online courses. During these times, my last meal is around 9 PM and aside from a cup of excellent black coffee (coffee is full of antioxidants and is a tremendous cognitive enhancer), lots of water and fresh mint tea (sometimes with organic ginger in it), I won't eat anything until 4 or 5 PM the next day.

The discipline of fasting has served to keep me deeply focused, highly inspired and full of energy, so I get many important things done. Good research has found that fasting increases the production of BDNF, which, as I've mentioned, boosts brain function. It also reduces neurodegradation and enhances neuroplasticity, which accelerates learning capacity, improves memory, and lowers your blood sugar and insulin levels. In one study, caloric restriction was shown to increase human growth hormone levels by more than 300%. Curbing your caloric intake even just a few times a week has further been found to turn on genes (remember epigenetics?) that instruct cells to preserve resources and push your system into a state known as *autophagy*, where your body goes into hyperdrive to clean out old, damaged cellular material and fix cells injured by stress.

I also use the ritual of fasting to help me make progress spiritually. As St. Francis de Sales wrote:

Besides the ordinary effort of fasting in raising the mind, subduing the flesh, confirming goodness and obtaining a heavenly reward, it is also a great matter to be able to control greediness, and to keep the sensual appetites and the whole body subject to the law of the spirit;

and although we may be able to do but little, *the enemy nevertheless stands more in awe of those whom he knows can fast.*

Let me ask you with sincere respect: How can we ever hope to master our impulses, produce our masterwork, lead gorgeous lives and materialize our mighty missions if we can't even control what we eat?

For me, fasting makes me more present, so much more creative, exponentially stronger, far more able to do the difficult things that are closer to my truest spiritual self.

Oh—I also drink a lot of water through the day, since proper hydration, which improves mitochondrial function, is essential to multiplying your energy.

The third and final element of *The Trinity of Radiant Vitality* is recovery. Rest is the elite producer's secret weapon. Recovery is not a luxury—it's a necessity and a priority that is beyond important for sustaining world-class productivity over not just years, but decades. Contrary to the dominant beliefs of our culture, hours spent renewing your depleted resources is time beautifully invested. Championship athletes all have one practice in common: they sleep a lot.

When I write of the rich value of recovery to fireproof your fitness and to protect pristine physicality, I not only refer to a good pre-sleep ritual, great sleep hygiene, naps and regular massage. Recovery can also be active—so long as it's away from work. Real renewal requires large blocks of time away from any influence that causes anxiety. This could include reading, conversations with interesting people, enjoying a great film, going to the gym, traveling and going out for dinner with someone you love. Personally, I also gain enormous refueling through visits to art galleries, my periods in nature, by making sure I'm having fun and via a morning routine that involves meditation, visualization and prayer.

———

One of the most powerful ways to win in business is to outlive your peers. So that you have another few decades to master your craft and polish your powers. One of the smartest ways to build your fortune is to extend the lifetime of your earning years. So that you have more time to allow the extraordinary phenomenon of compounding to work its magic. And one of the smartest ways to experience a life of sovereignty and genuine happiness is to make sure your life is a very long one. Implementing *The Trinity of Radiant Vitality* consistently will ensure this result. So you guard your good health like a pro athlete.

"Happiness is nothing more than good health and a bad memory," noted humanitarian and polymath Albert Schweitzer.

I do believe he was right.

17.

My Four Chocolate Croissant Evening

So ...

I sure don't want you to think that, because I exercise daily, eat cleanly, fast consistently and biohack to leverage the benefit of epigenetics, I never slip. Or treat myself. I do. Because I'm no guru. And *very* human.

Twenty-five hundred years—or so—ago, Aristotle articulated The Golden Mean Doctrine, which states that virtuous behavior requires one to walk the middle ground between asceticism and indulgence. To take the path of moderation between excess and deprivation. To avoid being an extremist in any dimension of one's life.

Here's a maxim that's worth remembering: *Restriction promotes addiction.*

Which brings me to a confession.

The other evening, after many months working on this book for you, rising before the sun most days to set myself up for prodigiously productive work sessions and fasting for extended hours so my thinking was clear and my energy was concentrated on this project, I decided to reward myself for my dedication. And give myself the comfort that I was vigorously craving.

73

So I ordered delivery of some freshly made Italian pasta. I then used it to make one of my favorite Italian dishes: *bucatini al limone*. The ingredients are the pasta, extra virgin olive oil, pecorino cheese, some black pepper, lemon zest and lemon juice and a little mint to provide a hint of sweetness (and a bit of good color on the presentation). Here's what the plate looked like:

Bucatini al limone made by me with love

How delicious it was! It soothed my stomach and serenaded my soul. When no one was looking, I even sang the *bucatini* a sweet little love song. Yes, I was that enamored with the pasta.

And—in that lofty state of carbohydrate bliss—I just had to keep going ...

Next, I ordered a pizza, with three types of cheese and a very thick crust (the size of Mount Kilimanjaro, it seemed).

And finally, I collected four—yes, four—splendid and divine and lavish and ethereal and marvelous and heavenly butter-made fresh-out-of-the-oven Italian croissants with chocolate inside them called *saccottini al cioccolato* (not that I was enthusiastic about them or anything).

And when no one on the street seemed to be looking, I ate each one. While I was walking. With a smile the width of a stadium pinned across my face.

Did I mention I'm not a guru? And that I'm *very* human?

I do have a point to this vulnerable oversharing.

... Everything in moderation *including moderation* is a sensible way to play. (Thanks for the tip, Oscar Wilde; he is also reported to have said, "I can resist everything except temptation.")

All I'm saying is this: in a civilization that makes us feel guilty, damaged and demeaned unless we are perfect, successful and running eighty-three advanced performance practices a day (with checklists to record our execution around each one), maybe—just maybe—we should make peace with *balance*. And be okay with Aristotle's "middle way," embracing the pleasures of this special world when it's the right time to love them. Life's just too short to be all rigid and machine-like, right?

Makes me think of the marathoners who've dropped dead of a heart attack, as well as the *nonnas* who had two shots of grappa each night and lived well past one hundred. I sometimes wonder if the positive neurochemistry that's generated by doing things that make you happy (like a "cheat meal") is a far better pursuit than the super-human strictness and überperson uptightness that likely produces more cortisol, which corrodes our vitality along with our longevity.

I overdid it because I had pushed myself too hard. A little less restriction and a bit more indulgence in those intense months on this project would have led to me enjoying a small plate of pasta, perhaps a slice or two of pizza, and maybe three fewer chocolate croissants. On that warm summer's evening.

18.

A Contrarian Philosophy for Mastering Unexpected Change

For more than twenty years, I've walked in the same forest.

During the positive periods of my journey, these woods have provided me with a place to regenerate my creativity, refuel my energy and restore my tranquility.

In those stages where I've suffered from difficulty, navigated tragedy and experienced groundlessness, this forest became a monastery of sorts—a retreat for my growth and steady transformation.

Along one of the trails, by a small pond favored by lively ducks, sits a sign bearing words that have helped me enormously to navigate uncertainty.

Here's what the important part says:

Forests renew themselves through natural disturbances such as wind, fire, insects and disease. These disturbances result in the creation of areas of dead trees within which a new forest will grow.

You see, the nature of Nature is unyielding change. And sometimes the foundations we stand on must fall so that they may be replaced with even stronger ones. Breakthroughs require breakdowns.

Progress cannot happen without upheaval and *the birth of something better always demands a death of something familiar.* Uncomfortable disturbance is essential not only for your evolution but for your very survival. Just like within my forest.

The sign in my forest monastery

To the untrained eye, turbulence is judged as bad and labeled as wrong. We wish things would go back to the way they were. So we would feel safer. Yet the discomfort of growth is always better than the illusion of safety. Seriously. Standing still is an immensely harmful act for anyone dedicated to becoming an everyday hero.

Your advancement as a leader and your optimization as a person are built around the doing of difficult things. *What is easiest to do is generally what is least valuable to do.* Lasting transformation happens during our stormy seasons, never during the days of our ease.

The great saints, sages and spiritual geniuses all understood that a main aim on the path to awakening was to stand in *any* mess that life sends and remain contented, courageous, serene and free. To stay tranquil while all appears to be falling apart. To construct an inner axis of power so strong, and yet so flexible, that *nothing* on the outside could shake its roots. Imagine this: making an interior life that stays graceful, quiet and grateful, regardless of what is happening outside of you. To have your strength depend not on worldly stability but upon your primal heroism.

As you release resistance to change in your personal life or professional career or external environment, and embrace the new circumstances that destiny has sent, you will come to see any volatility that has unfolded as a grand blessing. A necessary note in the soaring symphony that is the masterplan of the world. And a carefully crafted stepping stone into the growth and evolution that will make you into the leader, producer, warrior and loving citizen that true victory pleads with you to become.

"What the caterpillar calls the end of the world, the master calls a butterfly," the aviator and author Richard Bach once wrote.

Or as the eminent philosopher Friedrich Nietzsche observed, "One must still have chaos in oneself to be able to give birth to a dancing star."

19.

You're Absolutely
More than Enough

Eleanor Roosevelt said, "Comparison is the thief of joy."

And we sure do live in the Culture of Comparison, don't we?

... We feel happy about a work-win until someone on the team gets what we perceive to be more recognition than we received.

... We are content with our romantic partner until we see someone who looks better on the arm of another.

... We feel financially secure until we see a photo of someone sunbathing on their yacht, flying private whenever they wish and sniffing the roses in the colorful gardens that surround their opulent mansion.

... We feel confident about how we look until we spot an image of another with a leaner physique and a more model-esque face.

Much of my own emotional healing has centered around learning to feel good enough. Learning to be content with who I am, the way I live and whatever I have. And not comparing my life to the lives of others (which, I've discovered, often turn out to be nothing more than carefully crafted illusions designed to sell a brand and push a product).

I've also learned that *there are no extra people on this planet.*

Each of us has value. Everyone matters. And the cash in someone's bank account or the size of someone's home doesn't mean they are in any way better than you. Or more important to the world than you.

Why does our spiritually damaged society prescribe that a tycoon is more valuable than a ditchdigger? Or that a state leader should be considered more powerful than a teacher? Or an emergency worker? Or a sandwich maker? I really don't get this. And it bothers me.

Money is only one metric of success. It's only one form of wealth. There are many more, you know? Like being a good person and doing work that satisfies you, like having a fulfilling family life and being around friends who flood you with gratitude and hope. Many obsess over financial return on investment yet, tragically, ignore the value of character ROI and happiness ROI and spiritual ROI.

And I must tell you, from my experience as the adviser to a ton of captains of industry, billionaires and entertainment titans, that a lot of them have all the assets you could imagine, yet are troubled, unhappy and fraught with worry. Too much money can become a formula for complexity, difficulty and often outright misery. Personally, I place a vastly higher value on inner freedom than upon financial gain.

Consider the richness of a person who ...

... is always on time, has wonderful manners, is consistently considerate of the needs of others and cares about the environment.

... takes immense pride in doing their simple work with eagerness, high ethics and uncommon excellence.

... radiates positivity even in harsh conditions, sees the best in all around them and exemplifies thankfulness for whatever they have.

Isn't one such as this a hero of our society? A model of mastery? A representative of the extraordinary?

Own your specialness. Celebrate your virtues. Appreciate your goodness. Salute all you've gone through as well as the brilliant blessings that your future has in store for you.

Do. Not. Minimize. Your. Majesty.

Understand—once and for all—that there's no one exactly like you alive on the planet today. *No one.*

Since the beginning of the human empire, only one of you has been made. Amazing, yes? Just one of you—with your fingerprints, your gifts, your authentic ambitions, your way of talking, working, walking and loving. Good God, you're amazing!

Yes—the media you consume might send you photos of people who appear to have thinner tummies and videos of actors driving spectacular sports cars. But that doesn't mean you're not startlingly worthy. Because you are. Absolutely one of a kind. And while I believe it's very important to keep making every aspect of your life better, every single day, please also know and trust that who you are right now is more than enough.

So may I humbly suggest that you *give yourself* the words, praise and encouragement you are waiting for forces outside of you to give.

And become your own top cheerleader, your single finest supporter and your number one fan.

20.

The Starter's Activation Declaration

I've composed a statement for you to recite early in the morning while your neighborhood is silent, so you can access your brightest fire and most astonishing talents at the quietest time of the day. While the rest of the world is asleep, you have the opportunity to achieve a primary triumph: to associate with your purest self, to cultivate your dormant strength and to remember what you seek to stand for over the hours ahead.

At sunrise—when all is still, before the noise of the day has begun—you can access that side of yourself that has remained unwounded by discouragements of the past, that refuses to be conquered by negativity and defeat, and that wishes to exist in a way that makes a difference.

Reading this declaration *aloud* at dawn will—over time—reprogram both your conscious and subconscious mind to shed the false beliefs that have kept you small and scared. It will load in the thoughts and feelings that forge everyday heroism. And re-engineer the way you get things done.

Here you go:

This day is a blessing that I will honor, savor and make fullest use of. Tomorrow is an idea. Today is what's real. And so I choose to live it elegantly, patiently and immaculately.

Over the moments coming, I will show up as a leader, not as a victim. As an originator, not a copier. As a visionary, instead of a follower.

Today, I choose to be extraordinary rather than average. And brave, instead of timid. A hero in my own distinct way, instead of giving away my potent powers by blame, complaint and excuse.

Insecurity and meekness and the fear of rejection will not pollute my productivity, nor hinder my ability to uplift, respect and render value to other people.

This day, I will make time for reflection and deep thinking, resist all time wasters, remain in the present moment and perform labor that reveals mastery while remaining true to my highest ideals.

Today, I will keep each promise I make to myself, defend my hopefulness, exercise my best habits and accomplish the things that make my heart sing. For I have much music in me. And I will no longer disrespect myself by keeping that song within.

In the hours ahead, I will be supremely disciplined and incredibly focused, never confusing being busy with getting major feats done.

And should I need to rest, I will not measure this as a waste, understanding that first-class performance without honest recovery leads to the degradation of my native genius.

Today, I will not leave the site of a great insight without taking some action to implement it. I know that ideation without execution is the sport of fools. And that making amazing dreams real is an enormous act of self-love.

This day, I will be more valiant than yesterday, more optimistic than I was last evening and kinder than I was last night. I understand that big people are the ones who make others feel bigger. And that on my deathbed, what will matter most will be the human beings I've inspired, the caring I've delivered and the generosity I've displayed.

And so ...

... In the face of any chattering doubts, I will advance my most sensational projects and produce towering work that stands the test of time. Because I know that frustration is the child of stagnation. And steady progress is a testimony to my talent.

... Regardless of old challenges, I will take my next step into the ring.

... In spite of any self-doubt, I will continue the climb to my most aspirational summits.

I am more of a doer than a talker, more of a deliverer than a dabbler, more of a pro than an amateur.

I know that monuments are made one stone at a time. And so I start. And stay concentrated, grounded and centered. For many hours at a time, without being distracted by nuisances.

And in so doing—no matter what the outcome—I've realized a central victory. Over my darker self. And the weakness that once bound me.

And as I continue to make my small advances toward my highest ideals, my tiny triumphs introduce me to the truth and strongness within me. And this reconnection electrifies the once-damaged relationship with my most glorious self.

21.

The Very Good Bearded Man in the Really Cool Baseball Cap

I'm in Rome as I write you this chapter. Soon I'll leave to give a speech to business leaders in Sweden.

Two days ago, I delivered a leadership presentation to four hundred senior executives in Dubai. I know it might not seem like it, but I've chosen to speak at fewer conferences these days. I'm in a season of my life where I wish to travel less, improve my cooking skills more, and live more of a writer's life. So I'm enjoying my time on stages immensely.

Yesterday, I was at Dubai's humongous airport and happened to be in an elevator with a man who wore a cap I thought was neat. As a kid, I rode motocross bikes and the logo on his hat was of a brand that was cool.

I hesitated in giving him the compliment I wanted to give, scared of rejection. (Oh, the joys we miss and the marvels we lose stuck in the fear of being unwelcomed by others! I'll tell you a story about my brush with Hollywood royalty and my lost opportunity, in an upcoming chapter.)

Then I realized that I might not get the chance to appreciate this gentleman's baseball cap again. And so I did what I really wanted to do. So what if I looked silly? *Life's greatest risk is taking no risks, right?*

"Love your hat," I declared, unsure of the response I'd receive.

Amazingly, without any hesitation whatsoever, he removed the cap from his head and said, "Please take it."

In the past I would have refused the gift, out of politeness (and some insecurity around deserving the gesture).

This time I got it right. (I do get things right once in a while.) I acknowledged his unusual kindness with my sincere acceptance.

He smiled. A very generous smile. Quite lovely to witness, actually.

As we left the elevator, I asked him to wait for a moment.

I opened my carry-on case and plucked out a fresh copy of *The 5 AM Club*. I often bring a few copies of this book that has transformed so many lives on the road to give to flight attendants who overdeliver, hotel room service attendants who really care and taxi drivers who share a good story. The book was clearly destined for him.

I wrote his name, Mohammad, onto it with an inscription of good wishes to him and gently handed it over.

He beamed. Magnificently.

With my wonderful new friend at DXB (yes, that's his once-beloved hat gracing my once-hair-covered head)

I included that picture just to share the magic of what happened between two strangers on that Sunday afternoon in a crowded airport.

You know, there's a ton of negativity and toxicity and outright tragedy unfolding in the world right now. It hurts my heart to see the injustice, meanness, rudeness, greediness and hatred in evidence on the planet.

And yet I am also *really* clear that ...

... I've never seen so much decency being displayed by so many everyday heroes.

... I'm consistently *moved to tears* by the goodness demonstrated by so many diverse human beings, across so many different nations.

... I'm viscerally inspired by the random acts of nobility I've seen being performed by so many wise souls, even when they have little to gain for themselves.

This gentleman demonstrated powerfully what it means to be benevolent. To show goodwill to a stranger. To be friendly, kind and selfless.

Étienne de Grellet, a Quaker missionary, wrote of our duty to be considerate to others in the following terms: "I shall pass through this world but once. If, therefore, there be any kindness I can show, or any good thing I can do, let me do it now: let me not defer or neglect it, for I shall not pass this way again."

It's so easy for us to profess to stand for the virtues of generosity and kindheartedness. Yet what makes leadership over one's life real is the *doing* of what we believe to be right. This is the highest act of heroism.

I still wear that cap from time to time. To remind me of the man I wish to be. And to remember my bearded friend. At the Dubai airport.

22.

Train with Stronger Teachers

I do spin classes with a very fit instructor. She rides hard, moves fast and pushes all of us in the class to bring on our best.

When I first started taking her early morning classes a few years ago, I couldn't keep up.

I wondered if this was the right sport for me (and felt like quitting).

I couldn't cycle to the rhythm and was unable to stick with the beat. (You'd feel embarrassed just watching my awkward struggle, trust me.)

I looked out of place in a class full of what seemed to be superb athletes, and bumbled through the choreographed moves the polite yet tough instructor asked us to follow.

Yet everything that you now find easy you once found hard, right?

And consistency is the Mother of Mastery, correct?

And persistency breeds the longevity demanded to become legendary.

And so, I swallowed my pride, strapped on those biking shoes and kept on riding—session after sweaty session—in the face of intense embarrassment, immense exhaustion and obvious mediocrity.

Yet as I continued, something unexpectedly wonderful and uncommonly inspirational and maybe even genuinely beautiful (at least to my tired eyes) began to happen.

The classes with this very strong instructor started to feel a little more comfortable. The "game crash" I'd feel at 5 PM on the days I'd spin wasn't as exhausting. I became less goofy on the bike, more fluid in the class and a whole lot braver in that dark, candle-filled room.

As the weeks and months advanced, I cycled faster. I began to ride on beat. And I started to have fun. Serious fun.

All I'm trying to offer you in sharing this private scenario is this: we rise most not when we try to build Rome in a day, but when we steadily make the mini-victories that call on us to remember our lost powers and reclaim our sleeping strengths.

Small, consistent and regular always beats all fire and bravado at the beginning with a gigantic flameout at the end.

Please also know that growth you make in one area brings growth in every other area of your life. Because the way you do one thing sets up the way you'll do everything.

And remember, as well, that remarkable blessings always come to those who show exceptional loyalty to the promises they make to themselves.

The story gets better.

On the sunny Saturday morning that I write this passage for you, while here in TriBeCa in the quietude of a hotel room for thirteen days of writing, far from the demands, complexities and distractions that often invade my life, I went to a spin class run by the same gym that I go to at home.

I wasn't quite sure if I could keep up with the lithe, chiseled and fit instructor who looked like a pop star, or with the people in the room who looked like reigning fitness champions. I felt nervous, unsure and insecure. Like I did when I first experienced the sport.

Then the music started. The teacher pedaled. The candles flickered. And I pushed into gear.

As the class progressed, I began to ride hard, grew stronger as the minutes passed and felt happier as each song played. I danced on the bike earlier this morning, felt my soul soar and made my body sweat—as never before. Thanks to all the training with my superstrong hometown instructor, the class turned out to be a piece of cake. Delightful and enjoyable and fairly effortless, truth be told.

We humans are astounding creatures. Totally designed to adapt, flourish and advance.

You, I and all our brothers and sisters alive today bear a natural capacity to try something new, stay with the process, transcend the challenges and draw closer to mastery.

This journey is how we gain precious glimpses of what we truly are. This is how we play with The Gods of Our Incremental Growth and dance with The Angels of Our Greatest Selves. We must always walk toward the pursuits that frighten us. For there our gifts live.

Let me ask you something: *When was the last time you tried something for the first time?*

And if that time was a long time ago, what are you waiting for?

Who you were—even yesterday—need not limit all you can achieve today. So try something new. That pushes you to grow.

With a really great instructor showing you the way.

23.

A Red Flag Is a Red Flag

For my son's twenty-fifth birthday we planned a long weekend in Los Angeles, a city I love very much.

We'd go watch the Dodgers play. (I don't really like baseball, but my son does, and I really do love my son.)

We'd go for great sushi.

We'd walk the pier in Santa Monica.

We'd get our fortunes told at Venice Beach.

I'd been in LA for a few days before he landed, as I had some media appearances to make and some business meetings to attend.

Shortly after he arrived at the hotel, we headed to a renowned yet simple Italian restaurant. Great vibe. Nice people. Good *cacio e pepe*.

Before our main course arrived, two well-dressed men entered the trattoria and sat right next to us.

I said hello and we all began talking about current events, our favorite cities and observations we've made around the way the world is unfolding.

At one point, as the conversation turned to relationships, one of our new friends said something superbly insightful that I believe is worth sharing with you:

"A red flag is a red flag."

Hmmm.

It took me well over fifty years to learn that one. The hard way.

"When someone shows you who they are, believe them," said the celebrated poet Maya Angelou.

"Fool me once, shame on you. Fool me twice, shame on me," goes the wise saying.

Look, you and I are both good, trusting, decent and considerate people. And because we are good, trusting, decent and considerate people, we think that everyone we deal with in business and within our personal lives will operate in the same way. But that's just not true. A major pitfall of human perception is thinking that the way you see the world is the way everyone sees the world.

And you can get into a whole lot of trouble (that might take you years to get out of) if you fall into the trap of viewing someone the way you want them to be versus being brutally honest with your-self—and seeing them as they are.

Self-deception can cost you a fortune. Lying to yourself because you want to believe you've found the person you've always wanted as an employee, friend or lover can rip out your heart, terrorize your happiness and destroy your peace of mind (the costliest expense of all). Forever. If you're not careful.

Look, I'm an eternal hopefulist. By natural default, I just look for the greatest in people. German poet Johann von Goethe wrote, "Treat people as if they were what they ought to be and you help them become what they are capable of being." I've done my best to stay true to his words for many, many years. People do rise to meet your expectations of them. Often.

Yet not always.

Some people among us are very badly damaged. They have, generally through no fault of their own, been traumatized by harsh events, scarred from terrible tragedies and enormously injured by unexpected treacheries.

They deserve our understanding, our empathy and our good wishes.

Yet this doesn't mean it's in your enlightened self-interest to make them your business partner or your buddy or your spouse. Because people who are hurting badly commonly hurt people badly. And those in severe pain can cause you severe pain.

Such people are pretty much guaranteed to devastate your creativity, suck your productivity and drain you of your energy.

Because they can't stop being themselves. For you to wish that the red flags were green lights is just wishful thinking. And foolishness.

Sure, you can keep seeing their best and loving them. Just do it from *afar*. Enduringly successful human beings trade in the truth. Even when it disappoints them.

24.

The Shortest Chapter
in the History of Creativity?

"How long does a masterwork take?" the apprentice asked the master.

"As long as it takes" was the master's simple reply. "And don't stop until it's magic. Otherwise you might as well not even start it."

Handcrafting your tour de force is far from easy. It will call on you to develop extreme patience with the process, dig deep, pull out your greatness and come face to face with your dragons.

Yet if you continue to completion, you'll become a totally new person. And the confidence, expertise and self-respect gained in making the project will last an entire lifetime.

25.

The Rule-Bender's Hypothesis

Worrying too much about logistics keeps you stuck in logic—a place of great restriction rather than the limitlessness of your unbridled genius. All masterwork is created in a state of wild abandon, not cold reason. Focus on the *what* and the *how* will reveal itself.

Obsessing over perfection can be a major enemy of creativity. And a route to never offering any astoundingly good work to humanity.

Caring too much about what people think about your visionary venture—the one that is flooding you with energy—is an excellent way to ensure you do nothing that matters.

What I'm really suggesting to you is that artistry, ingenuity and your promise require that you step into your renegade nature, launching a rebellion against your intellectual loyalties. Your personal highness calls on you to activate the eccentric within, while you raise your freak flag on the pirate boat that you're meant to captain into the uncharted oceans of your potential.

Become a revolutionary. Launch your campaign against all that is normal and boring and un-fascinating. Initiate your invasion into the foreign recesses within your creative crevasses that the pressures and silly diversions of daily life have placed in lockdown.

Bend the rules that the conventions of your craft taught you were the only path to eminence. Split from the crowd. Stray from the herd. Your reputation as a change-leader, your destiny as a movement-maker, and the joy and ethical power that you seek, depend on this.

Be not average. Ever. When you produce work that makes your soul sing, you'll make our tired world come a little more alive. You'll make it more lovely. And spiritually sensible.

Of course, when you show up like this, you will be misunderstood, unappreciated, criticized and perhaps even reviled for your blatant display of authentic brilliance. When this happens, remember these words of Winston Churchill: "You will never reach your destination if you stop and throw stones at every dog that barks."

When I think of creative superstars, the names of Copernicus, William Shakespeare, Coco Chanel, Walt Disney, Hedy Lamarr, Philippe Starck, Jean-Michel Basquiat and Salvador Dalí appear in my mind.

Inside one of Dalí's workrooms

When I consider dazzlingly inventive luminaries and industry disrupters, I remember ...

... that Miles Davis copied his heroes, Charlie Parker and Duke Ellington, until he developed the chops (and, even more essentially, the confidence) to run his own race and create his own original style as a trumpet player.

... the Alexander McQueen fashion show where supermodel Shalom Harlow walked down the runway until—at the middle—she was sprayed by a series of paint machines that created a mesmerizing design on her dress. The audience roared thunderous applause. The dress is now legendary.

... Johannes Gutenberg's printing press, which radically transformed the world, allowing for the spread of ideas through books. Before this, generating a mass number of publications for many people to read was widely considered to be impossible.

... "The Physical Impossibility of Death in the Mind of Someone Living," that unforgettable magnum opus of English artist Damien Hirst, which shows a violent tiger shark that was killed and then suspended in a tank of formaldehyde. The creature was caught off the coast of Queensland, Australia, by a fisherman who was paid to do so. His only instructions were to catch a shark "big enough to eat you."

All true artistry—inspired work that challenges assumptions, pushes possibilities and gives you and me the permission to become the creative outlaws we secretly long to be—starts with a pioneering perception of reality.

My strongly held belief is this: *Exponential creativity demands abnormality. And requires us to deviate from ordinary company.*

To materialize your primal genius, you absolutely need to see the opportunities that exist on the other side of the shackles of normal.

To dominate your domain and create work that borders on incendiary, you really must commit to respecting your strangeness and steadfastly taking down the traditions that your teachers have taught you are essential to follow for winning.

To reveal your imaginative nobility and perform at the razor's edge of your talent, it becomes a necessity to be an activist against the status quo, operate within another orbit of inventiveness and *bend the rules* that existed before you entered the field to your own mystifying, mysterious and miraculous vision of a vastly more interesting tomorrow.

Makes me think of the words I read after I visited Dalí's bizarre house in the small fishing village of Cadaqués while on a speaking tour in Spain: "I do not understand why, when I ask for grilled lobster in a restaurant, I'm never served a cooked telephone."

Exactly.

The great maestro's paintbrushes

26.

Have Bravery like Swifty

Without a high grade of self-confidence, you'll never have the resolve to translate your silent fantasies into everyday reality. Or the valor required to stay with your most exalted enthusiasms when the going gets messy. And trust me, it will.

Makes me think of Irwin "Swifty" Lazar, the iconic Hollywood super-agent.

When he was just starting out, he was having dinner with a starlet he was hoping to represent.

He met the renowned singer Frank Sinatra while in the restroom and excitedly shared that he was a big fan. The crooner—then at the height of his fame—tried to brush Swifty off. But the young man had chutzpah, which is a Yiddish word for supreme nerve and audacious courage. He persisted in chatting with Sinatra with the intent of really connecting.

Eventually, Sinatra lowered his guard and warmed to the new agent.

"Would you please come to our table and say hello to us?" asked Swifty politely.

"I can't. I want to be with my party," said Sinatra.

"I sure would appreciate it, Mr. Sinatra," Swifty pressed. "It would mean so very much to me. And you'll enjoy meeting my dinner companion."

There was a lengthy pause, and then Sinatra said, "Okay. Give me thirty minutes."

Sure enough, about thirty minutes later—in full public view—the illustrious Frank Sinatra walked past the candlelit tables loaded with celebrities, political leaders and business moguls, straight to where Swifty Lazar was seated.

He tapped his new acquaintance on the shoulder, and with a broad smile said loudly, "Hi Swifty!"

The young man looked up and instantly replied: "Not now, Frank."

Duly impressed, the starlet signed with the agent that very night. And Swifty Lazar went down in history. For his bravery.

27.

A Teacher Called Trauma

Suffering is a school. And trauma is a teacher.

The dominant message we receive from those who show us how the world works is that trauma is the realm of the broken, damaged and defeated.

They say that it only relates to those who have lived in a war zone or experienced a random act of violence or for those who've been sexually abused, beaten up as a kid or suddenly lost someone they loved.

Not true. (And no human is broken; we're all just wounded, to various degrees.)

Part of what I need to share with you as I write this important chapter for you is this …

… *everyone experiences trauma.*

The fact that you're alive means you've gathered trauma, because it's an inevitable result of the journey that we all take as we move from birth to death.

Yes, some of us get hit by life's curveballs harder than others. And so have experienced the tragic events I've listed above. These people have endured what I call in my mentoring methodology "macro-trauma." It's serious. It cuts deep. And it's hard to shake off.

And some other equally good souls among us get off a little

easier—facing "micro-traumas," such as being yelled at by an angry motorist or having a fight with a spouse or losing a business deal to an undeserving competitor.

But the fact remains that no one gets out alive. (Thank you, Jim Morrison.)

Okay. Let's go even deeper.

Trauma is not a dirty word, best to be avoided at stylish cocktail parties and amid polite conversation.

No. Not at all.

Trauma has been my greatest teacher. It has blessed me with the ability to navigate adversity elegantly, helped me to access forgotten creativity that has infused my craft, moved me to become more relatable and humble, and torn down the shield that once protected my tender heart.

I wouldn't be the creator, father, partner, brother and son that I now am without the benefit of the hard times that Fortune has thoughtfully placed on my path. And I promise you that if you exploit your accumulated trauma for your artistic advancement, emotional growth and spiritual liberty, it'll be your greatest academy. *Trauma truly happens in your favor, never for your failure.*

Learning how to do the healing work to unfreeze repressed feelings and process through the stored pain of your ancient wounds will absolutely unleash your most special powers, grandest gifts and wisest self. This profound practice to purify your Heartset is also a sovereign act of self-love. Because you're making yourself into a healthier, happier and freer human.

Unlocking and displacing past trauma isn't a pastime for the weak. It sure isn't flaky, irrelevant and a waste of time. Actually, it's the pursuit of wise warriors. And genuine world-builders. Doing this healing is the finest way to ensure the rest of your life is successful and joyful and peaceful.

Dealing with your buried hurts and dissolving your suppressed emotions is so very practical and spectacularly relevant to a world-class life that soars, serves and knows its highest strength. This is the work that will magnify your prosperity, maximize performance and amplify your optimism. It really will, even if it seems like it won't.

Deep emotional clearing practice will make you far more creative, because trauma deforms the brain and working through your ancient wounding optimizes your cognition. Interesting, right? The stress of difficult events pushed down into your subconscious causes major perceptive blocks, stunts the full release of neurotransmitters (such as dopamine and serotonin) that are essential to peak artistry, and actually reduces the ideal connection between the right and left hemispheres of your brain. Release the past pain, anger, sadness, guilt, shame and regret that you've been carrying like an albatross around your neck and you'll begin to awaken the possibility that was previously hidden from your view.

Heartset healing will also guarantee that you unleash your fullest vitality. Holding on to trauma consumes a great deal of energy and natural inspiration. One of the results of ignoring what I call "accumulated scarring" is that you pretty much live in a state of limbic hijack, when the survival brain of the limbic system monopolizes your thinking and puts you into "fight, flight or freeze" mode. You lose the ability to rationally manage any threat (real or perceived) as your prefrontal cortex (the seat of higher thinking) is taken over by the amygdala, the less evolved and more primitive part of your brain.

Stress hormones such as adrenaline and cortisol are released and emotions such as fear, anxiety and anger are ignited. Note that the more severe the wounding of the past, the more intense will be the present-day response when an old wound is activated. You can always tell the size of your trauma (or someone else's) by the degree of the overreaction. If it's hysterical, it's historical.

The spouse who rages over spilled milk has regressed to an earlier age and is living out the smothered pain of the past. The boss who abuses employees and sabotages business associates is simply revealing the weight of their own baggage. The motorist who stops their car and threatens a fistfight because they think you cut them off is being driven by the Field of Hurt I mentioned earlier, made up of all the invisible collected trauma they allowed to remain at their core.

I once sat next to a senior executive on an airplane who asked me to move from my assigned seat because he said he preferred it. When I said I'd like to stay where I was, he began kicking my briefcase. And promised he'd "take care of me" when we landed. Such is the result of failing to work through and let go of emotional injury. Healing your Heartset wounds will ensure that you no longer lash out at people who did not mistreat you. And bleed on people who did not cut you.

Working through your micro-trauma and any macro-trauma will also increase the quality of your health beautifully. Trauma and the daily stress response it hardwires into your system make crisis-oriented living your default, which in turn reduces your immunity and increases inflammation, making you more susceptible to life-threatening conditions such as diabetes, heart attack, stroke and cancer. Process through your emotional pain and you restructure the architecture of your Heartset to produce less toxicity and more of the wonderful neurochemistry that will improve your physicality. And extend your longevity.

As you optimize your emotional life, you'll see a clear elevation of your happiness, gratefulness and capacity to *feel* versus intellectualize the miracles of life. Trauma causes a human being to disassociate from their body and run their days as an intellectual machine. Before I started doing this healing work myself, I'd *think* about the spectacle of a sunrise and *reason* about the gorgeousness of a piece of art rather than *feel* it—and *inhabit* it. Re-engaging your Heartset and reactivating your feelings, I promise you, is a completely different way of existing.

You begin to use your mind for those pursuits that the mind is good for. And you open your *heart* and fully experience the pleasure of everything else in your life.

What I'm really suggesting is that frozen trauma causes a human being to shut down intimacy with their emotional aliveness and retreat inside their head. This is done out of protection. We flee from our feelings as a trauma response because we don't wish to relive old pain when it is freshly triggered by a current event.

So we set up a series of escapes and detours designed to avoid our emotions, such as overwork or drugs or too much alcohol. Or online addictions and social media distractions. We begin to live our lives as attention seekers versus magic workers. And we wonder why we never feel the intense happiness we hear is part of the human path.

Many people, on encountering difficulty or tragedy, end up with PTS (Post-Traumatic Stress). Yet if we exercise our wisdom and make difficult choices, each of us has the ability to exploit setbacks for the benefit of personal transformation. Struggle can actually be used for PTG: Post-Traumatic Growth. Just look at the greatest men and women of the world. The Nelson Mandelas and the Mother Teresas and the Mahatma Gandhis and the MLKs. Each of these advanced souls had one thing in common: they suffered far more than what is ordinary, but rather than allowing the hardship to tear them apart, they leveraged it to remake them. To build them up. To remember their highest moral virtue and their greatest spiritual merits. To convert devastating pain into unusual power.

I'll walk you through tactics and tools to free trapped emotions, so you can liberate your greatness and activate the unlimited genius of your heart, in an upcoming chapter.

For now, simply remember that trauma—wisely used—can become the doorway into your most authentic, creative and heroic self. So see it as a teacher. Please.

28.

The People Builder's Mantra

A true story . . .

There was once a café that had a very good manager running the shop.

. . . She really cared about her customers.

. . . She greeted everyone she met with cheerfulness and politeness.

. . . She ensured that the goods on offer were the best in the community, always priced fairly, and that her employees were consistently friendly.

The manager's favorite customer was a woman who had been a schoolteacher. In her eighties, she always showed up at the café perfectly attired and looking exceedingly graceful.

Each morning she visited the café, holding the hand of an elderly gentleman, her husband. Whom she appeared to love very, very much.

Together they would carefully move through the coffee shop and make their way to the counter, always ordering the same thing: two cups of coffee and one small pastry, with two forks so they could share it.

Then they would travel to their usual table. And have a conversation. Because . . .

. . . Business is a conversation. Lose the conversation with your teammates, customers and suppliers and you'll lose your business.

... A splendid home life is a conversation. Neglect this because you're constantly playing with your devices or watching too much television or working all the time and you'll likely lose your family.

... And being an everyday hero begins with having a conversation with yourself, about who you wish to be and what you promise to do for the world. Lose the conversation with your finest you and you'll lose the intimacy with your authenticity.

So back to the coffee shop.

One day it occurred to the manager that her favorite client was no longer showing up at the café. She grew quite worried. Because she really cared.

A few weeks later she saw the lady standing in line at a bank. But the woman no longer looked impeccably dressed or remarkably relaxed.

No.

Instead, she now appeared disheveled. And confused. And frightened.

"What's wrong?" asked the manager.

"It's my husband. He suffered a massive stroke a few weeks ago. He died. I don't know what to do. I don't know where to go. I don't know if I can make it."

The manager paused. And then spoke in a low, gentle voice.

"Why don't you come back to the café? And have a good cup of coffee. I know it'll make you feel better."

"But who would I drink it with?" asked the woman, with a tremor in her voice.

"I'll drink it with you," said the manager. "It would be my pleasure."

So the two human beings—in a world in glaring need of greater humanity—walked back to the coffee shop, where the customer ordered her usual: two cups of coffee, one pastry and two forks.

And those two people had a conversation.

Maya Angelou once wrote this piece of wisdom: "People may

forget what you say and people may forget what you do. But no one will ever forget how you made them feel."

So build people up. Never tear others down.

Help anyone in need. If you don't have something good to say to someone, don't say it. Treat all with courtesy and kindness. I know that seems old school, but that was such a good school in so many ways.

Leaving everyone you meet better than you found them and feeling bigger than when they first met you is just a fantastic way to roll. And a good mantra to be guided by.

29.

The 7 Threats to World-Class

I'm about to walk you through the seven primary vulnerabilities that cause potentially legendary creators, leaders, entrepreneurs, athletes and movement-makers *not* to realize their promise. This is one of the most valuable chapters in this book.

The starting point is the following maxim: *The real aim of mastery is not reaching legendary but sustaining legendary.*

The main goal of a genuine everyday hero isn't just to create the conditions that take them to their loftiest aspirations. It's to *maintain* —and, of course, improve—that ideal state, as the remainder of your days unfold.

Fantastic if you do what it takes to arrive at world-class. The major focus, however, needs to be on *remaining* there. What makes an icon is the symmetry of optimized mastery and ironclad *longevity*. Few elements make you more undefeatable and of use to many than staying at the top of your field longer than any of your peers.

So how can you insulate the pre-eminence you generate so that it endures? Simple: become acutely aware of *The 7 Threats to World-Class*. And with this new awareness of the pitfalls you'll face, you can actively choose to fortify yourself against them.

Have a look at this learning framework:

THE 7 THREATS TO WORLD-CLASS

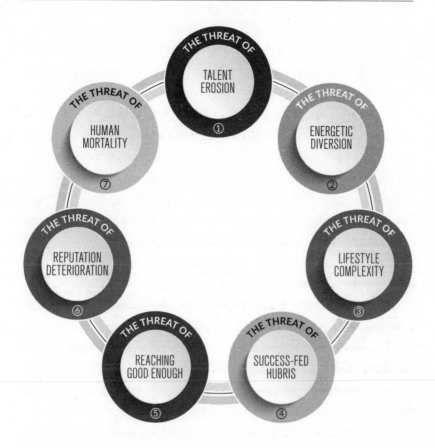

Based on more than a quarter of a century helping many of the world's top entrepreneurs, financiers, professional athletes and film stars not only rise to best-of-breed but also keep their position at the top, I've deconstructed the dangers you'll face on your ascent to domain dominance into the following seven threats:

Threat #1: The Threat of Talent Erosion

Oh my, this one is such a destroyer of outright genius. Just think of the musical giant who has a number one worldwide blockbuster or the actor who wins an Oscar. Amazing that they accomplished this. But what mostly happens—even though they reached this pinnacle—is that the skills that got them there begin to atrophy. The intensity of performance and output that getting to Best in World required leaves them exhausted. All the limelight, applause and adulation leaves them depleted—and often craving to "get away from it all."

Many superstars vanish from public view (sometimes for *years*) at the height of their powers. They stop caring about upgrading their craft. They no longer put in the daily practice time. They lose the fire to keep playing out on the jagged edges of their most luminous gifts and taking their craft into uncharted heavens. Because of what the intense and demanding journey to world-class, as well as the experience of superstardom, has drained out of them.

Threat #2: The Threat of Energetic Diversion

Fame, fortune and massive influence bring with them other unexpected dangers that you'd be wise to protect yourself against well in advance of reaching these conditions. (When I work one-on-one with a high-profile client, or in my *Circle of Legends* online mentoring curriculum, I provide a template that allows the leader to work through their "Threats and Vulnerabilities" when it comes to operating at world-class and then their "Pivots and Protections." I give you full access to this worksheet at the end of the chapter, so you get to do this powerful exercise yourself.)

As you travel in the stratosphere of rare air, you'll face enthusiastic attacks from jealous critics and angry trolls who were activated by seeing you soar to such heights. Your success triggers their pain at seeing their potential unfulfilled. And excites their self-loathing on not delivering on their own dreams. If you're not careful, these people will steal your energy.

As well, as you ascend, you'll receive exponentially more invitations to pursue amazing opportunities (that have nothing to do with your sweet spot). You'll attract new friends who want to hang with you just because it's cool to be seen with you. You might face lawsuits from business partners who want your money, and relationship hassles arising from the fact you spent so much time consumed with making your mesmerizing ambitions real that you neglected other parts of your life.

I've seen all of this happen with many of my clients. So I'm telling you the way it is. With all of this to deal with, just imagine what happens to the creative, productive and performance energy that caused the greatness to happen? Please think through how you will manage all of this far ahead of reaching the summits of your private Mount Everests.

Threat #3: The Threat of Lifestyle Complexity

Related to Threat #2 are the layers of complication that any world-class producer must face when it comes to their lifestyle. You see, when a superstar is just starting out as an anonymous performer, there is often an exceptional purity of focus. The startup entrepreneur is pretty much only concentrated on scaling their business. The pro athlete—not yet a champion—spends their days pretty much only training, eating, receiving coaching and sleeping. The brilliant musical artist—before virtuosity and adulation hit—is living in a spartan studio apartment, eating ramen noodles and working in the studio all night, generating the magic that will eventually entertain millions.

Yet once the company becomes a publicly traded unicorn (making the founder a multibillionaire) and the athlete's abilities make them an icon and the musician's gifts make them a global sensation, *everything* gets complex. The big money flowing often goes to buy homes, cars, private jet travel and an entourage of managers, security and other staff (each of whom has to be paid)—all based on the *false* assumption that the success they are experiencing will last many years.

113

It rarely does—leaving many once-successful people bankrupt.

I must repeat this one more time because it is so extremely important: one of the largest of all snares of superstardom is the belief that "once successful, always successful." So many A-Listers reach the apex and think that because they are at the top they somehow cannot ever be removed from the top. They fall into the psychological trap of believing that because they are winning now, they will always be winning; because they are selling a ton of albums, they will always sell a lot of albums; because they are generating a ton of income, they will always make a lot of income. So they stop improving, stop saving, stop getting up early, stop exercising and stop running their lives at excellence. This generally leads to disaster.

Threat #4: The Threat of Success-Fed Hubris

Perhaps the most common mistake I see some of the luminaries I work with make is becoming arrogant. *Gross inflation of the human ego is the largest occupational hazard of the world-class leader, whether they operate in business, sports, the arts and sciences, or politics.*

It seems to me that with all the fortune, elite achievement and people telling you that you walk on water, the ego gets fed to the point of hubris. "Hubris" is defined as excessive pride and exaggerated confidence. The mistake most successful companies suffer from is also descending into hubris. They forget that their customers are their real bosses and discount the fact that their competition could make them irrelevant *in an instant*—if they stop innovating, delivering extreme benefit and delighting the people who keep them in business; if they become more concerned with having an office tower named after their enterprise than enriching their clients.

Same thing can happen to titleholders and athletic champions. They fall in love with their win and think that because champagne was poured over their heads on the night of their monumental victory, next year's championship ring is already on their pinky finger.

114

They start missing practices, being rude to their fans, picking fights with peers, drinking too much, eating too much, gambling too much and failing to remain focused on advancing the genius that won them the crown. They lose what I call in my mentoring curriculum "the blue-collar mindset" and the white-belt mentality that made them masters. (I think of the captain of an NBA championship-winning team as I write this. Rather than taking the summer off, as is standard in the game, he showed up—*the day after his triumph*—at 5 AM to start practice. And begin the process of becoming even better.)

Threat #5: The Threat of Reaching Good Enough

So, to get to the top, you pretty much have to do what pretty much no one's doing. (Remember my brain tattoo: *To have what only 5% of the population have, you must be willing to do what 95% of the population is unwilling to do.*) Extremely hard work (an unforgettable work ethic beats natural talent every day of the week), tons of sacrifices (which really don't feel like sacrifices because you love what you do so much), installing exceptional habits, dealing with detractors and constantly having to find solutions to problems are the fees you must pay to gain admission into the very quiet (and mostly empty) halls of domain dominance.

Sure, the rewards make it *totally* worth it. And—absolutely— what the journey to world-class and living your heroic ideals *make you into as a human being* is a treasure more valuable than all the jewels in a diamond mine. Yet another major threat you'll face when you near the peak of success is that you'll start to coast. Guaranteed you'll experience this phenomenon. You've accomplished more than anyone you know. You've achieved more breathtaking results than even you thought you would. You're pretty much untouchable in terms of your craft, income, lifestyle and impact. A huge part of you will be attracted to simply enjoying the fruits of your labor. You'll want to play more golf or travel for most of the year or accept the level of performance you're at. You may even allow the deadly thought of retirement into your energetic orbit. (Please don't ever retire, I plead with you. It will age you and dim your bright light.)

Look, if you think and feel like this at the height of your powers, fine by me. It's your life. And one path isn't any better—in truth— than another. But accepting good enough won't keep you in the rare air of the grandmaster. Which means there's just no way you'll ever reach *legendary*. Just saying.

Threat #6: The Threat of Reputation Deterioration

When you reach the zenith of your field, people will try to take you down. Jealous competitors see a target on your back, detractors who are angry because you've done what they couldn't do will manufacture reasons to criticize you and attackers will come out of the woodwork. Be prepared for this. And know this isn't happening because you've done something wrong. *It's a sign that you've done everything right.* Just be aware there's a strong chance that malicious people with unhealthy agendas will try to degrade your hard-earned reputation and cancel your uneasily won good name.

I caution you to plan for this threat so you can put excellent protections in place. Because should you lose your reputation, you've lost one of your foremost assets. The other scenario to consider here is the case where, because of all your success, your ego consumes your better judgement and you actually do something foolish. That destroys your high standing.

Again, just think through all this so you can avoid these pitfalls that I've personally witnessed so many supreme performers fall into.

Threat #7: The Threat of Human Mortality

We're all going to die. *The key is to postpone your demise for as long as possible.* Just imagine applying the latest scientific breakthroughs on life extension along with time-tested habits such as early morning exercise, daily meditation, cold exposure, sauna and light therapy, forest bathing, intermittent fasting, therapeutic massage, acupuncture and nutritional supplementation to fireproof your health so that—via the transformational power of epigenetics—you recalibrate your longevity, giving you many, many, many more years to upgrade your mastery, scale your wealth, serve society and enjoy the personal rewards you've earned on your rise to—and lifetime at—monumental success.

All right. There you have them: the primary dangers to sustained domain dominance. I invite you to re-read *The 7 Threats to World-Class* and then deconstruct the framework as it applies to you. In my own strategy sessions, I often think through how I wish things to play out fifty years ahead. Then I reverse engineer it all—in meticulous detail on whiteboards—back to today.

You can access the worksheet my clients find so valuable here: TheEverydayHeroManifesto.com/7ThreatsWorksheet

I hope this helps you protect and amplify your superstardom. For a lifetime.

30.

Expect Ungrateful

Please don't judge me as cynical. But I've mentally conditioned myself to expect ungrateful.

Here's what I mean.

In Norman Vincent Peale's positive thinking classic called, well, *The Power of Positive Thinking*, this ceaselessly optimistic minister encourages us to "expect ingratitude."

As I understand it, his point is that most people will never truly appreciate your goodness and gentleness. It's just not generally human nature (at this stage of our species' evolution). So why lose peace of mind and valuable creative energy hoping to receive it?

I'll put it another way: *Avoid becoming an injustice collector*. That way of seeing the world just beats you down. And rips you up.

Accept the fact that the majority of people concentrate on what they *didn't* get versus all you gave and remember what you *didn't* do for them rather than the wealth of generosity you showered upon them.

And remember that someone else's lack of appreciation or good manners or grace or compassion or sense of fairness really has *nothing to do with you* and everything to do with them. People treat other people the way they treat themselves. So why make it about you?

Just stay true to your own moral instincts. Display the virtues of positivity, honesty, goodwill, excellence, humility, forgiveness and respect to all, with a clear understanding that very few will ever acknowledge your integrity and stainless character.

Do good anyhow.

31.

That Time I Was Left Alone at the Top of a Mountain

I can't make up some of the things that have happened in my life.

You may laugh at me when I share this one with you, yet that's cool with me if my story serves your ascension into your highest mode of operating.

And so ...

... When I was in my forties, I had the idea of becoming a professional ski instructor. I've always loved the mountains and the thought of skiing down them with some skill really spoke to me.

To breathe some life into this ambition, I enrolled in weekly classes with a wonderful mentor and worked enormously hard to increase my ability. The progress was slow, yet I steadily made improvement.

After two years of lessons, I spent a freezing week in the certification class on the slopes—and received my level one professional ski instructor qualification, which allowed me to teach beginning students. I still recall the day I went to collect my ski pro uniform—that blue jacket, those black snow pants! I brought my beloved children into the building with me. And as we left with my uniform in hand, I began to dance. Yes, I *danced*.

Although I still had a heavy international speaking schedule, I secured a job at our local ski resort, at minimum wage. And every few days, when I wasn't on an airplane, I'd rise at 4 AM, drive the two-hour drive (often in snowstorms) and help little kids learn to ski. It was a marvelous time of my life.

The day I collected my ski instructor uniform

Around that time, I decided to take a solo trip abroad so I could develop the technique of skiing big mountains. So I packed up my gear, got on a flight and flew to a faraway place with towering peaks, higher than I'd ever seen.

Each morning I'd hop onto a bus with chains on its tires that would wind its way through tiny villages and then up the thin and treacherous ice-covered road that led to the base of a vast mountain.

Each evening, after a nap, I'd quietly work on the book I was writing (it was *The Leader Who Had No Title*) and then, in solitude, cook a simple meal made of fresh ingredients in my austere kitchen, eating what I'd made while sitting on a weather-beaten chair outside under the stars.

After about a week, a friend I'd made invited me to heli-ski with him. If you're not familiar with the term, it means pretty much what it says: you climb into a helicopter and then fly over a bunch of summits until you arrive at the top of the mountain you're going to ski down. It's a pursuit reserved for experts. And by making the wrong move, one could easily die.

On the designated day, the helicopter lifted off in exquisite sunshine and amid fantastically blue skies. As we passed mountain after mountain, my heartbeat started to quicken. Droplets of sweat formed under my helmet and my goggles started to fog up. The aircraft landed at the absolute highest point of a colossally high peak. Four other skiers and I jumped out into the fresh snow. Then the helicopter flew away.

You won't believe what happened next ...

... The other skiers were total pros. And it was assumed that I was one as well. I was far too proud to reveal my fear and much too embarrassed to explain my relative inability. Here's the thing: thanks to my training at my local hill (yes, it was far more a hill than a mountain), I was a fairly skilled skier on regular snow. But skiing on the soft, billowy *powder* snow that you will find on giant mountains is a completely different game. It's similar to the difference between being a good swimmer in your community pool and navigating the ocean on intense endurance swims. And I'd never really skied under these kinds of conditions. Ever.

The guide went first—to ensure all was safe and to protect us against avalanches.

Next went my friend and his wife, both clearly superb at the sport. I heard them hooting with childlike glee as they made fresh tracks in the virgin snow.

Then a young but experienced ski pro took off. He must have been thirty. The way he skied made me feel like I was ninety.

I was left *completely alone*. On the top of a staggeringly tall mountain. Never having skied powder. I prayed for my life. Thought of my kids. And then wiped the buckets of sweat from my shiny forehead.

Here's the photo taken just before everyone else went down ahead of me, so you'll have even the smallest sense of my experience.

Life, I've discovered, sometimes (always) sends you scenarios perfectly designed to teach you the lessons you most need to learn to get to the next grade of your growth. Remember what I shared earlier about things never unfolding for your failure and everything always happening in your favor (even when it doesn't seem that way)?

I've also learned that: *We are most alive when we are closest to our fears.* Confronted with our doubt that we can get through a difficulty, we are pushed to own gifts we never knew we had. And once we are introduced to these special powers, we can choose to associate with them for the remainder of our days. And thereby eventually know the fullness of our human greatness.

And so ...

... I leaned into my terror and inched ahead, with legs shaking like teacups during an earthquake and a mouth drier than the Empty Quarter of the Arabian Peninsula.

I kid you not, I regressed *into the snowplow*, the first position of the starting skier. It just made me feel more secure.

What unfolded next was a hot mess. A middle-aged man skiing down an immense mountain, curled over my skis, mostly off balance and screaming for my mommy, at the top of my lungs.

(Okay, the part about screaming for my mommy isn't true; *everything* else is. I promise.)

Of course, I eventually made it to safety.

My companions were aghast. Yet they spoke no words. Their empathy for my calamity screamed so much louder.

On the helicopter flight back to the terminal, I reflected on the experience. I felt happy that I'd said yes to it. *Because real failure lies in not even trying.* And, as human beings, we become far stronger when we venture out onto the tough runs rather than coast along on the easy slopes. Sure, unchallenging trails appear to be so much safer. Yet they end up being far more dangerous. Because they smother the boldness, aliveness and bigness that is all we truly are.

I was offered an opportunity. I gave it my best. I looked foolish. I grew in wisdom, toughness and acumen. And I made it back to my apartment.

Just in time for dinner under the stars.

32.

The Peak Productivity
Strategies Pyramid

Full disclosure: this is a chapter for heavyweights or grandmasters-in-the-making only. If you are not interested in being one, no sweat—simply go ahead to the next chapter. But if you are—bravo, please roll up your sleeves, turn up your attention and fully embrace what you're about to learn. Because it's exceedingly valuable.

The learning framework I'm about to share will bring you superb tactical benefit as you electrify the productivity that will make your mark on history.

In this time of crushing digital addiction, unyielding superficial interruption and massive attraction to online amusements that don't matter, it has never been more essential to understand how industry titans and artistic champions shield their virtuosity so they become consistent producers of masterworks.

It's challenging enough to shift from performing fake work to real work. You now know how important it is not to confuse being busy with being productive. It's even harder to regularly send work into the field that represents genius-tier quality. And to ensure this keeps happening for you, decade after decade. (I call this practice being "a multiple-masterwork producer" and it's a wise standard to honor.)

Before I walk you through the system, I wish to provide some context and mention The Triad of Productivity Principles.

Principle #1: Cognitive Bandwidth Deserves a Fortress around It

"Cognitive bandwidth" is a term used by Princeton psychologist Eldar Shafir to describe the limited amount of attention the human brain has available each day. His research has found that people dealing with poverty, for example, experience "tunneling" such that their worries and stress consume much of their cognitive power, leaving little for other tasks. This, in turn, causes them to access less of their native intellectual brilliance and connect with lower amounts of their natural ingenuity (to solve problems, seize opportunities and materialize the wholeness of their inherent productivity that would raise them into greater prosperity). Worries, crisis and tragedy, as well as spending our concentration on digital escapism, drain our cognitive bandwidth, leaving us with less focus and genius to accomplish amazing feats.

Principle #2: Attention Residue Must Be Managed for Mastery

Closely related to cognitive bandwidth is the phenomenon of "attention residue" first advanced by Sophie Leroy, a business school professor at the University of Minnesota. Essentially, attention residue speaks to the molecules of your focus that you leave on one activity when you shift to another one. Every single move you make carries a creative cost with it. People who are constantly checking their devices, for example, soon suffer from digital dementia because each time they check for a message or look for a like, they leave a fraction of their valuable cognitive bandwidth on that activity. Do this daily (as many do) and you'll be installing Fragmented Attention Disorder as your general way of being. You'll never get anything sensational done.

Principle #3: Productive Exhaustion Requires Scheduled Renewal

"Productive exhaustion" is a phrase from my coaching curriculum that explains what happens when an advanced performer works intensely for long periods of time. Specifically, as you elevate your productivity and the expertise you bring to your arena, you will regularly experience cycles of vigorous intellectual, emotional, physical and spiritual fatigue. This weariness is not a marker that there's something wrong, but a signal that you're doing everything right. When you're showing up with incendiary passion and fiery commitment to produce nothing less than masterwork, you'll often be left depleted because you are fully using your capacities, gifts and primal assets. This will cause productive exhaustion. The solution? Regularly scheduled rest and refueling cycles. "A special ability means a heavy expenditure of energy in a particular direction, with a consequent drain from some other side of life," wrote the fabled psychologist Carl Jung.

Okay, let's study *The Peak Productivity Strategies Pyramid* together.

THE PEAK PRODUCTIVITY STRATEGIES PYRAMID

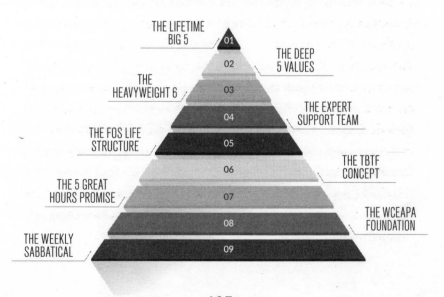

Strategy #1: The Lifetime Big 5

Many years ago, on one of my first trips to the South Africa that I so love, my client organized a safari for me. The guide who spent the day with us spoke of "The Big 5," the most powerful animals of all African wildlife. They are the lion, leopard, buffalo, rhino and elephant.

That evening, after an unforgettable day on the savannah, I pulled out my journal to download and deconstruct the day I'd been blessed to experience. I then asked myself this transformational question: *"What are my Big 5?"* In other words, what are the top five priorities that I needed to commit to spending the rest of my life hunting down.

I've lived under these five primary beacons since that evening and The Lifetime Big 5 idea has elevated my productivity enormously since then. Clarity breeds mastery, right? You'll never hit high-value targets that you don't even know about. Recording the five central aims to which you'll devote the remainder of your days will bring extreme purity of focus to your hours, days, weeks, months, quarters and years—insulating your cognitive bandwidth as well as promoting exceptional economy of your energy.

The foundation of exceptionalism is harnessing your genius around only a few things—so you get strikingly good at them. I've always loved the following advice of Thomas Edison, the standout inventor:

> You do something all day long, don't you? Everyone does. If you get up at seven o'clock and go to bed at eleven, you have put in sixteen good hours, and it is certain with most people that they have been doing something all the time. They have been either walking, or reading, or writing, or thinking. The only trouble is that they do it about a great many things and I do it about one. If they took the time in question and applied it in one direction, to one object, they would succeed.

Strategy #2: The Deep 5 Values

I know it seems obvious, but your most closely cherished values define what you most value. And knowing them intimately is completely essential to an existence of maximum authenticity and elite productivity. Betraying what your spirit wants you to stand for creates what I call an "integrity gap," because the way your worldly self is operating is inconsistent with how the heroic part of you wishes to behave. This major misalignment absorbs vast amounts of energy and creativity, which could be used to accomplish world-class results. Because your wisdom watches you not honoring the true you.

The key here is to become ultra-aware of your Deep 5 Values so you stay loyal to them. You never want to lead someone else's life—and arrive at your last day only to realize that you spent your finest hours on pursuits that were meaningless to you.

With the wish that it helps you, I'll share that my own Deep 5 Values are personal mastery, dedication to family, total craft artistry, the experience of ongoing beauty and humble service to society.

Strategy #3: The Heavyweight 6

Most of the exponential productivity gains and related income, lifestyle and spiritual growth of my clients comes through their near-religious practice of a handful of habits I've encouraged them to implement. I call these six regimes "The SOPs of AWC: The Standard Operating Procedures of Absolute World-Class." Train on these to the point of automaticity (where they become easier to do than not to do) and you'll receive what I call a "GCA: Gargantuan Competitive Advantage" that very few peers will ever be able to match. Extraordinary performance really is fairly easy to realize because so few are doing the things that extraordinary performance requires. There's just *not* a lot of competition in the rare air of virtuosity. Yes, the lower ground is very crowded. But there aren't many human beings inhabiting the stratosphere of their highest genius. Because so few among us know what to do—and then execute regularly with near-flawless precision around what needs to be done—to get there.

Here are the six daily routines that have given the luminaries I mentor the greatest productive results:

1. Joining The 5 AM Club and spending a Victory Hour upgrading your Mindset, purifying your Heartset, optimizing your Healthset and escalating your Soulset. The way you start your day really does have an outsized impact on each of the remaining hours. Begin your mornings with sixty minutes of self-strengthening and you'll experience consistently positive, prolific and beautiful days. And as the Spartan warriors used to say, "Sweat more in training and you'll bleed less in war."

2. Writing for at least ten minutes every day in a gratitude journal so as to crowd out the negativity bias of the human brain and make soaring thankfulness your automatic default. One of the most powerful interventions science confirms will make us not only more effective but happier is the daily Three Good Things exercise, where you simply note three small wins or uplifting experiences each evening. As Martin Seligman, the father of positive psychology, wrote in his book *Flourish*:

> For sound evolutionary reasons, most of us are not nearly as good at dwelling on good events as we are at analyzing bad events. Those of our ancestors who spent a lot of time basking in the sunshine of good events when they should have been preparing for disaster did not survive the Ice Age. So to overcome our brain's natural catastrophic bent, we need to work on and practice this skill of thinking about what went well.

3. Doing The Second Wind Workout (2WW)—ideally, a nature walk—that I mentioned in the chapter "Guard Good Health like a

Pro Athlete." I personally find that my life works a whole lot better when I train myself to be a whole lot fitter. And doing two fitness sessions a day will deliver this benefit to you.

4. Running The 60 Minute Student Regime, which means that you do not go to sleep unless you've spent *at least* an hour during the day immersed in study, such as reading a book that promotes your leadership growth, listening to an audiobook on relationship-building or empire-making, or taking an online course that enriches your domain knowledge so you have the ability to produce rich streams of reward for the customers you serve.

5. The 90/90/1 Rule, which is a habit I originally set up to help my mastermind participants block out the relentless distractions they were facing each morning. Essentially, for the next ninety days, create an ironclad and uninterruptible ritual such that the first ninety minutes of your work morning is monomaniacally focused on your single finest opportunity to lead your field. You never want to deploy your most valuable hours on least valuable activities.

6. The Weekly Design System, which is a methodology I developed to ensure that my coaching clients not only generate extreme gains in their productivity but also maintain a terrifically balanced life. Life balance is *not* a myth. I'll teach you the entire system in a coming chapter and I can confirm that the process will be a total game-changer for you. For now, simply know that the tasks that you schedule are the tasks that get done. And that consistently scheduling prodigy-grade weeks is a potent gateway into sustained superstardom. And a life of superb health, generous love and limitless joyfulness. If you would like to watch a video where I teach the entire procedure, visit TheEverydayHeroManifesto.com/WeeklyDesignSystem

Strategy #4: The Expert Support Team

Another early practice when I start a mentorship engagement with a CEO or an entrepreneurial heavyweight is to set up a team of expert counselors to ensure they transcend past victories and swiftly execute on the mission they have brought me in to help them achieve. This strategy is similar to the team enlisted to support a world-champion professional athlete. It's impossible to reach mastery-level performance alone.

Most top athletes invest in a mindset coach to keep their thinking at its best, a physical therapist to keep them injury-free, a nutritionist to calibrate their diet and supplementation plan, and a strategist to help them improve their play.

At the very least, I recommend that—budget permitting—you find the finest personal trainer you can to help you get into the strongest fitness you've ever been in. Yes, this will cost you money, and I learned this from Warren Buffett—while the average performers get stuck on the cost of something, superproducers focus on the return on investment that will flow from the spending. Going for what's cheapest will turn out to be very expensive. Or as Aldo Gucci said sagely: "Quality is remembered long after price is forgotten."

Engaging a superb personal trainer to push you to get über-healthy will completely transform your creativity, artistry and impact, along with dramatically increasing your income because you'll be more energetic, resilient and inspired. You'll never work out as hard alone as you will with a trainer, keeping you accountable. Working with a deeply skilled fitness coach has allowed me to experience the energy and good health to write my books, travel illness-free globally for decades and do all the things I love to do with my family (while still having time for myself).

I also instruct my clients to find a skilled massage therapist so they can run The 2 Massage Protocol by receiving two ninety-minute massages each week (which boosts their positivity enormously, allows them to get up at 5 AM more easily and extends their lifespan considerably). Along with all of this, we set them up with a premier psychotherapist so the repressed emotional baggage I mentioned in the piece on trauma no longer silently sucks their productivity, and we get clients attending a functional medicine clinic for biohacking so that they reverse aging and dissolve cognitive decline. Finally, we ensure clients work monthly with a spiritual counselor to access their highest self. Again, you can't get to Best in World on your own. Set up your support team of ultra-experts as soon as you can.

Strategy #5: The Forced Optimization Strategy (FOS) Life Structure

Another leading-edge life regime that will rapidly accelerate your productivity, income and impact is The Forced Optimization Strategy. One of the real reasons we don't execute on our intentions, commitments and deliverables is that it's just too easy not to, right? Fail to rise at 5 AM and do your morning run and you generally only have your unhappy conscience to deal with. Miss a session that you've scheduled to analyze your finances or increase your career performance or get the massage that will replenish your diminished reserves and mostly there's not much of a backlash. And so we get sloppy around our disciplines. And then find some feeble excuse for our failure to keep our promises (yes—of course—this happens to me at times, too).

The antidote to this weakness? *Force the optimization* of the routine that you want to integrate into your lifestyle. Just go ahead and FOS it. For example, let's say you desire to be in the best physical condition of your life ninety days from now. Completely possible. For sure. And let's say you want to get to this result via getting up at daybreak on weekdays and installing the habit of an intense morning workout so you consistently enjoy marvelous days. Most people will stop after a week. Maybe they'll last two. Yet by hiring an excellent personal trainer to show up at your home or at your gym (even if only twice a week) for three months, you *force the optimization* of the new routine. Because you now have some skin in the game by investing your hard-earned money. And because this human being will be at your front door at the time you've agreed, or at the exercise studio as scheduled.

Or let's say you wish to lock and load on my 2 Massage Protocol, then find the best masseuse in your community and pay for two sessions each week for the next quarter. Now you'll just have to go because you've booked the meetings and paid the fees. You've *forced* the optimization of the habit into your life.

Implement The FOS Life Structure across multiple areas of your world and you'll quickly and enduringly translate your current good intentions to lead an extraordinary life into the daily results that make glory real.

Strategy #6: The Tight Bubble of Total Focus (TBTF) Concept

This is another remarkably valuable mental construct to set yourself up for peerless productivity. This method will organize your workdays so that you defeat the war against distractions, interruptions and getting caught up in trivial pursuits. Celebrated artists, mighty billionaires, excellent athletes and world-champion scientists all have the same allotment of twenty-four hours each day as you and I. Yet *the way they interact with these hours* is diametrically different from how the majority manage themselves.

The TBTF Concept encourages you to build a metaphorical wall around what I call in my work "The 5 Assets of Genius." These are: your mental focus, your physical energy, your personal willpower, your daily time and your primal gifts.

Using the TBTF Concept, you fashion your entire professional life so as to work within a tight bubble of extreme focus, with a porous barrier that allows in only influences that protect your positivity, fuel your craft, nourish your talent and elevate your public service. Negative stimuli such as superficial social media influencers, videos of people performing silly tricks or awkward dances, the mainstream news, toxic people attempting to pour cold water on your bright flame, uninvited digital messages, endless notifications mostly about nothing, and pretty much any activity that doesn't allow you to make astronomical progress on your Lifetime Big 5 do not get to cross the barrier. A giant key to exponential productivity is battleproofing your focus. This powerful strategy helps you do it.

You'll become *fanatically* and *prodigiously* focused around the few major priorities that will allow you to make the whispers of your heart, the longings of your wisdom and the callings of your everyday heroism come true—before this precious window of opportunity closes (and it will). Once inside this figurative work pocket, your TBTF will make sure things that don't matter *never* begin to matter.

Here's the real point to integrate at the level of felt knowing versus simply an intellectual idea: one of the secrets of the immortal geniuses is *seclusion*. And the discipline of retreating from the world by placing themselves in a form of solitary confinement so they could produce their magic. All of history's great makers had this habit in common. They set up their workspaces to be completely diversion-free so they could get lost from society for extended periods of time, every day.

Think of Thomas Edison's Menlo Park lab. Or Telegraph Cottage, the small, private country house that General Dwight D. Eisenhower used as a refuge during World War II (his staff was very careful not to have anything in the cottage that would remind him of the war, so it would provide full relief from the pressures he was under, allowing him to think clearly about his strategy and campaign).

Your creative rabbit hole can be metaphorical: you can take the approach of simply blocking out distractions and locking away your devices so you create your magnum opus in a few solid time blocks each workday. Or you can actually set up a specific artistic space where you go dark—so no one and no thing can drain your cognitive bandwidth and productivity. Doing this daily is an extraordinary way to institutionalize flow state so your brilliance begins to visit you on demand.

Or you can go work in a library, in the study hall of a nearby university or within a spare bedroom. When I have a key project to complete, I'll often book a beautiful hotel room in a favorite city for a few weeks. Sometimes I'll book a suite in my own hometown just to get away from my usual responsibilities and the operational administrivia that never serves me in generating my best results. As a matter of fact, as I refine this paragraph for you, I'm in a hotel room an hour away from my house, with inspiring music playing, a "privacy" sign on my door, my phone on "do not disturb," and zero meetings or media scheduled. All I need to do here is work (real work), eat (room service) and sleep (good bed). Yes, it costs me money that I wouldn't have to spend if I were working at home this week. Yet missing the ideas and the creativity that are flowing would cost me a thousand times more.

Here's the photo of the current scene:

The work area in the hotel room where I'm writing this chapter

Strategy #7: The 5 Great Hours Promise

The old style of working is derived from an ancient era when people worked on factory lines and mostly toiled as manual laborers. By producing longer, more goods would be made (until the worker grew fatigued and the next shift took over).

We live now at a very different time. Many of us are paid to think and invent and to find splendid solutions to the planet's greatest problems. Many of us are *cognitive laborers* rather than physical workers. Working longer, therefore, does not serve us better, because working long hours depletes our creativity and degrades our mastery. This is why I don't resonate with the whole "hustle and grind" culture—at all. The most productive people on the planet *do not* "hustle and grind" 24/7/365. Instead, when they work, they work with supreme intensity. They do not snack on digital amusements or foolishly chit-chat about TV shows when they show up to advance their craft and pursue their trade. They are serious. They are professionals, not dabblers. Specialists instead of generalists. They go super-deep versus really wide when they work. When they sit down to produce, they bring the fullness of their human genius to the table and *spend it all* on their occupation.

Then, once done with the work session, they renew. They nap. They play. They enjoy the fruits of their industry and the joys of their effort. This way of working—in cycles—is one of the utmost of all secrets to peerless productivity and a gorgeous life.

I'm a huge fan of the Indian painter M. F. Husain, often called the "Picasso of India." When a reporter for *The Guardian* asked the artistic legend how he organized his days, he replied: "I work early. Get up at five or six. I always feel it's my first day. I don't get bored with sunrise. I then work hard for three or four hours."

And what would he do for the rest of the day, the interviewer asked. "Ah, the rest of the time I think it is very important just to loiter around."

Just to loiter around. Love it!

And so, I recommend that my clients work only five hours a day (to me, *five* hours of undisturbed, fierce, steady and exquisite work is ideal) on those days reserved for work. Anything more *is completely unnecessary* and actually leads to diminishing returns because you're tired (so you won't produce anything substantial, so why waste the time?). Just five hours of glorious, majestic, monumental achievement on your workdays. Then recover. Regenerate. Refuel. And savor the rest of your day.

Those I advise almost always initially resist The 5 Great Hours Promise as it's so unorthodox (heretical, actually). Yet once they observe that they are actually getting more world-class work done in a week than they'd previously accomplished in many months—*by working less*—they thank me. And use the enormous amounts of time they've freed up to be with their family, read the books in their home library, visit art galleries, commune with nature or pursue their sporting passions.

Strategy #8: The World-Class Executive Assistant + Personal Aide (WCEAPA) Foundation

Okay. Almost done on this chapter, which I know has been intense yet will be priceless once you implement it.

Titans of industry have told me that this particular strategy I'm about to walk you through has multiplied their financial fortunes, activated explosive gains in their performance and genuinely revolutionized their personal lives, bringing far more happiness, balance and spiritual peace.

It continually astounds me how many super-elite executives, revered billionaires and standout entrepreneurs still do many of the things they did when they first started out, like booking their own travel, making restaurant reservations, supervising home repairs and going to the store for their daily supplies. Why would they do this at the level they are at? Force of habit. They've done it so many times it's all become unconscious. Yet this behavior—which served them well in startup stage—now consumes many hours each day that could be used in advancing their Lifetime Big 5, making their masterwork, polishing their skills, accelerating their empires, growing their movements and making a difference in the lives of many other human beings.

Hiring a talented and trusted person—a World-Class Executive Assistant + Personal Aide—to organize and orchestrate your professional life as well as elegantly manage your personal life will free up immense bandwidth, energy and time for you. Your WCEAPA can manage all scheduling, answer all calls, deal with all complexity and essentially handle every single one of the activities that you dislike.

Just imagine the improvement in your productivity, happiness and serenity as you concentrate *purely* on all those things it's smartest for you to do. That you're excellent at. And that you love doing. This method is a major way to create a life you adore.

Strategy #9: The Weekly Sabbatical

During a simpler period in history, one day a week—known as the Sabbath—was reserved for a vacation of sorts from one's labor. Families united, the plows were paused, books were read, and meals were shared.

The final standard operating system of *The Peak Productivity Strategies Pyramid* is to get exceedingly good at taking days off. At least one day each week (and then—I hope—one week off every month and eventually at least two months away from work every year). Shift from being a human doing to a human being—and relax a lot more. We really do receive our best ideas when we're not working. And you'll never lead the field if you're really worn out. As I've shared, longevity is a primary ingredient to become legendary, and by taking an uncommon amount of weekly, monthly and yearly sabbaticals to be with your family, take great trips, read great books, develop great friendships and simply rest, you'll ensure that you're creative, inspired, skilled and ultra-strong for many, many more decades.

Okay. That's it. Many of my best strategies for peak productivity offered with high encouragement and sincere enthusiasm. So you can explore your cathedrals of possibility. And inhabit your temples of promise. I pray it helps you raise your game exponentially.

P.S. To download a tactical worksheet that will help you implement *The Peak Productivity Strategies Pyramid* swiftly and effectively, go to TheEverydayHeroManifesto.com/Productivity

33

Join the Hope Brigade

I'd like to share more of my poetry with you. So, as Ben Harper's song "Excuse Me Mr." shakes the floor of my writing room, I gently offer you these words:

Where there is darkness and doom,
And the people feel defeated,
Know that doubt is the great swindler.
And join The Hope Brigade.

When you are punished for your truthfulness,
Where you are misunderstood for your genius,
Rebel against such cowardice.
And join The Hope Brigade.

In times of misfortune, when you think of quitting,
When fear enchants your counterfeit self,
Where despair does its violence, silence the enemies within.
Recall your ability to perform acts of wizardry.
And join The Hope Brigade.

The flock will beckon you to become like them.
To live noisily and to crave well beyond plenty.
To disregard your nature and dishonor your power.
To stifle your instinct for simplicity
To allow the attractions of ordinary to invade your hours.
Refuse this request of the majority,
By knowing the fury of your sovereignty.
And join The Hope Brigade.

When you wonder if you matter,
While remembering that you are mortal
In the mornings of your delicious angst
Consider the serenity
At the root of your bravery
Proceed resolutely amid any uncertainty.
And join The Hope Brigade.

Has love torn your heart?
Does life seem too hard?
Do you feel alone?
Is adversity more common than triumph?
Has worry welcomed you more than cheer?

A new dawn is coming.
The fruits of your goodness will soon be showing.
Have faith in Fortune's fairness.
And join The Hope Brigade.

34.

40 Things I Wish I'd Known at 40

1. That family, flowers and walks in the woods would bring me more happiness than cars, watches and houses ever would.

2. That getting super-fit would multiply my creativity, productivity and prosperity considerably.

3. That your choice of relationship partner is one of the main sources of your success (or failure), joy (or misery) and tranquility (or worry).

4. That I'd do my finest work when I'd be working in hotel rooms and flying on airplanes rather than when chained to an office desk.

5. That good friendships are priceless treasures. And that old friends are the most precious ones.

6. That heaven helps those who help themselves. So do your best and let your higher power do the rest.

7. That people putting you down is a sign of your increasing success.

8. That the priorities I thought were most important in my youth are actually the pursuits I'm least interested in as I mature.

9. That silence, stillness and solitude form the sweet song that most attracts the Muse.

10. That small daily victories, performed with disciplined consistency over extended periods of time, lead to revolutionary results.

11. That when I didn't get what I desired it was because the universe had something a whole lot better in mind.

12. That being scared just means you're about to grow. And that frequent discomfort is the price of accelerated progress.

13. That if you risk all for love and it doesn't work out, there is no failure because all love stories are, in truth, hero tales. And no growth of the heart is a waste. Ever.

14. That working diligently without concern for the rewards is the very behavior that brings the rewards.

15. That just because someone is aging doesn't mean they are growing.

16. That life has a fabulous feedback system showing you what you are doing right by where you are winning (and what you need to improve by where you're frustrated).

17. That it usually takes twenty years of working anonymously before you acquire the wisdom and expertise required to know what to leave out of a piece of work so it becomes extraordinary.

18. That the humbler the person, the stronger the character.

19. That your income will never exceed your self-identity. And your impact will never be larger than your personal story.

20. That we get what we settle for. (So stop settling for what you don't want.)

21. That sometimes silence is the loudest reply you can give.

22. That the way people make you feel when you interact with them tells you everything you need to know about them.

23. That taking a lot of time off would make me twice as productive.

24. That feeding the trolls is a waste of your time. Most critics are jealous because you did what they couldn't do. Ignore them. And allow mastery to be your response.

25. That bullies become cowards once you stand up to them.

26. That journaling is praying on paper. And every prayer is heard.

27. That a genuinely rich life costs a lot less than you think.

28. That some people in business will tell you they'll do amazing things for you, but once the deal is signed, they'll end up doing nothing for you.

29. That the activities and places that fill you with joy are the activities and places where your wisdom wishes you to be.

30. That the best use of money is to create experiences and memories and not to secure objects and possessions.

31. That willpower is built by doing difficult things. So do more difficult things. (Daily.)

32. That it's better to read a few books deeply than consume many books lightly.

33. That hardship is the birthplace of heroism. Honor your scars as they have made you you.

34. That the majority of human beings have wonderful hearts and they'll show them to you if you make them feel safe.

35. That elderly people have the best stories. And deserve the highest respect.

36. That all life has huge value. Don't ever step on a spider.

37. That when you feel most alone, your higher power is closest to you.

38. That not every hour of the day and not every day of the week needs to be used "productively" and "grinding." Taking naps, staring at the stars and, sometimes, doing nothing are pursuits absolutely necessary for a life of unlimited beauty.

39. That respecting yourself is vastly more important than being liked by others.

40. That life's too short to play small with your highness.

35.

The Misty Copeland Confidence-Making Technique

Misty Copeland, a hero to millions of humans, is one of the best ballerinas our civilization has ever produced.

She was the first African-American woman to become principal dancer at the prestigious American Ballet Theatre and has held audiences spellbound through her performances at the Metropolitan Opera House in New York, the Bolshoi Theatre in Moscow and the Bunka Kaikan in Tokyo.

She's also a shining example of using a mean childhood filled with parental alcoholism, regular uprooting and relentless adversity as fuel to achieve the apparently impossible.

As a young ballerina, she would rise before dawn to start her practice regime, understanding that outworking everyone around you is how dreamers transmute potential into power.

Naturally blessed, along with exceptionally dedicated (a formidable alchemy), she was able to stand *en pointe* (on her toes in special ballet shoes to perform specific dance moves) only months after her first ballet class, in a field where it generally takes practitioners many years to arrive at this ability.

When no one else had faith in Copeland's ability to realize

awesome results as a performer, her first teacher caught glimpses of her prodigiousness and encouraged her unusual pupil to continue when she wanted to quit.

"The perfect ballerina has a small head, sloping shoulders, long legs and a narrow rib cage," the instructor said, echoing celebrated choreographer George Balanchine's much-respected statement on the attributes of a ballet superstar.

"That's you," whispered her teacher one day in class. "You're perfect."

As the days passed and Copeland's training dedication deepened, the way her mentor saw her gradually re-ordered the way she saw herself.

As Copeland gained skill, refined her prowess and upgraded her performance, her self-identity rose in the process.

She began to accept that she was special and talented and perhaps even gifted.

World-class is very much a game of confidence. *And becoming a sensation in your arena begins by strengthening the trust you have in yourself.* The quickest—and most sustainable—technique for building such psychological undefeatability and emotional hardiness is to behave as the person that you most seek to become.

As esteemed psychologists suggest: *It's easier to act yourself into a new way of thinking than to think yourself into a new way of acting.* (Please read that maxim twice.)

… You'll build your own confidence through relentless practice rather than mere hopefulness.

… The smallest of actions is always better than the noblest of intentions.

… Ideation without execution is the doorway into delusion.

… And a breathtaking vision not backed up by pristine daily implementation is the primary mistake of promise neglected.

36.

The 40 Copies of a Single Book Habit

Our home is filled with books.

I really don't know of any investment with the same yield as a book. For a small amount of money, you are granted access to the world's most valuable ideas and the planet's wisest minds. Whenever I visit the residence of a business heavyweight, I see very few televisions. And nearly always an enormous library. All it takes is one book—the right one—to transform your entire life.

I often buy many copies of a single book.

Six copies of James Allen's classic *As You Think* rest on the shelves of my library at home; eight copies of Shel Silverstein's *The Giving Tree* can be found on a desk in my office; eleven copies of Paulo Coelho's *The Alchemist* sit on a table in my workroom so I can give them out to anyone who visits. I've purchased forty copies of *Meditations* by the Roman emperor Marcus Aurelius.

Why, you wonder?

Because as English philosopher and statesman Francis Bacon once wrote: "Some books are to be tasted, others to be swallowed, and some few to be chewed and digested; that is, some books are to be read only in parts; others to be read, but not curiously; and some few are to be read wholly, and with diligence and attention."

I'll share a story to hopefully amplify your love of books. (I buy more books than I know I'll ever read in my lifetime and my guess is you have the same addiction, too. But an addiction is only unhealthy if it's an unhealthy addiction, right? A great legacy would be gifting my library to my children.)

Anyway, every time I land at Fiumicino airport in my beloved Rome, I head to the apartment where I stay, drop my bags on the floor, take a quick shower, then head straight to a tiny, charming bookshop just off the Spanish Steps where the dusty volumes are piled up on the floor, texts on sale are noted by a sign that seems left over from the Roman Empire and soul fills the room like you haven't felt since you last visited the Vatican.

I walk directly to the philosophy section that I know so well, search for my favorite edition of *Meditations*, chat with the always smiling manager in my primitive Italian, which I'm certain sounds more like Mandarin to him than his mellifluous native tongue.

Then I head back to my place. And I read.

Then I nap. Then I read. Then I sunbathe. Then I read. Then I chill with my pals over homemade plates of *amatriciana* or *carbonara*. Then I'll read some more as the sunset makes the sky go all pink and wispy over Trinità dei Monti, the magical church in the center of Rome.

I invest in that same book every time because I've learned that *wisdom meets you where you're at*. You won't understand anything above your current level of comprehension. And you and I can't appreciate any work that's beyond our immediate understanding.

Here's what I mean ...

... When I first read *The Alchemist*, I didn't get what all the fuss was about. Now I read it and I see the spiritual genius that's embedded within it. The book didn't change. But over time, I grew. And with more knowledge and experience I became able to see and embrace the knowledge and experience with which Paulo Coelho wrote.

When I first read *Jonathan Livingston Seagull*, I thought it was just a book about a bird.

Now I see it as a masterpiece about standing in one's highest self-expression. And the importance of staying true to yourself. At any cost.

And when I first flipped the pages of the *Meditations* about fifteen years ago (after hearing that it sits on the bedside tables of many of the world's greatest presidents and prime ministers, maestros and gurus, stateswomen and humanitarians), I found it dense, confusing and utterly uninteresting. I put it down after only a few moments.

But as I've read it more often, lived longer and grown as a human being, my ability to understand the meaning of what the benevolent emperor wrote in his private diary (while Europe was enduring one of the worst plagues in its history) has grown with me.

Again, these books didn't change. I did.

And, far more importantly, so can you.

37.

The Meaning of Disgrace

One of my all-time favorite lines in the *Meditations* of Marcus Aurelius is this: "Disgraceful: for the soul to give up when the body is still going strong."

Become a poet-warrior is what I'm suggesting.

Live quietly and gently. Show tenderness to all. Cherish simple graces, know when enough is enough and enjoy the hypnotizing enchantments of a spartan, minimalist and creative lifestyle. Just as a sincere poet would.

And yet, when it comes to taking difficult action to materialize your mighty mission and showing ferocious dedication to delivering on your dreams, *never* give in.

Live by a warrior creed, always staying faithful to your vision, crusade and self-promises, while remembering that tiny triumphs made with sincere regularity stack into heroic transformations when done with consistency over a lifetime. You will get to where you aspire to be. With resolve and patience.

For laziness, apathy and surrender are the parents of regret.

Throwing in the towel is the realm of the defeated. And quitting in pursuit of your goals, desires and ideals is a vicious slap in the face to your primal genius. You deserve so much more than a relationship with the experience of giving up—and thereby fitting in.

Sure, you'll get scared along your journey. I get scared, too. Yet fear creates more damage than the actual things that strike fear within our hearts, doesn't it?

Forgive me for bringing up mortality but I did assure you that I'd always be honest with you ...

... And so I must remind you that death is in the cards for all of us. Any one of us could die on any day.

Given this truth, isn't it best that we make the changes we need to make and pursue the course we know we must follow? So we know our eminence.

And avoid disgrace.

38.

A Basic Motto
for Stunning Prosperity

Here's a powerful motto to keep at the front of your mind and at the center of your heart: *Just because you can't see a solution doesn't mean a solution doesn't exist.*

When riddled with stress, our perception contracts and our ingenuity closes. We lose the capacity to see opportunity. It's almost as if the fear places a set of lenses over our eyes so we are blocked from noticing possibility. We start seeing through "timidity goggles," if you get what I mean.

One of my best friends just came off the single most profitable twelve months of his career. I asked him how he did it.

"Easy," he replied, as he sipped his espresso. "My team and I were all about finding solutions to any problem that appeared. We refused to be stopped by trouble. We'd talk about what you and I sometimes talk about—how a lotus flower blossoms in the swamp. So we stayed positive, resilient and agile, no matter what came up. That's how we won."

This is why he's one of my best friends. And why he also happens to be super-rich.

39.

Hug the Monster

There was once an old spiritual master who was visiting a mystical monastery. As he walked up the mountain path, he was followed by onlookers and those who wished to learn the secrets of his sensational powers.

Before entering the monastery, the group had to pass through a large courtyard that had been decorated with colorful flags and carefully crafted stone sculptures.

As they walked through the front gates, they immediately saw that three vicious dogs had broken free of their thick iron chains and were sprinting toward them.

Everyone gasped. Stopped. Then started running—in the opposite direction.

Everyone except the old master.

Instead, he smiled. And then yawned. And then did something you might find quite extraordinary: he darted directly toward the dogs.

The dogs increased their pace, moving more swiftly through the courtyard. The master yawned once again, and then increased his speed as well.

The dogs ran even faster and the master pushed even harder. Now he was singing as he sprinted, and raising a fist into the air, a

155

gesture that seemed to give testimony to his insurmountable faith in his victory.

The onlookers were spellbound.

As for the dogs, they grew frightened of the master who was stronger. Soon they turned away, to go back to their corner.

Fear works like this, I have found.

Run from it and it will come closer to you, with even more force.

Go directly toward it and it will turn to go, like an uninvited guest who realizes they should not have shown up.

What I'm encouraging, with much respect for your highest heroism, is that you hug your monsters, as regularly as possible.

Keep them in the basement and they'll brainwash (and heartwash) you into thinking (and feeling) that they are really vicious. But go down the steps, turn on the lights and look them in the eye. They'll look more like little cartoon characters. Not harmful at all.

I used to be incredibly frightened of public speaking when I was in university. The thought of giving a presentation to even ten people made my heart pound and my voice shake. When I'd have to speak in class, my mind would start racing and my pulse would be throbbing. I sure was a hot mess. Back then.

And then I realized that any important achievement is essentially a triumph over fear.

I had great dreams and mighty ambitions that I refused to allow my insecurities to rule. I wanted to make a better life for myself and to take as many people as possible on the ride with me.

And so I made a decision to no longer operate as a victim. In a single moment, I made a life-changing choice.

I went to the library and took out a few books on overcoming the fear of public speaking. I still recall staying in my bedroom for the better part of many weeks, reading those books, line by line. Locked in my room.

I didn't go out with friends. I didn't watch television. I didn't play games and I didn't fool around. I just studied strategies on how to build my confidence in front of an audience. And how to become good on my feet while presenting before people.

Next, I signed up for a Dale Carnegie course on public speaking. I gave little speeches to a roomful of participants. Every Monday night in the meeting room of a quiet motel. I still remember it so very well.

I know this sounds obvious, but here's what happened:

… The more talks I gave, the easier it became.

… The more I ran toward those dogs, the more they ran away from me.

… In time, with deep practice and steadfast patience, speaking in public became fun. Really fun.

Now, I can walk onto a stage before ten thousand or twenty thousand people or thirty thousand or even forty thousand human beings and it pretty much feels like I'm at home in our family room.

Such is the power of staying with your program to turn fear into fuel and your campaign to transform weakness into valor.

 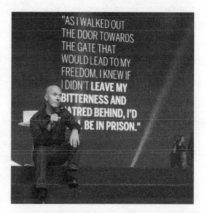

At a leadership event in São Paulo, Brazil, before forty thousand people

On stage in a stadium of tens of thousands of senior business leaders

I adore this quote by Frank Herbert in *Dune* that makes the point so eloquently:

> I must not fear. Fear is the mind-killer. Fear is the little-death that brings total obliteration. I will face my fear. I will permit it to pass over me and through me. And when it has gone past I will turn the inner eye to see its path. Where the fear has gone there will be nothing. Only I will remain.

So when you feel timid, recall the story of the wise old master. And make certain that each day, for the remainder of your very long and richly blessed life, you chase your mean dogs. And hug your biggest monsters.

So they *all* run away.

40.

The 4-Figure Dessert Rule

The Hôtel du Cap on the French Riviera is one of the preferred places on the planet for the jet set.

The property is beautiful, the location is magnificent and the hotel's service is renowned.

One morning a guest requested a *tarte tropézienne*, which is a brioche bun filled with cream. Brigitte Bardot named it while she was in Saint-Tropez making the film *And God Created Woman*.

The client was politely informed by the kitchen that the pastry was not on the menu, as it was the specialty of the Saint-Tropez region, some sixty miles away.

Yet the guest insisted. He stated firmly that he had to have what he wanted.

So, get this, the concierge *chartered a helicopter* and asked a member of his team to fly to the finest bakery in Saint-Tropez and purchase a fresh *tarte tropézienne*.

Just in time to savor with coffee, the dessert was placed on the guest's table. Along with the bill.

The amount? €2,005. The tarte was €5; the rest was for the helicopter.

The guest was *delighted*. And so Hôtel du Cap scored another win. As part of its dedication to remaining legendary.

In an era where most enterprises don't even deliver on what their marketing promises, differentiate your organization by making it standard operating procedure to *astonish* customers and completely overdeliver on their expectations.

At a hotel I once stayed at in Prague, I asked the front desk clerk if it was possible to get an extremely fast turnaround on the dry cleaning of a dress shirt. Her reply was unforgettable: *"Anything* is possible."

At another hotel, this one in the tropical paradise of Mauritius, the staff is trained to abide by a simple mantra: "The answer is yes. Now ask me the question." Exquisite, yes?

So the next time you're faced with a challenging customer, consider that every displeased patron can be remade into a fanatical follower, with some caring, understanding, ingenuity and appreciation. And that movements truly are built one relationship at a time.

All it takes is a shot of inventiveness, an impressive amount of enthusiasm for brand protection and the clear love in your heart to make another human happy.

Like the concierge. Who found the €2,005 tarte.

41.

Don't Be a Sloth

Real confession: my best friend adopted a sloth.

The sloth (a strange animal that appears to me as a cross between a raccoon and an orangutan, in case you don't know what a sloth is) doesn't actually live with him.

Because that wouldn't be pretty. Would likely be very messy, if you ask me.

No.

He found a way, through a wildlife organization, to help a sloth in need lead a much better life. By sending the little guy some money every month.

Now, my buddy's commitment provides me with an endless source of humor when we enjoy our regular dinners together. I make joke after joke and for some inexplicable reason find his sloth-supporting decision terrifically amusing.

He rolls his eyes, justifies his decision by his affection for the creature and then generally ends up laughing with me. And having another glass of wine.

(Please don't send me a complaint that I should show sloths more respect; I adore all living creatures—except sloths. So I'm not going to read your message pleading with me to join Sloth Supporters United. I'm just not interested.)

All kidding aside, did you know sloths are the slowest-moving mammals alive?

It's true.

That's why the vice of being lazy is referred to as "sloth."

My point in this tiny chapter about sloths? Simple. Don't be one.

42.

Ben Franklin's 13-Virtue Habit Installer

Superb daily habits will get you so much further than exceptional natural talent. You know this to be true, after spending so much time with me on these pages.

I've seen so many genius-grade humans do nothing with their potential.

And so many people of average ability work their way up to spellbinding mastery.

Yes, I'll agree that consistently keeping the promises you make to yourself, putting in long hours each day to practice and improve, and operating with great discipline can be hard. Yet I propose to you that a life spent choosing hard feats over effortless moves turns out to be the easiest way to live.

Why, you wonder?

Because the regular doing of hard things—like rising with the sun, exercising instead of couch-surfing, saving instead of overspending, optimizing your talents and treating everyone you meet with consideration—guarantees you a life of creativity, productivity, fine health, financial abundance, professional eminence and reverence from many (along with a clean conscience). All of which makes your life exponentially *easier.*

I also wish to remind you of another primary principle of

heavyweight habit installation: *It's far easier to maintain an excellent habit than to restart it after you've stopped.*

One of the books that most shaped me as a young man was *The Autobiography of Benjamin Franklin*. What still stands out to this day is his method of installing the thirteen virtues he believed to be most important for a life of success, well-being and lasting influence.

As context, I'd like to share a passage from the book:

> It was about this time that I conceived the bold and arduous project of arriving at moral perfection. I wished to live without committing any fault at any time. As I knew what was right and wrong, I did not see that I might not always do one and avoid the other. But I soon found I had undertaken a task of more difficulty than I had imagined.

Although Franklin knew what he had to do to become a deeply moral man, he often found that he slipped. The solution was to build a system to break weak habits by meticulously installing stronger ones.

The statesman's primary virtues for a great life are:

1. **Temperance.** Carefulness in food and drink.
2. **Silence.** Avoid trivial conversations and using words that are harmful.
3. **Order.** Practice austerity in physical spaces and perform each pursuit precisely.
4. **Resolution.** Do what you promise yourself you'll do, without fail.
5. **Frugality.** Be cautious with your expenses and avoid waste.
6. **Industry.** Manage your time well and avoid unnecessary activities.
7. **Sincerity.** Never deceive anybody and be yourself under all conditions.
8. **Justice.** Treat everyone equally and do nothing wrong.
9. **Moderation.** Avoid the extremes of both sloth and asceticism.
10. **Cleanliness.** Keep your body, living space and environment immaculate.
11. **Tranquility.** Maintain inner peace and do not ruminate over small matters.
12. **Chastity.** Don't participate in meaningless sexual pursuits.
13. **Humility.** Model the great saints, sages and seers.

Franklin created the following table for each of the thirteen virtues, which he placed on the pages of a journal he named his "little book." As you can see, in the left column are initials for each virtue and at the top are letters for the days of the week.

THE 13 VIRTUES OF HUMAN GREATNESS

	S.	M.	T.	W.	T.	F.	S.
T.							
S.							
O.							
R.							
F.							
I.							
S.							
J.							
M.							
C.							
T.							
C.							
H.							

Every night, before sleep, he'd measure his behavior during the day against his commitment to embody the habit he was working on integrating by doing some focused reflection on how he had conducted himself.

Franklin would concentrate on one virtue per week and in this way could "complete a full course of the program in thirteen weeks and four courses a year."

Also know that Franklin believed that the thirteen virtues are progressive. Spending a week working on temperance will then give you more willpower to become stronger in being silent. After a week concentrating on the virtue of silence, you'll have more self-control to maximize the order in your life. And so on.

My favorite edition of *The Autobiography of Benjamin Franklin*

This method is an excellent example of the transformational power of working daily on your self-awareness and *The 3 Step Success Formula* that you'll discover in an upcoming chapter.

For now, simply spend some time over the coming hours considering Benjamin Franklin's essential virtues. And how your performance, prosperity, serenity and spirituality would be improved by applying his fascinating system regularly.

P.S. To access The 13 Virtues Worksheet I give to members of *The Circle of Legends* online mentoring program and start integrating them into your weeks, go to TheEverydayHeroManifesto.com/13Virtues

43.

The Peacock's Complaint

I love reading Aesop's fables. The parables guide me on my path, reminding me of what's important and helping me live with more knowledge, conviction and clarity.

This morning I read the one called "The Peacock's Complaint."

One day, a lovely peacock submitted a complaint to the goddess Juno.

It said that the voice of the nightingale was so much more melodic than hers. This was completely unfair, argued the bird.

Juno replied that the peacock's blessing was beauty and that all living creatures were given their own unique talents.

The eagle was powerful; the parrot could mimic people; the dove was exceptionally peaceful.

And the peacock was eye-catching. Alluring.

"They are all contented with being themselves and unless you want to be miserable all the time, you had better learn the same," counseled the goddess.

The peacock understood the lesson. And soon grew enamored with its attractiveness, proudly showing its plumage.

For all the world to behold.

44.

The Most Costly Conflict

I've seen people get into fights that consume the most valuable years of their lives.

I know of one gentleman who took on a large organization. Because he felt he had been treated unjustly. And he knew he was right.

He could have settled the matter with some astute negotiation and intelligent discussion and perhaps a little compromise.

But he needed to be vindicated. Fully and completely.

And so he spent twenty years fighting his war. *Yes, twenty years.*

And guess what? He won.

And guess what? He suffered a stroke, lost most of his fortune and ended up in a wheelchair.

He could hardly speak by the time the whole battle was over, but he did manage to mumble to me: "See, I taught them a lesson, didn't I?"

Of course, I viscerally believe that one must fight for what is right. Martin Luther King, Jr., once said: "Our lives begin to end the day we become silent about things that matter."

To stand for your principles, remain true to your values and defend that which is important to you is what strengthens your character, fuels your everyday heroism and escalates your self-esteem.

I get that. We are on the same page on this.

And yet, through my own trials, I've also learned this: *No fight is worth the loss of your creativity, productivity, happiness and peace of mind.*

Lose these treasures and you've lost *everything*.

And so, it's all a fine balance, isn't it?

Pick your battles carefully. Sometimes you must uphold your honor and come out swinging. And sometimes you need to see the larger picture, prefer the protection of your prized joyfulness over the vindication of being right and play a wiser game, moving ahead by avoiding conflict—trusting that taking the high road will serve you best in the long run.

45.

Kill Your Darlings

Yes, I do remember what I mentioned to you earlier about using words that uplift, encourage and inspire.

Yet I needed to use this title. To explain how I roll as a writer.

It's been twelve long and arduous and strenuous months—months that have also been exhilarating and exuberant and euphoric—to get to this stage of this book.

Here's a picture of the granularity and obsession with detail that consumes me during my creative process:

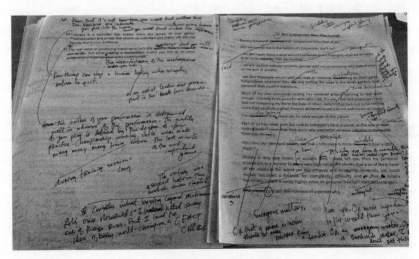

A sample of how I work on a book

You might ask why I work so extremely hard on a project (*The 5 AM Club* took me four years) and why I spend so much time trying to get every line painstakingly right.

Advertising icon David Ogilvie once wrote: "I'm a lousy copywriter but I am a good editor. So I go to work on editing my own draft. After four or five edits it looks good enough to show to the client."

My answer to your question about why I am so absorbed and dedicated and fanatically faithful to the highest of standards as I write would contain a few of my dearest artistic rules:

1. It's because I deeply respect my readers and so must give them the best I can possibly make, because this is what they deserve.

2. It's because pushing my craft on a new work beyond what I've produced in the past, out onto the jagged edges of its limits, expands those limits. And increases my game.

3. I must never rest on my laurels, for this would be the beginning of the end. To repeat what worked in my last bestseller without venturing into the danger and glory of my next level of performance would be a formula for irrelevance.

4. My family name is on the front cover, so I mustn't send anything out into the world that doesn't represent the result of one going all in.

5. Karma is real and our higher power watches all we do. By working under the intention of love for my readers and the spirit of sincere helpfulness to make their lives better, my personal dreams will become real and great things will happen for my loved ones.

6. Our civilization needs more truth and beauty, so if I am able to pour more of these into the world, I have a duty to do it.

Which brings me closer to the title of this chapter ...

Below is a photo from yesterday's work session in the little seaside cottage where I'm polishing the manuscript:

Look closely, please. You'll see a note resting against the candle holder, sitting close to my manuscript so I can see it as I write. It says, "Kill Your Darlings." The sentiment is sometimes altered to "Murder Your Darlings" and is often attributed to Nobel Prize laureate and novelist William Faulkner.

It's a really, really, really valuable rule. For any serious creative producer. And heavyweight artistic leader. (And whether you're refining a screenplay, advancing a startup, running a team or launching a movement, you *are* a creative producer.)

The phrase, to me, means that mastery demands that we remove what we believe is good or even magnificent yet not absolutely necessary to the magic of a project, for the greater good of that work.

The note was my reminder that less is often more and that even though there were chapters I *loved* in the manuscript, I had to be willing to take them out to make the book better.

Doing your masterwork really is, in many ways, a lot more about what you have the guts to leave out than all you allow to stay in.

Making something look simple often takes ages to do. A measure of genuine expertise is removing all except what matters. Because it takes tremendous acumen, knowledge, courage and skill to only include what's essential.

"Kill your darlings, kill your darlings even when it breaks your egocentric little scribbler's heart," advised writing legend Stephen King, words I've inscribed on the most available part of my spirit.

My enthusiastic prayer is only that you do the same.

P.S. I've assembled a number of those chapters that I decided not to include at TheEverydayHeroManifesto.com/LostChapters

46.

Avoid the Third Reward

Giving a gift and expecting a return is not a gift at all. It's an exchange.

What makes giving an act so blissful that it borders on the mystical is the intention with which you give.

And if you want something back, you corrode the splendor of the present you are delivering.

Before I wrote this particular piece for you, I—yet again—read a passage written by Roman emperor Marcus Aurelius. You now know this philosopher warrior is a great hero to me.

He used the term "benevolent," which finally landed on me in a way that I've long hoped it would.

I got it. Took me many years to get here. Where the meaning beneath the word became a felt knowing versus an intellectualized understanding.

To be a benevolent person (or leader, creator, maker) is to do what you do in purity. For the right reasons. In complete integrity. Mostly for the good of other people.

I'm not saying there's anything wrong with also doing good for yourself. Self-love is a wonderful maneuver. And win-win is a superb game to play.

And yet you'll ascend into higher reaches of your triumphantly happy nature, enter the Edens of your most glorious nobility and experience the Nirvanas of your most sacred success when you give primarily for the sake of giving. Not getting.

The wise and courageous ruler (back to Marcus), who thoroughly cared about the welfare of Rome (then the most powerful empire on the planet) and the state of its citizens, also wrote in the passage I read: "When you have done a good act and another has fared well by it, *why seek a third reward*, as fools do, be it the reputation for having done a good act or getting something in return?"

... Philanthropy to get your name on a hospital wing isn't real philanthropy, is it? It's vanity.

... Helping a good cause and then advertising your donation everywhere you go for brand building isn't real helping. It's self-promotion. (I don't know about you, but I'm growing weary of all the companies insincerely doing things to show "a social conscience" when—out of the spotlight—they could not care less.)

... Doing something kind for a loved one, a neighbor or a team-mate and waiting for even a thank you destroys the magnificence of the marvelous move that you had the wisdom to make.

Just give them the reward and let go of the longing to be repaid. *The service you have given is your dazzling bounty.*

Deliver benefit with zero strings attached. No reply required. No applause necessary. Only then is your generosity innocent. And, therefore, honorable.

And every time you act like this, you'll increase as the ruler over your neediest desires, your ego's relentless demands and any disloyalty to the inherent powers that your heroism requests that you continue to express.

And wouldn't this be the finest gift to receive in return?

47.

To Heal Your Once Wide-Open Heart Makes You a Great Master

Our society suggests that to open your heart and exhibit your emotions is a manifestation of meekness.

Actually, it takes a genuine warrior to do the principled and dangerously brave work required to tear down the fortress built around a once wide-open heart and reunite with the emotional intimacy that allows a human being to feel empathy for humanity, awe over the gorgeousness of life and enthusiasm for the magic of one's deepest dreams.

When we were kids, we were emotionally naked. We held our vulnerability in our open palms for all the world to see. Yes, we were that strong. We spoke honestly of our fears, cried innocent tears, risked taking risks, stayed true to ourselves and felt safe revealing our brilliance to anyone who cared to see it.

And because we were peaceful feeling any pain that we naturally felt as human beings participating in the human experience, we also had complete access to the happiness we all are meant to know.

The poet Kahlil Gibran made the point superbly in his masterpiece, *The Prophet* (one of my favorite books):

Your joy is your sorrow unmasked. And the selfsame well from which your laughter arises was often filled with your tears. The deeper that sorrow carves into your being, the more joy you can contain. Is not the cup that holds your wine the very cup that was burned in the potter's oven?

Then, as we proceeded through life—and met with disappointments, difficulties and discouragements—we gathered the emotional residue of our challenging encounters. To protect ourselves, we unconsciously began to construct a suit of armor over our tender, wise and powerful hearts. To escape the hurt. To avoid the suffering. To forget the trauma.

... Yet in dismissing our pain, we also disassociated from our light.

... In fleeing our sadness, we also betrayed our hopefulness.

... In running away from that which we fear, we caused our ability to hug our monsters and destroy our demons to atrophy.

... And in resisting the beautiful befriending of all that we truly are, we unintentionally suffocated the wisdom, mastery and wonder of our sovereign selves, which remain locked in a closet, deep within our most unvisited parts.

A primary principle in my Heartset philosophy is this: *To heal a wound, you need to feel the suppressed emotion under it.*

A second principle I need to reinforce (so you interact with it at an even more profound level of unforgettability) is this one: *If it's hysterical, it's historical.* In other words, the size of any overreaction to any particular situation in real time indicates the depth of the much earlier emotional injury.

A third Heartset principle worthy of your higher consideration is: *Feelings left unfelt form a subconscious Field of Hurt that degrades your genius, cheats your promise and blocks your greatness.*

Psychologist Carl Jung wrote of the willful blindness the majority

178

of human beings show to what he called our "shadow," that counter-feit portion of ourselves that we stuff into the unconscious so we don't have to deal with it, in the following way:

> Unfortunately, there can be no doubt that a man is, on the whole, less good than he imagines himself or wants to be. Everyone carries a shadow and the less embodied in the individual's conscious life, the blacker and denser it is. At all counts, it forms as an unconscious snag, thwarting our most well-meant intentions.

He added:

> One does not become enlightened by imagining figures of light but by making the darkness conscious. The latter procedure, however, is disagreeable and therefore not popular.

Sigmund Freud wrote to this very point even more directly: "Unexpressed emotions will never die. They are buried alive and will come forth later in uglier ways."

To dismiss Heartset work as foolish, and to concentrate on improving your Mindset while neglecting to heal old wounding and process through the pain stored within you, is to ignore the open door to your supremacy. And to create a state of self-sabotage that will keep you glued to the place that you currently are.

All of that suppressed micro-trauma—and possibly macro-trauma—that you probably aren't even aware of because it's lodged so completely inside your subconscious—is the real reason you might not be awake to your gifts, intimate with your talents and fully alive to your potential to cast stardust into the world.

That Field of Hurt, trapped within your psyche, is the main reason you are procrastinating on producing your magnum opus, resisting the installation of virtuoso-grade habits, sabotaging healthy relationships (or attracted to toxic ones, because traumatized people don't know what healthy looks like—and, incredibly, a drama-soaked lifestyle seems safer to them than a peaceful one, because it's so much more familiar), or increasing addictions that range from too much time on social media to too much time shopping or drinking or complaining and basically missing out on the opportunities right in front of you to realize your giant promise, lead a phenomenal life and serve many people in the process.

All the repressed pain of our past also explains why most people retreat into their heads, forgetting the truth that instinct is always much smarter than the intellect. And the heart is always wiser than reason.

And since so many of us are now living in our minds and are stuck in our *thinking* rather than enjoying our natural capacity to stay present to what we are *feeling*, we have forgotten how to sense (and cherish) all that is life around us.

This, in turn, means:

... We are unable to *feel* remorse on harming another human.

... We start wars that kill our brothers and sisters (because we no longer *feel* any connection to them).

... We disrespect a neighbor because of the color of their skin or the nature of their gender or the name of their religion because we can't *feel* the terror of such violent behavior.

... We pollute a once-pristine planet with chemicals, garbage and other toxins that destroy the oceans, degrade the forests and annihilate our animal friends because we have shielded ourselves to the bodily sensations of sorrow any fully awake human being would *feel* on killing anything living.

Such is the behavior of a civilization that no longer associates with their emotions, numbed to their bodily sensations. Such is the way of a people who are locked in robotic reason and machine-like intellectualization, preferring to manufacture more information than to grow in wisdom.

Such is the result when worldly egoism triumphs over human heroism.

I need to end this chapter (which I happen to be writing in a clapboard cabin on a rugged and sparsely populated island in the Atlantic Ocean, as the wind howls, the waves crash and the windows tremble).

I'll leave you with a specific technique that has transformed the creativity, productivity, prosperity and impact of the clients I mentor. It's called The AFRA Tool.

The A stands for *awareness*. The F stands for *feel*. The R stands for *release*. And the second A stands for *ascend*. Let's look at the learning framework related to it:

THE AFRA TOOL FOR HEARTSET PURIFICATION

1 AWARENESS
FIND THE FEELING

2 FEEL
STAY WITH THE SENSATION

3 RELEASE
LET THE HURT GO

4 ASCEND
MOVE FORWARD HIGHER

The next time your weaker self gets negatively activated by a person or a situation, rather than playing the victim and blaming the other person or outer condition, begin to *exploit* the circumstance for training to purify your Heartset by working with the suppressed emotional injury and old trauma that the scenario has beautifully raised from the hidden recesses of your subconscious life into your conscious attention. You'll know that blocked emotion from the Field of Hurt has risen to the surface where you can now deal with it by the very fact that it's bothering you, confirming that it has left your unconscious realm and has entered your conscious world. "Everything that irritates us about others can lead us to an understanding of ourselves," said Carl Jung.

If you didn't have pre-existing anger within you, nothing could ever make you angry, right? So that frustrating romantic partner or difficult coworker or aggressive driver who sends you into a fury is—in truth—a spiritual friend, heaven-sent to deliver your growth and help you own more of your supremacy. Because they have triggered an ancient wound, made it conscious for you so you can look at it and, if you choose, heal the hurt so it no longer sabotages your creativity, productivity, prosperity and joy. If you didn't have old, undealt-with sadness, shame, resentment, jealousy, disappointment or regret left over from former events inside, no one and no thing could ever get you off your genius today, right?

As you run The AFRA Tool more and more, you will not only be *using* so-called "difficulty" to your advantage by leveraging every hard situation for your growth and self-mastery and turning all stumbling blocks into stepping stones, you'll also be transforming wounds into wisdom and any problems into the power that you get to take with you along the rest of your lifetime.

Okay. Please allow me to walk you through how to apply the tool.

The next time you feel a *strong* reaction to something that unfolds, begin training yourself through steady conditioning to think of the AFRA acronym. I emphasize "strong" because—again—it's only when your emotional reaction is an *overreaction* to the event that you know a pre-existing wound has been struck. Of course, the arising of various human emotions in *proportionate* response to circumstances in our days is normal, healthy and doesn't suggest any old wound has been activated, like getting angry during a mean conversation with a family member or feeling sad when a client fails to appreciate your hard work or scared when a demanding professional opportunity presents itself or feeling insecure about your finances or feeling put down by the way a friend speaks to you or inferior when it seems someone is doing better than you from their social media images. Next, run the four-step process below to get the healing:

Step #1: Awareness

Begin building awareness around the inner wound by locating the feeling in your body. The original hurt is trapped in there because you were taught not to feel through it to completion (most people were told as children that feelings are wrong or for weaklings). We didn't feel safe to acknowledge the emotional cut so we denied it, causing it to freeze within us, blocking our truest power to be amazing and accomplish the sublime.

At first you may not be able to locate the sensation related to the emotion because emotional fluency is so foreign to you. But remember: you're starting a new skill. Mastery requires practice and patience. Keep searching for the physical response the challenging person or situation has caused. It might be a tightness in your chest or a heaviness in your throat or a pain in your stomach or a throbbing in your head. See yourself as an emotional detective of sorts, investigating more of the universe within your Heartset and getting to know this essential part of you better. Place all of your attention on the feeling within your body. This will automatically bring you into the present and out of any worrying and intellectualizing. Do your best to stay out of your head and remain with the actual sensation that has been lodged in your body. Note its texture and sense its color. Be one with it.

183

Step #2: Feel

The fact that you're now feeling the old, once-repressed emotion that the current scenario has activated is not bad at all and completely good. Yes, society says if we're not feeling happy all the time something is wrong. What nonsense!

To be a fully alive human is to experience *a range of emotions*. To repeat to reinforce: the fact that you're feeling an unpleasant emotion means that it has surfaced from your unconscious and is now within the conscious part of you. Fantastic! It no longer secretly owns you, running and mostly ruining your creativity, productivity and happiness. So at this step of the process, the goal is to *stay* with the sensation. Don't run from it. Don't escape by distracting yourself with a device. Because to heal a wound you really do need to feel the repressed condition under it. And the fact that the feeling is now awake to you by being an actual sensation in your body means that it's on its way out, no longer stuck in your Field of Hurt where it can create havoc in your life without your even knowing it. Just breathe into it, sit with it and accept it rather than judging it as wrong. Trust that the quickest way out of this pain is to go directly *into it*.

Step #3: Release

I know this seems vague, yet at this point in implementing The AFRA Tool all you need to do is set the intention to let go of the old wound. By feeling the buried emotion fully and by then *desiring* to release it from your system, you dislodge the frozen pain. And it *will* start to leave your body. Leaving you freer. Sometimes the release will take a few minutes or a couple of hours. Sometimes the stuck emotional baggage is bigger, so it takes longer to work through it. Trust this process. And know that as the hurts of the past clear you are experiencing a major healing. This exercise will leave you more intimate with your gifts, more friendly with your strengths, more connected with your courage, more awake to your aliveness, more trusting of your instincts and much closer to your loving nature. Forever.

Step #4: Ascend

Each time you run this Heartset purification protocol, there is a pay-off, making you move forward higher and healthier. Every time you run The AFRA Tool and release some of the previously ignored toxicity (it's *not* all from past hurts we have sustained, by the way; some of it is also from the guilt, shame and regret we feel at the ways we have treated others) that has been stunting your performance and keeping your heart closed to being able to love at a level beyond all reason, the Field of Hurt becomes less dense. You will feel lighter. You'll grow nearer to the limitless happiness, unchained excellence and spiritual freedom that is your essential nature. You'll experience more energy and confidence. Continue practicing this method daily in response to any "problems" life sends, and you'll soon begin to see that life never really hinders you. All that happens is working to help you rise and reclaim your primal genius.

Keep doing this Heartset work—as hard and messy as it can be at times—and the vast reservoir of self-loathing (made from all of the stored low-energy feelings we've denied) that sits within the emotional systems of so many of us on the planet at this time will steadily vanish.

Automatically, the higher order emotions of hope, gratitude, joy, empathy, compassion, bravery, inspiration and awe begin to occupy you, reuniting you with the higher power and daily greatness that is your essential nature. And you at your finest.

Yes, healing your once wide-open heart will make you a great master. The practice is a direct route to scaling the self-love that electrifies you to honor your ethical ambitions, materialize your gifts, treat yourself with respect and make our world a better place. Because of your shining light.

185

Every situation that the voice of fear (known as your ego) claims is bad is, in truth, a blessing that will serve your ascension into the artistic force, productive giant and servant hero that the call on your life is asking you to be. And as you steadily release all emotional impurities by wisely leveraging all that happens to you as part of your process in becoming a warrior-sage, you will reawaken the wonder, majesty and ability to see possibility that you once knew as a child. Before the world caused you to close down.

And neglect your magic.

48

What I Learned from Leonardo's Private Notebooks

One unforgettable afternoon, as I was walking the streets of Rome in springtime—as I so love to do—I ducked into the easy-to-miss museum that sits at the edge of Piazza del Popolo. It had a simple sign outside advertising an exhibit of the works of Leonardo da Vinci.

Leonardo, a maestro of range, generated work in the fields of architecture, painting, anatomy, sculpture, engineering and aeronautics.

The productivity of this unusually creative soul was clearly special. As his most famous biographer, Giorgio Vasari, wrote: "Sometimes in supernatural fashion, a single person is marvelously endowed by heaven with beauty, grace and talent in such abundance that his every act is divine and everything he does comes from God rather than from human art."

And yet as I walked through the museum looking at the instruments he had developed and diagrams of the insides of various creatures, and studying—for a few careful hours—the etchings, markings and words within the private notebooks he meticulously kept, one insight became strikingly clear: his so-called "genius" was less a genetic blessing and more the result of self-teaching. And continuous daily improvements. And enormous degrees of discipline, devotion and training.

Supreme artists, architects, inventors and leaders are not born into their skill. Their mastery truly is self-made (as I've done my best to affirm throughout this book, so it becomes a default belief of yours once you put the book down).

This luminary would spend day after day obsessively (and passionately) studying the seemingly smallest of subjects that would contribute to the advanced perception and optimization of skill that would later lift our civilization.

He taught himself about the way the jaw of a crocodile works, the nature of the placenta of a calf, the anatomy of a woodpecker's tongue and how moonlight radiates through a crisp winter sky.

He understood that pre-eminent creative leadership requires careful focus, workhorse-like effort and uncommon tenacity. Not good genes, a famous school and the right social connections.

In one of his notebooks, Leonardo wrote 730 of his hard-won understandings on the physics of water flow. Another page revealed 169 precise versions of trying to square a circle. A scribbling showed his messy list of 67 words that he had discovered to describe running water.

Leonardo worked utterly tirelessly when he worked. He also wasted a ton of time as all creatives do (this isn't a misuse of the resource—it's incubation of your next grade of ideas). Real professionals trust their natural rhythms of productivity, alternating stunning intensity with deep recovery so that their prowess expands over a lifetime instead of experiencing a bright and quick flameout.

The more I considered the body of work of this grandmaster, the more inspired I grew. The more I observed this great man's prodigious output, the clearer it became that we each have amazing talents within us—abilities that, when developed and refined relentlessly, would allow us, too, to offer works that inexperienced eyes would label as divinely gifted.

Let's have a look at six of the daily habits that made Leonardo the virtuoso he's now considered to be:

Habit #1. He Wrote Things Down

That which you write down is amplified within your mental clarity. And clarity of thinking breeds mastery of production. Keeping various journals on the subjects on which you seek excellence is a potent way to upgrade your ideation, capture your inspiration, imagine on paper and record your rising knowledge.

Habit #2. He Mined His Natural Curiosity

I'll never forget the day my extraordinary daughter and I were driving home from a visit with my brother. She was five years old at the time and sat quietly in the back seat, looking up at the vast blue sky as I drove along the highway. Spotting a group of clouds, she said enthusiastically, "Look, Dad—it's a lion in the sky!" As kids, we were intimate with our artistry. Unfortunately, as we leave our playful years behind, too many of us lose that natural access. Because we become serious. And adults. "It took me four years to paint like Raphael, but a lifetime to paint like a child," observed Pablo Picasso.

Habit #3. He Was Ridiculously Patient

Vigorous patience is one of the behaviors of all world-class performers. When Leonardo was creating *The Last Supper*, his ritual was to sit in front of the canvas for long periods of time, simply looking at the painting—studying the piece as a whole, along with the intricate nuances. Then, he would get up, make a single stroke and walk away. Sometimes for weeks. South African artist Lionel Smit, one of the most remarkable artists alive today, does the same thing. (If you can ever get your hands on one of his paintings, do it.)

Habit #4. He Blended Multiple Disciplines

Leonardo married his learning in aeronautics with his love of the arts, his immersion in engineering with his dedication to sculpture. His supposed giftedness was actually in large part the result of intense

189

concentration and radical innovation in many different fields of interest. Engaging in many disciplines will allow you to connect dots that few others can see.

Habit #5. He Took Time Off

"Men of lofty genius sometimes accomplish the most when they work the least," Leonardo once wrote. Allowing time for dreaming, playing and living life was part of the formula for his prodigious productivity. Disruptive and history-making insights rarely show up when you're in a cubicle. So travel, explore, have fun and rest.

Habit #6. He Adored Natural Beauty

Many of our civilization's top imagineers spent considerable time in the wild. Long walks in the woods. Extended hours in a cottage by the sea. Quiet evenings staring up at the stars. In a documentary I watched about Greek shipping tycoon Aristotle Onassis, I discovered that after the stylish guests he entertained on his yacht would retire to bed, Onassis would remain on the deck, sipping cognac and simply staring up at the heavens to work through problems and download inspiration that would grow his business empire.

Being near nature is a time-honored way to relax your mind. So your greatest ingenuity flows.

As I neared the exit of the museum and the sunshine streaming across the cobblestone street outside, I spotted the following quote from Leonardo da Vinci that I'd like to leave you with:

I love those who can smile in trouble, who can gather strength from distress and grow brave by reflection. 'Tis the business of little minds to shrink, but they whose heart is firm, and whose conscience approves their conduct, will pursue their principles unto death.

Beautiful, right?

49.

The "You Won't Win If You Don't Even Try" Attitude

Such a simple insight: *You won't win if you don't even try*.

So often, we get a big idea. One that will raise our career into a new orbit. One that will take our life to the next league. One that will really make us feel fully awake (and most intimate with our wonder). But then, guess what happens next? The voice of reason takes over, beneath which often lives an emotion called fear.

… We start to sell ourselves on all the things that could happen that will ensure we'll fail.

… We start to worry about whether we have what it takes to fulfill the dream, realize the aspiration and materialize the accomplishment.

… We seduce our fantastic excitements into believing they are no longer worthy of our attention.

Eventually, that marvelous and audacious idea that made our heart roar and our spirit soar seems foolish and ridiculous. And so we don't take action. Actually, *we don't even try*.

Imagine an athlete wishing to win—but not even entering the tournament. Imagine a business manager wanting to lead her team to the rare air of absolute world-class—but not even showing up to the

191

first strategy meeting. Imagine a brilliant inventor aiming to turn his field on its head—yet not even starting the tinkering.

Nothing happens until you move. You'll never become a headliner if you wait. Destiny awards the starters. Fortune rewards the driven. And you'll never know victory if you allow yourself to be paralyzed by apathy.

In the moments of my own life where I find myself resisting initiating, I'll reread this wisdom of the Indian sage Patanjali:

> When you are inspired by some great purpose, some extraordinary project, all your thoughts break their bonds. Your mind transcends limitations, your consciousness expands in every direction and you find yourself in a new, great and wonderful world. Dormant forces, faculties and talents become alive. And you discover yourself to be a greater person, by far, than you ever dreamed yourself to be.

And so I enthusiastically champion you to:

… never leave the site of a great idea without taking some action to make it real.

… always remember that it never hurts to ask (the worst thing that will happen is you'll hear a sound called "no," which is just a "maybe" in the making).

… not lose your nerve when the thinking and feeling of defeat show up.

… know and trust that rejection is the tuition demanded of everyday heroes to remain honest to their gifts and greatness. And that if you wait until you're qualified enough and skillful enough and confident enough to go for what you want, you might be waiting a long, long time. Perfect conditions don't exist and waiting for them is often simply an excuse because you're really, really scared to begin.

You might say: "But Robin, what if I try and fail?"

I'd gently reply: "What if you don't try? And then spend the rest of your life in regret, smoldering over all that could have been, should have been, and failing to catch a glimpse of who you truly are?"

"We know ourselves only as far as we've been tested," wrote Polish Nobel laureate Wisława Szymborska.

The Gods of Advanced Achievement adore those who launch their visionary venture and only reward the ones who step into the ring.

You really can't lose when you lean into your heart's desires and luminous dreams, you know. If you get what you want, you win. And if what you desire doesn't happen, you grow.

50.

The Hard Worker
Who Never Got Any Better

I was in an exercise class earlier this morning, before returning to my hotel room in the city I'm staying in to write this section of the book for you (yes, I need to be in a lot of different places to keep my creativity, energy and inspiration high; the Muse loves *variety*).

Slightly after sunrise, I headed to the gym for a fitness class where we lifted weights, did sets of push-ups, performed sequences of planks and pretty much sweated out any residue from the day before.

It was fantastic and wonderful. To me.

In this particular group workout, the moves need to be made to the driving beat of dance music. The idea is to do the exercises as a choreographed whole so everyone's moving in unison. So we all become united. So we all are as one.

At the beginning of the class the instructor celebrated one participant. "This is Joel's one thousandth class," she announced merrily.

Joel beamed, picked up his pace and lifted his weights like a man on fire.

Here's the thing, though ...

Throughout the class and through each of the exercises, the

recipient of the honor was completely off-beat, totally out of synch and not highly athletic.

He'd shown the commitment, will and persistency to attend a thousand classes. Awesome feat. Amazing—for sure. Nice work on this part, Joel!

Yet I did find it fascinating that after all those sessions he still wasn't displaying even the slightest hints of the mastery shown by the instructor.

The lesson for us? *Let us not confuse mileage with mastery. And time invested with skill optimized.*

The real principle? *Training that's not intentionally programmed to make you better won't make you any better.*

Anders Ericsson was a pioneering researcher on exceptional performance. I first read of him and his 10,000-Hour Rule more than twenty-five years ago, well before the concept was made famous by other authors. The 10,000-Hour Rule, drawn from Ericsson's studies of elite athletes, chess prodigies, musicians and other creative geniuses, is that one needs to invest approximately 10,000 hours of conditioning before the first signs of world-class performance begin to present themselves.

Ericsson also pioneered the term "deliberate practice." His work has confirmed—and this is *very important* to note—that mere training around a particular ability over a long period of time doesn't necessarily lead to mastery. What makes The Great Ones such standouts is that they commit to *a particular type of practice.*

When advanced performers show up to capitalize on their talent, the session is precisely designed to improve their skill. They train with the clear intention of getting incrementally better. And each practice matters, as it's a stepping stone to their vividly imagined ideal of becoming legendary at what they do. Each slight advancement at every conditioning bout stacks up into a revolution of expertise when done consistently over an extended period. The tiny, deliberately made triumphs eventually become major behavior transformations and those days invested in optimizing the area of their focus inevitably morph into decades of domain dominance. The process is intentional and deliberate rather than random and accidental.

... Athletes who just showed up, did the drills and ran the plays without the conscious commitment to upgrading their power did not rise to the next level.

... Painters who just went to their studio and painted as they'd always painted did not refine their art or accelerate their ability.

... Brain surgeons who merely performed more operations over the length of a career never became superstars. They simply remained ordinary brain surgeons.

So practice that's not carefully calibrated and passionately executed to lift your game and magnify your mastery isn't really practice. It's simply phoning it in.

Like the sweaty man in my morning exercise class. Whom I genuinely applaud for his one thousandth appearance.

51.

The Dark Sides of
Your Upsides

Every gift carries with it a curse of sorts. Every heroic character of Shakespeare's tragedies possessed both a special talent that made them great as well as a tragic flaw that led to their downfall.

The very blessings that make us amazing are the same qualities that can cause us grief. Every single one of your strengths also contains an associated weakness. Human beings are such experts of duality.

A few examples to bring this insight into sharper focus:

… The critical eye that allows someone to handcraft their magnum opus and make their bright light shine is the same eye that causes them to criticize the faults in others. And become hypervigilant in noticing every imperfection of their environment, prompting them to complain and spend a lot of time in frustration.

… The incendiary drive to get big things done, in an era where very few can break free of the iron chains of diversions and interruptions, to deliver awe-inspiring output, often brings with it the tragic flaw of being extremely impatient with others and brutally hard on yourself.

... The artistic integrity that makes your work so honest, excellent and powerful can also lead you to becoming fanatical about perfecting its quality, leading others to call you difficult.

... The obsession of holding yourself to virtuoso-league standards, operating at excellence and relentlessly growing your craft, is the same way of doing that makes you feel as though you've never achieved enough.

... The supreme confidence that causes an individual to believe in their enthusiastic endeavor and splendid capacities is also a trait that can unfold into arrogance. And the false faith that you can do no wrong.

... Being ultra-competitive can lift you to the apex. It's also a behavior that—unchecked—can destroy good relationships, create ambient anxiety and significantly erode your serenity. Because everything becomes a contest. And losing annihilates your self-identity.

... Wiring yourself, through infinite practice, to become an uncommonly hard worker can lead to vast productivity. Yet this very virtue can prevent you from enjoying life's small pleasures and sitting silently in your well-won joy. Because you've become addicted to doing. And you've forgotten how to simply be still.

... The self-discipline that breathtaking success requires can also lead to the rigid, robotic behavior that genuine soulfulness dislikes.

So does all this mean you should shrink from your eminence, stunt your brilliance, or do violence to your masterwork by neglecting your gifts? And slowing the pursuit of your enchantments?

Of course not.

The fact that your inherent genius comes with saboteurs and downsides just means that each of us—as creators, productives and leaders—needs to allow the daylight of our awareness to enhance our clarity around those acts that don't serve us (and those around us) and manage these less-than-ideal behaviors in an intelligent, responsible and precise fashion.

Illuminate your human talents, applying them to accomplish crowning results. Always be a person of unusual ability and a genuine magic worker for the world (yes, you work for the world). Yet may I humbly suggest that you never allow the shadow sides of your peak abilities to defeat positivity, moral authority and advanced spirituality.

Because your best self deserves to prosper.

52.

The 3 Step Success Formula (and My Broccoli-Eating Behavior)

If you've been following my work for a while, you know *The 2x3x Mindset* maxim well.

Simply stated, the principle recommends: "To double your income and impact, you must triple your investment in two core areas: your personal mastery and your professional capability."

Education truly is inoculation against disruption. And the leader who learns the most wins.

Because as you know more, you'll be able to do better. Knowledge—when capably applied—yields exquisite power. You don't have to be the biggest talent to lead your field and make a rare-air life—just the best student.

"Education is the kindling of a flame, not the filling of a vessel," observed Socrates.

"Wisdom is not a product of schooling, but of the lifelong attempt to acquire it," contributed Einstein.

On the subject of transcendent growth, I teach a model that readers of *The 5 AM Club* from around the world have found to be exceedingly helpful in raising leadership, productivity and positivity. And so I wish to share *The 3 Step Success Formula* with you:

THE MECHANICS OF DAILY HEROISM:
THE 3 STEP SUCCESS FORMULA

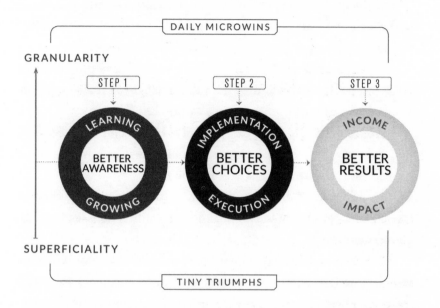

The main thesis behind the framework is that, with better daily awareness, you'll put yourself into a position to make better daily choices. And—of course—as you start making better daily choices, you'll automatically start experiencing better daily results. To state it simply, *The 3 Step Success Formula* is this: *Better awareness breeds the better choices that deliver better results.*

The more you learn and thereby increase your awareness, the greater wisdom you'll have to become the kind of person who makes smarter decisions. And enhanced decision-making guarantees more exceptional outcomes.

Some examples:

... Learn what the world's longest-living people eat and you'll gain the new awareness to make better daily choices that will generate better daily results within your energy, vitality and longevity.

201

... Study the best routines of fabled artists and you'll gather the insights that, when monomaniacally acted upon, will magnify the beauty of your exuberantly imagined results.

... Read about the psychology, emotionality, regimes and rituals of the ultra-rich and you'll be armed with the unusual awareness that you can apply to give you better financial consequences.

... Explore the methods that empire-makers have used to build great companies and you now have the intelligence that—superbly practiced over time—will result in a world-class company.

... Discover how the great spiritual masters achieved what they did, and through devoted decisions to implement this learning, you'll gain access to the same states they inhabited.

Yes, education, when elegantly used, produces immense creative force. (And, conversely, ideation without execution does lead to dangerous delusion.)

The "superficiality to granularity" arrow on the vertical axis of the visual model is also important. Study *any* elite performance and you'll learn that there was *zero* superficiality in their approach to their area of expertise. *They know a lot about very few things.* And as they advance along the journey of their mastery, their approach consistently grows more and more granular.

... Scientist Charles Darwin studied barnacles exclusively for eight long years. But this obsession was mission-critical to his journey as a naturalist and was central to the game-changing theory of evolution he arrived at later.

... The manager at Eleven Madison Park, which received the "World's Best Restaurant" title, required all staff to place the emblem of the restaurant in a specific orientation on the place setting, even though it was out of sight to every diner because it was on the underside of the plate. It was thought that this degree of granularity put the server in the correct state so that the service that followed was equally precise.

... Championship Formula One teams vacuum the floor of the garage in the pit area so that not even a molecule of debris can enter the race car's engine, causing a catastrophe.

Here's a bit of a weird example from my own life (which instinct told me I should share) on the value of lifelong learning for better daily results.

... I've been into broccoli lately. Really into it, actually.

After watching a podcast, I grew fascinated with the wonderful benefits of a compound that it contains called sulforaphane that include the neutralization of bodily toxins, the reduction of free radicals, lower levels of inflammation and enhanced brain function.

The fresh stuff that you see in the vegetable section of your local grocery store just seems too big for me. Hard to eat. Feels like I'm stuffing a brick in my mouth. Same for my family. I get one-star reviews every time I make it. Seriously.

So I kept on experimenting and remained relentless around finding a solution that gave us the rewards of the vegetable without the downsides of the fresh version of it. And eventually purchased a bag of *frozen* broccoli.

I bought it because the pieces looked smaller in the picture on the bag. The heads didn't appear to be the size of my head. The stalks didn't resemble the Eiffel Tower. Seemed like it would be better for us. At least three-star reviews could exist in my future.

I brought it home, defrosted it, cooked it in a wok with some avocado oil, some fresh garlic, a little turmeric and bits of Spanish onion. Then sprinkled in a little Himalayan sea salt and black pepper. A delicious side dish for the dinner I made that night. My family loved it.

But then I wondered: Does frozen broccoli have the same amount of sulforaphane as the fresh goods?

On doing some research, here's what my study taught me: freezing broccoli removes the sulforaphane from the vegetable. Or to be more precise, it blocks its release.

But here's the beautiful thing that I discovered through some vigorous reading ...

By thawing the broccoli and then sprinkling mustard seeds over it or mixing some Dijon mustard into it, the enzyme of myrosinase is produced. Which then sets off a chemical reaction that increases the bioavailability of sulforaphane. Cool, right?

I *loved* learning this. Made me so happy to figure out this hack. See the raw power of learning? And the value of *The 3 Step Success Formula*? (Getting great at research is another GCA—Gargantuan Competitive Advantage—in this world of superficiality and people unwilling to invest the focus, passion and time to *rigorously* study something.)

The advanced and more granular information developed the better awareness that has allowed me to make better daily choices for myself and my family when it comes to our health. Delivering better daily results.

Strange example, perhaps.

But I hope *The 3 Step Success Formula* makes more sense to you now. Because when it comes to making any improvement in a skill, habit or other important area of your life, it works. Really, really well.

53.

What I Think About When I Think About Difficulty

I used to be a runner. Then I got hurt. So I'm no longer a runner (except on a treadmill; I guess that still makes me a runner—now that I think about it).

Anyway, a book I love is by Haruki Murakami, the famed Japanese novelist, marathoner and former owner of a jazz bar named Peter Cat. It's called *What I Talk About When I Talk About Running*.

In this chapter for you, I wanted to spin his words into a new title called *What I Think About When I Think About Difficulty*. I'll walk you through nine of the core beliefs I've rehearsed psychologically and emotionally—to the point of automaticity—to help me personally find victory over adversity. The very nature of a life lived mightily and without holding back means you will often face upheaval and, sometimes, serious suffering. So it makes a good deal of sense to develop your expertise in navigating storms well.

Groovy. Let's go.

Belief #1: This, Too, Shall Pass

Many years ago—as I endured a painful divorce—a respected mentor offered me this wisdom, for comfort during my crisis. It wouldn't

205

seem like these four words could make a difference. Yet they totally did (and I remain most grateful to him for his generous advice). They were to me as balm on a tender lesion, serving to remind me about my brighter future. And of the reality that hard experiences never endure, but patient, steadfast people always will.

Belief #2: Every Seemingly Terrible Situation Inevitably Ends Well

The philosopher Arthur Schopenhauer wrote to this principle when he suggested that life must be lived with foresight, yet can only be understood in hindsight.

It's only when we look back on our lives that we can connect the dots and see how everything that happened was for our highest good. And finest growth. What we saw as a burden—in the heat of the difficulty—through the passage of time turns out to be a blessing. That makes our lives vastly better. Please never forget this idea. It has served me so well.

Belief #3: If It Helps You Grow, It's Not a Problem, but a Reward

To me, the primary purpose of a life lived fully is healing our ancient wounds, fully stepping into our native talent and ascending into all that we were built to be, while being helpful to as many human souls as possible. That was a long sentence. Yet it states what I believe to be truth.

One of the main aims of being in earthschool is to capitalize on *every* condition that you experience to remake weakness into wisdom, fear into faith and pain you're still carrying into unconquerable power. And, yes, the process of reclaiming lost heroism in becoming stronger, braver and more noble is fraught with many messy, uncomfortable and difficult times.

Yet I've grown the most when my life has looked its worst.

It's been *thanks to* my troubles that I've been introduced to my virtues. Misery is the very fire that forged courage and persistency, patience and gentleness, the optimism to forgive and the devotion to work for the world. These priceless benefits were developed not in the days of ease, but in the seasons of my deepest suffering. They have been the rewards Fortune has sent me for remaining present to the difficulty and for converting hardship into healing, purification and spiritual ascension. Everything that the ego claims is "negative" and "a problem" is in your life for a highly positive and awesomely helpful reason. You just can't see the payoff yet. Because you're not supposed to. You're meant to fully experience what you're enduring. Then the boundless blessings will flood into your days.

"What doesn't kill us makes us stronger," wrote Nietzsche. My experience with living tells me he's correct.

Belief #4: Adversity Shows Up to Test How Much We Desire Our Dreams

"When life seems tough and you wonder why, please remember, the teacher is always quiet during a test," goes the proverb.

Life sends hopefulists, exceptionalists and possibilitarians such as you and me disappointing and uncomfortable experiences to measure our commitment to our most gorgeous goals. And most euphoric ideals.

When destiny sends me a curveball, I'm now much more able, thanks to all my years of prayer, meditation, visualization, autosuggestion, journaling, breathwork and growth with spiritual advisers, to remember that a problem only becomes a problem when seen as a problem. And so I take a long inhale, roll up my sleeves and get busy showing the situation that I've come to play.

Belief #5: Chaos Carries Opportunities

When I was in my early thirties, I read Napoleon Hill's classic *Think and Grow Rich*. That book changed my life. (It's less about making a lot of money and far more a treatise on handcrafting a rich life, by the way.)

One of Hill's phrases has remained with me: "Every adversity, even failure, every heartache carries with it the seed of an equal or greater benefit."

When things get super-hard, I encourage you to default into being an opportunity seeker. Ask yourself how you can *profit from* the setback to reveal the peak of your powers, turn calamity into victory, and rework the apparent failure into an *even better* life than you previously enjoyed. This is how warriors operate. And how heavyweights roll.

Belief #6: Heroes Are Born in Hard Times

Heroes are not made during periods of stability, but during days of discomfort.

... Mandela became Mandela on Robben Island.

... Rosa Parks became a legend while facing mistreatment.

... Martin Luther King, Jr., evolved into Martin Luther King, Jr., while fighting the brutality of racism.

... And Gandhi grew into Gandhi as he battled an empire.

What tries to break you also offers you the life-altering chance to know your unseen strengths while making new skills that will serve you for the rest of your life. The novelist Jennifer DeLucy addressed this insight neatly:

> But there was a special kind of gift that came with embracing the chaos, even if I cursed most of the way. I'm convinced that, when everything is wiped blank, it's life's way of forcing you to become acquainted with and aware of who you are now, who you can become. What is the fulfillment of your soul.

Belief #7: To Live without Adventure Is to Not Really Live at All

A great Hollywood story needs both tragedy and triumph, loss and love, and a dark villain who ultimately loses to the flawed victor.

That's been the narrative of my life so far. And very likely the hero story of yours as well.

The higher you reach, the harder the fall. More risks, more stumbles. More influence and impact, more stone throwers and arrow slingers. That's just how the sport works, yes?

And yet I'd rather reach bravely for those ambitions—and fail— than arrive at my last day, full of regret and rage at the realization that I'd watched the game from the stands rather than playing in a championship match.

True defeat is choosing not to go all in. And playing small with the gifts the universe has given to you. Getting bloodied is just part of winning. So wear your wounds as medals of valor.

Belief #8: Life Always Has Your Back

Even when you don't feel your higher power is protecting you and your guardian angels are watching over you, they are. As a matter of fact, you'll be closest to the heavens of your strongest self at the very time that you feel most alone. (Also remember that the ego screams loudest when its death is closest.)

I've discovered that dark nights of the soul are—in truth— faithwalk experiences. In other words, they show up at the perfect time to help you trust in a force larger than yourself. When things in my life have looked like they were completely falling apart, they (and I) were simply being reassembled in what I later realized were the most wonderful (and intelligent) ways.

... So that I'd have more easy trust that whatever was happening was actually for my best.

... So that my egoic self would have less of a say and my heroic side would have a clearer voice.

... So that fear would become confidence, pain would know peace and selfishness would learn the art of giving.

... And so I'd let go of control over all that unfolds and learn to allow in the wisdom of a source more sovereign than myself to lead me where it was best for me to go.

I believe that life unfolds as a magical orchestration of seemingly random events that are absolutely for your greatest progress. And largest gain. So why fight it when it's actually taking you to a better place? Simply embrace it. And enjoy the ride.

Belief #9: Life's Too Short to Take Tragedy Too Seriously

I've worked hard on myself over the past many decades. I still have a long road ahead of me. Much learning left to do, many weaknesses still to attend to and more insecurities yet to be released. But if you'll permit me to say so: I feel good about how far I've come.

As I shared with you earlier, one of the most valuable lessons my struggles have delivered is that of becoming more comfortable when things are most uncomfortable. I've been granted a lot of practice at letting go. Difficult cycles have taught me to detach from outcomes. To do my part and then allow nature to do the rest. To build such an unconquerable inner core that my joy, peace and freedom depend less on anything in the outside world.

I still care (somewhat, yet surely less than ever before) about what others think of me. I still long to do big things in society and am partly fueled by what I achieve in the world. I still feel stung when someone treats me poorly. Yet not that much, really. And far less than before, when I was a younger man. With a smaller sense of self.

I'll go even deeper …

… I still have a fire in my belly and am immensely ambitious. But I'm ambitious in a very different way now. And around very different things.

… I'm ambitious to raise my game around self-mastery and to escalate my craft with quiet audacity.

… I'm ambitious to become less needy for approval, applause and appreciation and become more humble, steadfast and true to myself.

... I'm ambitious to inspire, encourage and protect my family, improve the environment and give even more of myself to causes that move me, such as reducing illiteracy and helping children with leprosy lead better lives (that's such a tragic affliction—even more so for a little kid).

... I'm ambitious to use whatever remains of my life treading the earth lightly, being considerate to all and doing all I can to be a loyal public servant to others.

... I'm ambitious to deepen my relationship with my maker and derive more happiness and excitement through the exploration of my inner world than through my wide-ranging travels through this outer one.

This very philosophy—which is my moral compass, my towering spiritual lighthouse—was forged by heartbreak. By the betrayal of people I trusted and loved. By being mistreated by humans I'd helped and been generous to. By being dramatically let down by individuals I'd sincerely lifted up. And opened my heart to. And so how dare I put down these mean, wonderful and wise teachers? How dare I say that all the difficulties I've gone through have been a brutal battle when they've actually been a perfectly organized training camp to sculpt me into a better version of my former self? I see it all (mostly) in a positive light ...

... and I don't take it all that seriously. Anymore.

Sure, I've been through some real horror. Yet I still laugh when my buddy updates me on his adopted sloth, and I still cry while watching a romantic comedy, and I still know that I'm just a relatively insignificant man who will have no place in the pantheon of history. No one special.

Taking yourself too seriously guarantees that no one will take you seriously.

Be in the world, yet not too much in the world. I love being in it, yet I don't require its rewards to lead a satisfying life. I enjoy what I do, the benefits I have earned and the graces of my days. Yet they absolutely don't define me. More and more, my sense of self, axis of agency and foundation of might come from what is within me rather than what is outside me.

And this has brought me great tranquility. The kind of peace I truly pray for you.

As a matter of fact, one of the most glorious gifts one past trial delivered to me was getting to a place where even if I lost *everything* I had earned and *all* I possessed, I'd still be *completely* fine. Now, I'm so grateful for that "tragedy." Because it freed me.

One last quote as we close this chapter. I think it's worth your attention. And I believe that it'll give you hope and strength when you're down. It's from John Lennon:

"Everything will be okay in the end. If it's not okay, it's not the end."

54.

Why I Write to Heartbreak Country Music

I once sat next to an artist on a flight to Paris.

Here's what he said: "I pick women who break my heart. It's good for my art."

Made me laugh. And then made me think.

Great creativity demands deep sensitivity. And deep sensitivity comes from growing intimacy with your emotionality. With your Heartset. With your feelings.

No masterwork was ever produced by a craftsperson stuck in their intellect. It's the human heart that makes wizardry real.

One of the methods I use to open up doorways into my loftiest creativity is the strategic use of music.

I make playlists for each of my artistic projects. And I often curate ones that dig deep into long-forgotten hurt. For a mountain of creative gold lives there. Suffering is such fertile ground for any artist, holding the seeds of your most ego-free, sincere, unlimited and therefore influential work.

As I write this piece for you, I'm listening to heartbreak country music.

You know the kind. The musician sings of drinking too much whisky, wishing that he had loved you like he now misses you, and days of misspent youth in the back of pickup trucks. Drinking Bud Light.

So why do I follow this eccentric productivity practice, you wonder?

Because music really does open my heart. It floods my soul with a beyond-the-reasoning-mind kind of wisdom and outside-the-everyday sort of inspiration that upgrades my craft. And fuels my jam.

The right kind of music electrifies access to the Muse within you, me and every other creative. A good song opens me up, gets me going and once in a while—with a special track rolling—breaks my heart in the tiniest of ways. Because that rupture can be so good for my rapture. And the art I'm aiming to deliver.

Your job as a consistent producer of monumental enterprises is to battle your demons, slay your dragons and fight the lies that have limited your dreams. Great tunes will help you do this.

It's been said that music is the strongest form of magic.

I do believe this to be true.

55.

The Patient Who Blinked a Book

Jean-Dominique Bauby was a man who loved the high life—and had it all.

The editor-in-chief of French *Elle*, he adored fast cars, enjoyed excellent food and appreciated his powerful friends.

Then—suddenly—while driving with his young son, Théophile, in the countryside outside Paris, he suffered a major stroke that left him completely paralyzed.

Except for his left eyelid.

The condition, known as locked-in syndrome (or pseudocoma), did not affect his mind, which was left strikingly clear to record his experiences.

So that he could communicate, his therapists at the Berck-sur-Mer hospital taught him a code called the Silent Alphabet, which involves blinking, letter by letter, to form words. The process to explain even the simplest of needs was painstaking and grueling. But Bauby did it, showing exceptional heroism in his cruel situation.

The patient decided to share the account of his circumstances, his thoughts on life and his reflections on the human condition in a memoir. So, over a period of months, he blinked 200,000 times to complete the book, with a trusted assistant capturing his words.

The Diving Bell and the Butterfly became a massive bestseller. Here's a passage:

> By means of a tube threaded down my stomach, two or three bags of brownish fluid provide my daily caloric needs. For pleasure, I have to turn to the vivid memory of tastes and smells ... Once, I was a master at recycling leftovers. Now I cultivate the art of simmering memories. You can sit down to a meal at any hour, no fuss or ceremony. If it's a restaurant, no need to call ahead.

Bauby died of pneumonia two days after the work was published. Leaving us with a memory that is an unforgettable testimony to positivity, possibility and the fullest expression of humanity.

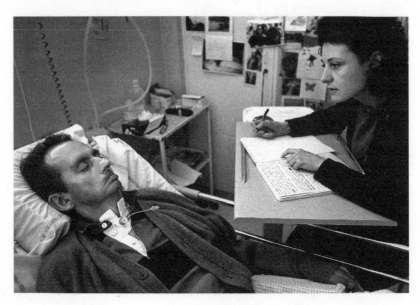

56.

The Possibilitarian's Secret

We live in a period of tremendous volatility, uncertainty and high-velocity change. Disruption is tearing at the foundations of a lot of organizations. And hurting the spirits of many good people.

Many of us have lost our confidence in a predictable future. The majority of people face constant worry. Most of the population has been overwhelmed with a most unhelpful negativity.

Yet a spectacular minority of human beings are able to remain strikingly positive and profoundly bullish in the face of exponential upheaval. And amid challenging personal times.

One of their primary strategies to stay centered on possibility rather than descend into toxicity is to fill their minds with such great dreams that there's simply no room for stressful concerns.

I'll reinforce the idea again so we can process it together: *Fill. Your. Mind. With. Great. Dreams. So. There. Is. No. Room. For. Petty. Concerns.*

Think of your mind as a well. Fill it to the brim with thoughts of your noble aspirations, enchanting enthusiasms and the uplifting information that insulates your energy around your visionary ventures, the good you've been blessed with and the dazzling goals that speak to the possibilitarian within you. You'll *crowd out* all dark and doubt-filled anxieties. "Sunlight is the best disinfectant," said Supreme Court justice Louis Brandeis.

Here's another fundamental principle for personal leadership: *Human prowess is manufactured in moments of restraint.*

By this I mean every time you exercise your self-control muscles (no matter how weak they might currently be) to restrain an impulse you know doesn't serve you, your willpower grows stronger. Every time you do what is correct instead of easy, courageous instead of meek, excellent instead of mediocre and benevolent instead of selfish, you ascend in your mightiness. Do this daily and you'll eventually reach mastery within the key areas of your life.

Do that which is right over that which is easy. Such a simple instruction to follow. One that would restructure our results. Yet one that is also so simple that it's easy to forget. And neglect.

One of my favorite habits is night walking. Late at night when I'm in the mood, I'll explore the streets—of my hometown or the city I happen to be visiting to give a presentation. These are my beloved "wisdom walks," because over the course of two or sometimes even three hours, under the stars and in the dark, I reflect on who I'm becoming, what I'm learning, ideas I'm finding fascinating and those elements of my professional and private realm that I wish to improve. Last night I witnessed something I need to tell you about.

There—in the darkness—was a man. Picking up after his dog. Using the light of his phone. To find the debris.

Maybe what I saw doesn't resonate with you as much as it did with me. (I couldn't stop thinking about the gentleman and his consideration for his neighbors for many hours afterwards.)

Yet here's the point: he did what was the right thing to do in a culture where many people prefer the easiest thing to do.

The dog owner did not know I was watching him. He didn't behave as he did for any recognition. He did it because it was correct. And this is what makes him great.

And so, each time you push out thoughts of apathy, weakness, mediocrity and defeat and replace them with reflections on achievement, beauty, goodness and victory, your human power will rise. Considerably. And your mind will become even more full of the positivity that disinfects fear, lack and insecurity.

What makes a fabulous wine so fantastic is the *terroir*—the environment—the vines are raised in. Elements of a terroir include climate, soil, terrain and farming practices. Similarly, your mind has its own terroir—the surroundings that shape each thought you produce. A negative environment breeds degraded thinking. A pristine terroir promotes positive thoughts. So choose yours well. Please.

Here are four specific tactics to help you become a possibilitarian who sees awe, wonder and opportunity in circumstances where the majority sees only negativity:

Tactic #1: The Inspirational Index Card Technique

Write those quotes that most uplift you—whether from holy books, heroic autobiographies or marvelous poetry—onto a series of 3 x 5 cards that you carry with you everywhere. When you have a free moment, perhaps while standing in line at a grocery store or while commuting on a train, memorize the phrases. And allow their words to repopulate the thoughts that inhabit your consciousness. Yes—of course—you can deploy this strategy on your digital device. But it's less effective because then you'll be tempted to check for messages, snack on social media or scan the news.

Tactic #2: Implement The 3 S's: Silence, Solitude and Stillness

These three potent influences provide the kind of ecosystem that quiets a worried mind and a turbulent heart. Noisy surroundings create a noisy psychology as well as a fear-filled emotionality. The more time you spend in quietude, the more you'll dissolve toxic energies and organically replace them with hope, happiness and spiritual liberty. Meditation will help you enormously here. I've created a series of very powerful guided meditations that will significantly optimize your positivity, increase your productivity and help you let go of past grievances you might be carrying. Feel free to access them at TheEverydayHeroManifesto.com/PositivityMeditations

Tactic #3: Deploy Value Chain Gratitude

Reflecting on your blessings instead of your burdens alters your neuro-chemistry, which in turn elevates your moods. Remember that brain cells that fire together wire together, so *actively* seeking out things you can appreciate in your life will create stronger neural pathways around gratefulness. And the more appreciative you become, the more there will be no space for discouragement to show up and distort reality toward the perception of negativity. Yet don't just practice gratitude by writing a few quick items in your gratitude journal. Go deep by engaging in what I call "value chain gratitude," displaying thankful-ness from the beginning to end of any benefits that cause your life to be better. For example, at a grocery store checkout, say a prayer of silent thanks to the cashier who is assisting you, the stock clerk who put food on the shelf, the truck driver who carried the supply to the store and the farmer who raised the crops that you and your family will eat. Run this strategy across all areas of your daily experiences and soon your entire life will be one giant immersive experience in granular gratefulness. And, therefore, inescapable joy.

Tactic #4: Become a Solution Noticer

Every problem comes with a factory-installed solution—whether you can currently see that solution or not. This is an *extremely* important principle to understand and implement as you free your-self of burdens and banish demons of defeatist thinking. Make the commitment to improve your acuity as a problem solver and your worries will vanish, allowing you to express your highest gifts to a welcoming world.

I want to share with you something very special to me.

220

When I was a lawyer in my twenties, living in a city far from my parents, my father wrote me a note on his old-school prescription pad, which he tucked inside a book that he sent by mail. He explained that the Sanskrit symbol for funeral pyre looks almost identical to the symbol for worry.

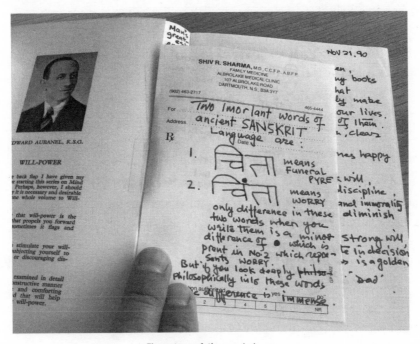

The note my father wrote to me

Hmmm.

If you look really carefully at his script, you'll see he writes that "the only difference in these two words when you write them is a minor difference of •." The dot.

That's a pretty interesting distinction, isn't it?

Dad explained that although the only technical difference between the two Sanskrit characters was a single dot, the real difference was this: *A funeral pyre burns the _dead_, while worry consumes the living.*

So avoid it at all costs.

Wise words for us as we navigate the tides of our days.

And in case you're wondering what his writing beneath the note says, it reads:

Many times many books come in our way that positively and surely make a positive dent in our lives. This book is one of them. Resolution, meditation, clear thinking enhance one's happy treasures in life.

Self-doubt, weak will, lethargy, lack of discipline, lack of purpose and immorality are sure ways to diminish life strength.

Character, honesty, strong will, consideration, resolute in decision and forthrightness is a golden road to a golden life.

Dad

The book mailed to me by my father is called *Will-Power* by Edward Aubanel. And it sits neatly at the front of my library so I can read it often. And ward off worry.

57.

The Big Lie of Positive Thinking

All right. I'm going to go out on a limb (yet again) and offer you another insight that I think you might say is quite a contrarian one and perhaps a contradiction to the chapter you just completed. The idea is this: positive thinking doesn't really work.

To be more precise: positive thinking doesn't really work (and last) *unless* certain conditions are put in place for it to work (and continue). Allow me to give you some context for these unorthodox statements.

I've read a lot of the classic (and not-so-classic) books on how to reframe setbacks into setups, reperceive hardships into advantages and reprogram troubles into triumphs. I've honestly learned a lot from these works and sincerely appreciate the wonderful efforts of these authors to help those experiencing challenges.

Yet something never felt quite right to me with their recommendations to look for the reward within the problem, to be grateful for all the good you still have during painful periods and to move ahead as quickly as possible from a crisis, without giving the worry any more energy.

Yes, to lead a happy, serene and inspired life, we can't dwell on our misfortunes. On this we agree. And it *is* a complete waste of time to stay stuck in the past, obsessing over a scenario that disappointed you. Nothing good will happen if you refuse to let go.

But it never made sense not to deal with what is. It never felt right not to acknowledge how I was feeling when my heart was hurting and my feelings were sinking during a rough spot. And to just race straight into positive thinking without honoring (and then processing through) the emotions that the difficulty generated. Manipulating my thinking without embracing and staying with my authentic feelings seemed fake, forced. Like pure denial.

What I mean is that if you're going through a messy time in your life, restructuring your thinking to spot all the benefits and highlight all the positives ignores all of the emotional realities that have naturally come up.

... If you've lost a job or are facing any other kind of financial sorrow, focusing your Mindset purely on the opportunities inside the adversity causes the anger or sadness or fear or shame or embarrassment to be suppressed within your Heartset, creating a whole range of future problems (disease is the result of dis-ease).

... If you're dealing with heartbreak from the end of an intimate relationship or another form of loss of a loved one, pretending that you're not grieving by putting your head down, keeping busy (as many counselors will advise) and practicing a false optimism betrays the fact you're feeling anguish that needs to be worked through.

... If you're suffering the emotional injury caused by a serious illness or a potentially catastrophic lawsuit or a severe accident, rushing into intellectual exercises designed to reveal the silver lining disrespects the very real sentiments that any human being who has not buried their emotions would feel. And increases the invisible toxicity already within your system from past unprocessed hurts (which you now know about very well).

To run to positive thinking without performing emotional healing is to make things worse. This sets up a wall between you and the wisdom, vitality, creativity, productivity, compassion and courage that is your truest nature. (The word "courage" is derived from the Old French word *cuer*, which means "heart," by the way.)

By not dealing with the organic feelings arising, you'll close down the enormous power of your Heartset and live only within your head, becoming more like a coldly logical automaton instead of a high-functioning human being connected to the collective as well as to your own native magic. Disconnect yourself from your pain and you'll also disconnect yourself from joy—and primal genius. Conversely, feel through your pain and you'll reclaim your ability to experience the awe and wonder that destiny has in store for you.

I'll go even further: a lot of the problems on the planet right now, such as wars, racial and gender injustice, environmental decay and financial greediness, are caused by people disassociated from their hearts, locked in their minds. (Maybe "locked-in syndrome" can happen psychologically as well as physically?) Because no one ever taught them to do any better ...

... And because society schooled them into thinking that "mindset is everything."

... And because experts taught them that positive thinking is the ultimate salvation.

... And that positive *feeling* is for the foolish, weak and unproductive. And should be swept under the rug.

If you can no longer feel (because you've avoided doing so for so long), how will you ever be able to sense the compassion needed to treat another well? If you can no longer access your delight and aliveness, how will you ever be able to gather the inspiration and spiritual chemistry to launch your movement or produce your masterpiece? Too many people—in business and society—suffer from what I call in my mentoring curriculum "dysfunctional optimism." We try hard to think uplifting thoughts, but are at war with the reservoir of toxic emotions hidden within us. That's a perfect formula for total self-sabotage.

If you can no longer experience your emotional universe, each move you make becomes a form of mental calculus. You become more like a machine than a human, more like a bot than a person. If all you do is accumulate micro-trauma and macro-trauma, you'll be wearing a suit of armor each day, out in public. Yes, it can protect you. But it will also block you—from hearing the whispers of your greatness, feeling the deep inspiration that drives your masterwork and interacting with every single human being you encounter with politeness and patience, compassion and love.

Repress uncomfortable emotions and you'll create a vast subconscious world of darkness, anger and guilt that chains you to victimhood—and gets you addicted to escapes such as overwork, drama, digital distraction and rampant consumerism because you're fleeing yourself. It's just too difficult to be alone with you. So you need to be too much in the world.

I'm not sure these words of Dostoevsky really fit here, yet my intuition is begging me to place them here, so I will:

"You sensed that you should be following a different path, a more ambitious one. You felt that you were destined for other things, but you had no idea how to achieve them and in your misery you began to hate everything around you."

Unconsciously managing all these unprocessed feelings also consumes huge amounts of energy (making you far less productive) and sends toxicity through your body, creating disorder within your organs and diminishing your health. It's really, really important that you know this.

"So is positive thinking a waste of time, Robin?" you ask.

My reply? "It's a *superb* use of your time—*once* you've worked through the natural emotions and physical sensations that arise in a crisis. Otherwise, you'll simply add more trauma to your emotional system, weighing down your optimism, performance, impact and essential caring for humanity, via the Field of Hurt and all of its heavy energy that will radiate through your body and into your mind to degrade its native power." Actually staying with and befriending the feelings surfacing during any difficulty, until they release and dissolve, powerfully raises your spiritual energy, which then *automatically* raises your positivity naturally. Ironic that the best way into sustained positive thinking is dedicated emotional healing, isn't it?

"And how do I know when to stop the emotional processing and shift to cognitive reframing and writing gratitude lists to improve my mindset, along with doing all the things those positive-thinking pundits instruct me to do? I can't be feeling those uncomfortable feelings forever, right?" you question.

"Right," I'd reply to you, with lots of love and respect. "It's wise to experience the emotions so you avoid suppressing them and can initiate the exercise of releasing them, yet you definitely don't want to *wallow* in them. You'll know when it's time to make the shift and to start the intellectual process of counting your blessings and looking cheerfully into the future. Trust your instinct."

Because you are wiser than you understand, more powerful than you can fathom and meant to live a delightfully positive life.

58.

That Time I Went Camping

I'll confess right now that I'm not much of a camper.

A morning without a shower isn't much of a treat for me.

Evenings with flies, bugs and bears just aren't my cup of tea.

But I did have one camping experience ...

In preparation for the big trip, my two friends and I went to a supply store. We purchased a lantern, canteens for water, lightweight pots and pans, waterproof matches, sleeping bags and a sleek tent.

We drove for four hours. Out of the city. Past the countryside. Into the wilderness. It was lovely.

We found the campground. Laid down the ground cover, planted the metal stakes and set up the tent.

It was hard to do, as I'm likely the most un-IKEA person you've ever met. (Meaning me and instruction booklets are like oil and water. Or like tuna and jam.)

Eventually, we got the tent up. It looked misshapen. Rickety and disjointed. Yet it was our tent, so we were happy, and proud of our accomplishment.

As the sun started to set, I started a little campfire. I felt like an explorer. Like those daring and adventurous survivalists who discovered new lands.

... Like Vasco da Gama or Amerigo Vespucci.

... Or maybe Ferdinand Magellan, with a little of John Cabot and Christopher Columbus.

It was an exhilarating moment in my life. I felt a bit invincible. If you know what I mean.

Of course—true to tradition—we pulled out a bag of marsh-mallows and found sticks so we could roast them in the flames. We snacked on the sandwiches we had carefully prepared and warmed some hot chocolate as the air grew crisper.

We started telling stories and making each other laugh.

It was quite a special sight. Bordering on the magical, in a way. But then something happened that I'd love to tell you about ...

I heard a rustle in the trees. Then a breaking of branches that began to trouble me. Then a bunch of strange animal shrieking noises that left us frightened.

A coyote? A wolf? A gigantic black bear?

Not sure what it was (or they were). All I know is that I had no plans to stick around to find out.

And so—I kid you not—we tore down the tent with the energy of a hippie with his hair on fire, stomped on the flames like we were members of Riverdance and gathered our lantern, canteens, pots and pans as if we were fleeing for our lives.

We ran. To the car. Fast as Jesse Owens. As swiftly as Flo-Jo.

As I ran, all I could think of was that I didn't have to outrun the violent animal. I simply had to outrun my friends.

So there we were. Three young men in our twenties with all our stuff in our hands. Racing to the vehicle. The scary sounds still shriek-ing. Under the stars in an incredibly dark sky.

We made it. Got into the car. Locked the doors. Took off like Bond avoiding the villain. Relieved to be alive.

It was late, yet heaven cooperated and soon we spotted an old motel, just off the main road. All the lights were off, except for one in the lobby. We each booked a room and spent the night there. Away from the coyote. Or the wolf. Or the grizzly bear.

My lesson? Don't camp. Ever again.

And … that life's such a precious ride. Make sure you never hold back. And always have time for fun.

The journey you and I are on offers such adventures and chances to explore, enjoy enchanting experiences and learn more about yourself.

Occasions to discover more about what you love and what you don't. How to manage surprise and ways to appreciate the treasures of great friendships. Invitations to celebrate the rapture of star-filled skies, the gorgeousness of nature and the genuine friendliness of our universe.

"Whenever you are creating beauty around you, you are restoring your own soul," wrote American novelist Alice Walker.

So say yes to new prospects and raise a victory sign when you sense a sensational opportunity to more fully respect your destiny. Don't ever postpone really living. Never put off something until a better time in the future. Because there is no better time to step into adventure, growth and excitement than now.

Just get a good tent. And avoid the black bears. If you know what I mean.

59.

The 13 Hidden Traits
of the Billionaires I've Advised

Being around many billionaires and other financial heavyweights (I will only work with the ethical ones) for so many years has shown me that most of them have a series of common qualities that cause the culture to label them as gifted and otherworldly, when in reality they just think as few think and operate as few behave. Remember: to have the results that only 5% of the population have, you need to do what 95% of people are unwilling to do.

Given that economic prosperity is such a struggle for so many people, I thought it would be valuable for me to share thirteen of the dominant traits of the moguls I've advised.

Trait #1: A Foolhardy Degree of Self-Faith

The super-wealthy remain steadfast in their belief that their creative ambitions and enthusiastic aspirations will be made true in the face of everyone around them claiming their visions are ridiculous, impractical, nonsensical and impossible. They are doubted, mocked, rejected, condemned and opposed. And yet they stay faithful to the beauty of their ideals.

Trait #2: A Blinding Vision of a Brighter Future

Related to the first point, yet slightly different, is the quality of entre-preneurial masters to see magnificent possibilities where the majority incorrectly thinks that the only things that can happen are the things that have already happened. The very nature of invention and innovation is that it decimates the normal. And degrades the status quo. I call this capacity to unlock value and magic where none is seen by the majority "The Visionary's Gift." Where most view a problem, these brave souls see possibilities. And a greater future for humanity.

Trait #3: A Terrific Thirst for Rebellion

The billionaires I mentor are path-blazers, way-showers, often rebels and always outright revolutionaries. They have a consistent disregard for rules, are closet freedom fighters and pirates disguised as business luminaries. They have the brazen bravado to bend their world to the vision that they've set for it. And the endurance to do whatever it takes to make their vision real.

Trait #4: A Childlike Level of Curiosity

You and I were sorcerers as kids. We dreamed heroic dreams, colored outside the lines and saw life as an amusement park. We loved to learn new things and try new skills. We constantly asked "Why?" and wanted to know the answers to our biggest questions. Yet as we grew up, our holy curiosity got torn down. The financially richest people on the planet have insulated their inquisitiveness from a bored, ordinary and too often gloomy society. They are *extremely* devoted students. They read constantly (I can't tell you how many times I've heard a tycoon say, "I read everything I can get my hands on"). They eagerly invest in coaches and guides. They take educational courses, attend conferences (often sitting in the front row and taking diligent notes) and relentlessly upgrade their skills. *They understand that the better you get, the more value you can give.* And the more masterwork you push—to as many people as possible—the more money you'll make (money is simply the marketplace's return on benefit delivered). This is part of what makes them great, economically.

Trait #5: An Acute Carelessness about the Opinions of Critics

You can crave to be liked by everyone around you. Or you can set the world alight by your genius. I doubt you'll be able to accomplish both. The opinions of others are nothing more than their opinions, as I mentioned earlier. That's it. Don't invest more power in them than that. Someone's opinion is just their statement about what they think is possible, based on their entrenched belief system and past experiences. *It's really none of your concern*, so don't let it sabotage your success. And don't allow the limited perceptions (and jealousies) of those who feel threatened by your radiance to rent space (for free) within your mind, heart and spirit. That real estate is far too precious to let them squat on it. The icons of vast wealth vigorously refuse to allow their ambition to be limited by fear-based, jealousy-fueled beliefs. They are like world-champion racehorses with blinders at the sides of their eyes. Tunnel vision around their mission. Distractions don't matter.

Trait #6: A Gargantuan Commitment to Consistency and Persistency

All world-class producers are *enormously consistent*. They understand the power of mundanity—repeating the same routines, rituals and methods of performing, day after day after day—to create superhuman grades of productivity, value and impact. Consistency truly is one of the surest highways to legendary. Along with this, my ultra-high-net-worth clients also display unusual amounts of persistency. Knock them down and they get back up. Put up a wall and they'll tear it down. Tell them a trouble cannot be overcome and they just might never speak to you again. These types meet with rejection and hear only a yes in the making. To these human beings, failure is nothing more than a gateway into higher success. They are unstoppable, undefeatable and unkillable. Regularly. At a live event I held a few years ago, a participant—a truly wonderful young man with a smile that could light up an arena—approached me at the end of the weekend experience. "I have to hand it to you, Robin," he said in a complimentary tone, "you're really *consistent*." I felt I had delivered content of blazing inspiration, along with insights of unusual richness and all he could say was, "You're really consistent?" But later that evening, in the stillness of my hotel room, I got what he meant. He was a celebrated collegiate football player, an elite-level athlete, and he'd been to many of my live events. To witness me operating at the same level each time, honoring the same virtues and holding true to the same philosophy, represented *consistency*, the DNA of any great athlete.

Trait #7: A High Love of Winning and Being Best in World

Oh, how the ultra-prosperous adore the feeling of progressing, advancing and translating their passionate designs into daily evidence. Many of them are former athletes. Their drive to win the title and secure the championship has helped them install an obsession to achieve victory in every other area. And they don't just want to be sort of good and mildly successful. These individuals completely need to be the absolute best. In the world. (I've never forgotten a line on the mission statement of one of our organizational clients: "We are committed to being the best in our field. *By far*.")

Trait #8: A Deeply Trained Ability to Resist Instant Pleasure

Nearly every billionaire I've ever worked with has had otherworldly-grade personal discipline. Their self-control capacity is pristine. Herculean, even. They stay with their ethical ambitions, refined plans and high-value targets not only when they are full of startup energy, but also long after that energy has turned into the necessary drudgery

234

of doing hard things. Their dogged perseverance is marvelous. Many of these financial titans eat less than most people, rise at dawn to gain a head start on their day, care *enormously* about staying fit and run their days like a precisely calibrated military campaign. Importantly, they put off the easy pleasures, understanding that with daily focus, patience, a supreme work ethic and unyielding dedication they are guaranteed to reap steady, small rewards for their efforts over the passage of time. I call this way of being "sustained incrementalism." Economic superstars play the long game. While the lightweight wants the win in a moment.

Trait #9: A Learned Skill of Multiplying Wealth

Most people are consumers. They buy things all the time, often when they need them least. It fills an emotional hole and unmet need, which makes them happy—for a minute or two. Until they realize they are now in deeper debt, which makes them unhappy—for many years. The heroes of prosperity are creators. They make the things that most people buy. Further, as their economic fortunes grow, they make their money work for them while they sleep. By making smart investments. And avoiding the doom loop of unserviceable debt. Now, please don't fall into the snare of thinking that the development of passive income that compounds exponentially over time is the only way to world-class wealth. I'd like to call your attention to a term not so often used: *active* income. My clients enjoy unusual fortune because they focus on the generation of *both* passive income (where their money is made to work for them, rather than working for their money and trading labor for cash) *and* active income (money made by contributing rich streams of value to their marketplace).

Trait #10: A Refusal to Be around Negative People

The great visionaries armor-plate their optimistic energy. Every inspirational achievement was created by a wildly inspired human being. Lose that state and you'll lose the fire that makes your star-dust real. And so, the maestros of money avoid excuse-makers and complainers like the plague and spend their time with hope-shouters, world-builders and other empire-makers.

Trait #11: A Near-Infinite Sense of Agency over Accomplishment

The victim says society owes them a living. They plead for help from the government and their relatives and anyone who they happen to meet who will listen to their story about how hard it is for them to survive in a turbulent economic climate and how much of a struggle it is to win. The visionary leader owns their human power to execute around their aspirations and has *a sense of agency* that makes them sure of their abilities. They have the wisdom, courage and creativity to know that the true axis of power of a fully alive human being comes from within, never from some outside force. I've seen these types refuse to purchase a lottery ticket because of the message such an act would send to their strongest selves, a message that, in order to experience vast wealth, luck would have to intervene rather than success unfolding as a direct consequence of their actions. These types understand that the more you deliver on what you promised to yourself, the more your confidence will grow to realize even more challenging enterprises. And that being monomaniacally focused on one's priorities, out-innovating everyone in your field, producing goods and services that are distinctive and precious, working harder than anyone you've ever met, and doing all this with lavish integrity will get you into the Hall of Fame of Prosperity a whole lot easier than hoping for a handout ever will.

Trait #12: An Application of the Asymmetric Risk-Reward Paradigm (ARRP)

ARRP is a term I employ to describe the practice of billionaires to invest their acumen, energy and time purely in opportunities where the upside is *exponentially* larger than any downside. In other words, the possible rewards have absolutely no symmetry or proportion to the risks if the venture or investment fails. It's a myth that magnates are foolish risk-takers, consistently making ill-considered moves and flying by the seat of their pants. No. The ultra-rich tend to be more conservative, thoughtful and deliberate than one would expect, seeking out enterprises where astonishing returns are available without having to bet the farm.

Trait #13: A Contrarian Mode of Deploying Capital

Finally, the billionaires I've advised mostly operate under a completely different way of spending (and seeing) money. I call this a "maverick investing calculus." Essentially, this describes their rare (yet earned and developed, not innate and gifted) ability to *spot hidden value*. Whether their asset class involves equities, art, real estate or precious metals, they see a treasure where the crowd sees a loser. The A-Listers of Abundance are *prescient*, looking well into the future and wearing badges of honor for being ahead of their time. They get that by the time the mainstream media is reporting on a financial opportunity, it's too late to get in. Again, their gift of being able to see around corners and get to where the puck is going instead of where it currently is (à la hockey great Wayne Gretzky) is actually no gift, but the eventual result of patient study, preparation, testing and training that most people are simply not willing to do.

I'll leave you with the philosophy of John D. Rockefeller, the richest person to have ever lived, after adjusting for inflation:

> I believe in the dignity of labor, whether with a head or hand; that the world owes no person a living but that it owes every person an opportunity to make a living.
>
> I believe that thrift is essential to well-ordered living and that economy is a prime requisite of a sound financial structure, whether in government, business or personal affairs.

I believe that the rendering of useful service is the common duty of mankind and that only in the purifying fire of sacrifice is the dross of selfishness consumed and the greatness of the human soul set free.

I believe in an all-wise and all-loving God, named by whatever name, and that the individual's highest fulfillment, greatest happiness, and widest usefulness are to be found in living in harmony with His will.

I believe that love is the greatest thing in the world; that it alone can overcome hate; that right can and will triumph over might.

P.S. To receive a digital version of The Billionaire Blackbook, a manual for creating a hypergrowth company, accelerating your financial fortune and battleproofing your prosperity in volatile conditions, go to: TheEverydayHeroManifesto.com/BillionaireBlackbook

60.

The 8 Forms of Wealth

My mentoring methodology has, as one of its philosophical foundations, a transformational concept called *The 8 Forms of Wealth*, which I'd like to offer to you, as it's been so very helpful to my clients in organizing and orchestrating a life that can truly be classified as world-class.

Our culture trains us to believe that wealth only comes in one form: money. I disagree. There are a lot of people who have a lot of cash—and not much else. Such souls are cash rich, but joy poor. They have economic liquidity, but poverty of positivity. And spiritual scarcity.

JPF (joy, peace and freedom) are a million times more valuable than FFA (fame, fortune and applause), at least the way I see life.

There are *eight* major dimensions of wealth to work on if you're serious about a life of genuine abundance. And true riches.

On a private advisory assignment, or on the initiation of one of my online coaching groups, an early step is to have each client rate their current performance in each of these eight areas from one to ten, one being extremely low and ten being world-class.

THE 8 FORMS OF WEALTH

This exercise gives them a powerful visual assessment of precisely how they are doing in each of the fields of *authentic* wealth. Clarity precedes mastery. You can't remedy a problem that you have no awareness about. So much of elite performance and handcrafting a gorgeous life is about building intimacy with your blind spots. And ending the hypnosis of self-deception.

If you would like to do this transformational online analysis and access a helpful training video for *The 8 Forms of Wealth*, head over to TheEverydayHeroManifesto.com/The8FormsofWealth

Okay. Now, let's go through each form of wealth together:

Form of Wealth #1: Self-Mastery + Sincere Heroism

This sphere represents your progress when it comes to knowing, reclaiming and expressing your heroic nature. Personal mastery is about calibrating your Mindset, purifying your Heartset, optimizing your Healthset and escalating your Soulset—maximizing *The 4 Interior Empires* I introduced you to earlier. Install a practice to do this mission-essential work each morning while the rest of the world is asleep and you are guaranteed to see major gains in your outer empires of creativity, productivity, prosperity and public service to many. Remember: leadership, greatness and impact are an inside job. You will never make an exterior life that's higher, stronger and more noble than the one you build within. Materializing your finest self really is a true form of real wealth.

Form of Wealth #2: Physical Fitness + Longevity

This life dimension relates to all aspects of your physical status, including brain health, personal energy, stamina, the ability to recover quickly, the quality of your immunity, sleep hygiene and longevity. Giving the time and resources needed to flourish in this segment of your life will cost you, I agree. Disease (or death) will cost you more.

Splendid health is a key element of genuine fortune. Invest in it (like any excellent investor) as the returns that will flow will be in an order of magnitude beyond anything you can fathom. As the elders of one wisdom tradition say: "When young, we are willing to sacrifice all of our health for financial wealth; yet once we grow old and wise, we are willing to give up all of this wealth for even a single day of excellent health."

Yes, Healthset appears in this category as well as being part of Form of Wealth #1. I do this intentionally because although great health is part of personal mastery, it also deserves its own kingdom. So you make it a top priority as you build a world-class life. Because without it you have nothing.

241

Form of Wealth #3: Family + Friendships

No one, at the final hour, wishes they had spent more time with their lawyers, corporate suppliers and golf partners. No. We all hope, at the end of our lives, to be surrounded by family and friends whom we have treated well and who are overwhelmed by their appreciation and adoration of us. Too many in their twilight are filled with giant regret that they didn't spend enough time with those they love. If this priority will matter at the end, wisdom instructs that you make it *essential* now. This is especially true when it comes to children. As parents we have a tiny window of opportunity to show unconditional love and shape our kids before they go off to lives of their own. Once that window closes, it's hard to open it up again, if you haven't done the work to make this important relationship deep.

Form of Wealth #4: Craft + Career

Every human being has the promise to realize soaring levels of joy, meaning and internal peace from becoming splendidly skilled at what they do for a living, so they operate at the height of their powers, talents and capacities. Few pursuits provide as much psychic satisfaction as doing your work at mastery, becoming Best in World (*by far!*) at your craft, solving hard problems that enrich a ton of people and having the time of your life growing into the producer your inner heroism is pleading with you to be. Definitely devote great energy to raising your performance in this region.

Consider your devotion to the maximization of your craft and the related amplification of your professional career as a massive form of wealth worthy of celebrating (and increasing).

Form of Wealth #5: Money + Net Worth

Yes, of course, your income and your net worth (believe it or not, some people think these are the same; they are *so* different) are a form of wealth within your life.

To realize a beautiful life balance, having enough money to create fantastic memories for your family, easily handle their needs (as well as your own) and enjoy the fruits of your labor by buying the material goods (and experiences) that fill your heart (and soul) with happiness is fundamental. So much stress is caused by a lack of economic prosperity. And so much good can be done in the world once you have a fair amount of money.

I'd love for you to note that one of the biggest mistakes people make in their financial lives (after accumulating too much debt and failing to practice the time-tested yet usually broken rule of living within their means) is to upgrade their lifestyle each time they increase their income. Huge error. If every time you make more money you increase your expenses, you'll never build any net worth. You'll always be on the hamster wheel.

I also recommend that you avoid being hypnotized by "Top Line Seduction," the psychological attraction to being impressed by personal (or corporate) income rather than looking at the *profit*. Your annual and monthly inflow matters a lot less than how much you have left over to save and invest, once expenses and taxes are paid. Don't confuse gross income with net profit. Ever. Please.

Finally, on Form of Wealth #5, trust and know that money is not evil. Only people who have no money say that, to justify their poverty. Prosperity *can* bring you—and yours—happiness. If used with wisdom, enthusiasm, consideration and the disciplined exercise of your integrity.

Form of Wealth #6: Mentors + Influencers

We do rise to the level of our conversations, associations and relationships. *Your inner circle absolutely drives your external mastery.* The sixth form of wealth, then, involves spending more time with people whose lives you dream of living. People who—by the way they think, feel, operate and contribute—reveal to you a whole new way of working and living. Influencers who *push you*, by their example, to show up with even greater optimism, excellence, originality and decency.

And if you're really serious about rolling at world-class, make sure you regularly hang with human beings who are behaving at such a level of amazingness that you'll never ever be able to catch up to them! Their model will kindle an un-put-outable fire in your belly and fuel your magnificent ascent into the magic you are meant to be, sprinkling your starlight into the universe. If you're the most successful person you know, maybe it really is time to know some new people. Finding exceptional role models to mentor you will create a total right-angle turn in your life. This, I promise you.

Form of Wealth #7: Adventure + Lifestyle

Humans are happiest when we are progressing. And exploring. And venturing out into the vivid blue oceans of previously imagined places, potentials and pursuits that set our spirits aflight. You and I, at a primal level, are nomads. We are travelers. Voyagers. Pioneers, of sorts. We long to learn new skills, embrace novel experiences, enter foreign cultures, turn strangers into friends and advance through life with sparkling eyes and dancing hearts.

To realize optimal life balance, it's important to inject some sort of "institutionalized adventure" into your weeks, whether that's a trip to an art gallery or a visit to the library or a trek to a restaurant that makes a type of food you haven't yet tried. As well, nourishing your inner explorer on a regular basis will fuel your inspiration and upgrade your creativity.

Part of raising your game on Form of Wealth #7 also involves the consistent escalation of your overall lifestyle. Committing to the building of a world-class level of living is such a splendid goal. Consider the ideal home you wish to live in, the quality of the material things you own, the amount of renewal time you want to take off, living in multiple countries that energize your artistry (rather than buying a second or third home that drains capital and makes you feel compelled to spend time there, consider the strategic use of great hotels), and the overall grade at which you exist. Doing something weekly to optimize your lifestyle will yield superb dividends over time.

Form of Wealth #8: Impact + Contribution

I know we agree that a life that doesn't make the lives of others better is a terribly empty one. So commit yourself even more diligently to investing in this final form of wealth by making sure that each week you've planned some activity that will scale your usefulness and increase your public service, in some small (or large) way. So when you exit the world, you will know the honor and dignity of a life lived for so much more than yourself.

———

All right. That's it. *The 8 Forms of Wealth* framework. So you experience genuine and enduring life excellence—rather than reaching the end of your days only to discover that you spent your finest hours climbing mountains that led to the wrong summits. You never want to live the life modern society sells you as being successful, while neglecting what universal wisdom has taught us that living wonderfully truly involves.

Sharing my thoughts on the multiple forms of wealth prompts me to recall these humorous words from the diary of literary lion Henry James:

> When one has fair health, a fair fortune, a tidy conscience and a complete exemption from embarrassing relatives, I suppose he is bound, in delicacy, to write himself happy.

245

61.

The Algorithm for a Beautifully Balanced Life

Please note: This chapter contains calibrated information on my weekly planning process. I've done my best to make it clear and have also created an instructional video that I mention at the end of this piece. For years I've been asked to share this procedure publicly—so I'm doing so here.

Okay. Let's start.

Now that you know there are actually *eight* forms of wealth (money being just one of them), I'd like to walk you through a transformational method that will help you integrate them into your life beautifully so that your good intentions translate into terrific results.

This system is also the one I personally use for my weekly planning. The process is one of the single most valuable tools I've used to construct a creative, productive and helpful life. To fully understand the methodology of this chapter and gain its complete value, please go to TheEverydayHeroManifesto.com/WeeklyDesignSystem and print out the tactical worksheets so they are in front of you. Also watch the video I've carefully made, walking you through the eight steps of the planning process. Doing this will make what I share here more clear and much more beneficial to you.

There are three fundamentals when it comes to building absolutely world-class weeks that are both immensely industrious and uncommonly balanced:

1. The things that get scheduled are the things that get done.
2. Vague plans produce vague goals.
3. World-class weeks soon morph into the sensational quarters that lead into the spectacular years that generate sublime decades.

With these core insights in mind, let's have a look at the learning model below that offers you a high-level view of the system that will substantially increase the caliber of your performance, happiness and inner freedom.

THE WEEKLY DESIGN SYSTEM

I set aside an hour early every Sunday morning to plan the week ahead. (As American novelist Saul Bellow said, "A clear plan relieves you of the torment of choice.") My family is sound asleep, the neighborhood is overwhelmed with quiet, my devices are at a lovely setting called "off" and I'm granted the fine luxury of contemplation. To consider what's most important. And script out the seven days in front of me so that I lead them ideally (as ideally as possible in an unpredictable world, of course).

It's also worth noting that one of the best ways to multiply your self-discipline and ability to stay consistent is by getting really, really good at weekly scheduling (and then keeping the tiny daily promises that you've set).

Now let us go through each step of the process:

Step #1: Go Macro + Connect to Your Vision

Your starting point is to fast forward and think about what you will have wished your life stood for and what you need to have achieved by the time you become old in order to feel satisfied that you were true to your ideals. This will ensure that the week ahead is strategic rather than reactive, intentional rather than automatic.

The first time I explain the system to a client, I ask them to create their Tombstone Statement—four paragraphs detailing what they hope their family, friends and colleagues will say about them after they die. This is based on their Lifetime Big 5 targets, a concept I walked you through in the chapter on *The Peak Productivity Strategies Pyramid*. Then I have them write out their Top 10 Daily Devotions—those habits and daily routines that, when routinized, cause them to perform at their best.

Every Sunday morning, with high intention and complete presence, they review these two documents in a heartfelt way to reconnect with what's most important, before they start building their blueprint for an ideal week ahead. This provides them with a visit to

248

their personal lighthouse, to guide them with clarity. Again, I've provided the actual worksheets I use in my coaching for you at the digital site mentioned at the beginning of this chapter. Or you can write your Tombstone Statement and Top 10 Daily Devotions in your journal. Please do what feels right for you.

Step #2: Reflection on Your Weekly Story

Next, write out a Weekly Story that explains in detail how you lived out each day of the previous week. Once you begin using the actual weekly planning template that is part of this method, you can perform this step far more easily because you'll have a neat schedule of each of the past six days. For now, just think through what you did each day last week, then list the work accomplishments, exercise sessions, periods spent learning, time with family and friends, and so on.

Writing your Weekly Story will give you strikingly high levels of awareness about where you're winning. It will codify, wonderfully, where things went well so you can repeat your winning formula over the week ahead (just imagine the inspiration, momentum and productivity you'll enjoy week after week when you do this consistently). And the practice of reviewing your entire week in fine detail will identify which opportunities for improvement are most available to you. With better awareness of how you're performing, you will be fueled to make the better daily choices that guarantee better daily results (recall my broccoli eating habit and *The 3 Step Success Formula*).

Step #3: Celebrate Your Weekly Exceptionals

Once you start using The Weekly Design System one-page scheduler (I provide this for you online), you'll be noting three truly exceptional professional goals and three truly exceptional personal outcomes that you fully commit to accomplishing by the end of the coming week. At this stage of the Sunday morning planning process, you celebrate the accomplishment of these targets. By passionately writing about what it was like to achieve them and how it feels to have completed them.

Step #4: The Weekly Rating and Measurement

As you can see if you've downloaded the template, a measurement index has been provided for you to rate, from one to ten, the week you just lived. This will further enrich your awareness of what's working in your life (so you can replicate and then amplify it), and what needs to be enhanced.

Step #5: The Coming Week's Truly Exceptionals

At this point of the weekly planning process, you get to note the three Professional Truly Exceptional goals that you need to achieve during the fresh week ahead for it to feel like it was a very successful one. On the professional side, these could include finishing an essential creative project, delivering a key sales presentation skillfully and scheduling a diversion-free evening to study an aspect of your craft that will raise your domain expertise. Personal Truly Exceptionals could include "five strong workouts," "meditate on four mornings," "three family meals with my full presence and zero devices" and "Saturday until noon all to myself."

Step #6: Best Human Practices and Prioritization

Next, you quickly look at the inventory of best practices in each of *The 8 Forms of Wealth* that you'll record when you first set up the system. This will allow you, before your week begins, to remember those behaviors in the eight key areas of your life that, when you do them, cause your life to operate at its finest.

It's such a simple insight, isn't it? To enjoy more success and happiness, schedule and then do the activities that experience has shown will bring you success and happiness. For example, when it comes to the Self-Mastery form of wealth, your inventory might include "rising at 5 AM and running my morning routine," "applying The 2 Massage Protocol," "an hour for prayer in silence," "a two-hour nature walk," "a three-hour reading and study period" and "a journal and future-planning session."

Do the same sort of inventory for every remaining form of wealth and you'll then have a clear and potent list of all the greatest behaviors in the primary parts of your life to schedule onto your plan for the seven days in front of you.

Each Sunday, you review, then select one, two or maybe even three of the pursuits from the inventories of the form of wealth that you most wish to advance or improve and then actively write what you've come up with onto your printed one-page scheduler. This way, you'll ensure that you never miss doing activities that are highly important because you've fallen into a rut of being busy being busy.

Step #7: Integration and Building Your Template (for a Beautiful Week)

Using the one-page scheduler I'm sharing with you online at TheEverydayHero Manifesto.com/Scheduler, you now finish your complete calendar for the week ahead. This is key: record your work meetings and each of your professional deliverables. Yet also note your workouts, nature walks, family meals, massage sessions and meditation times, and so on, and all those personal items that ordinarily do not get scheduled onto an elite producer's schedule (and so they don't get done). This ensures that *everything* that's essential gets onto your plan—not only what you need to be ultra-productive, but also what you need to stay connected to your family and get über-fit, as well as financially strong and spiritually confident.

At the top of the one-page scheduler is a box for your three Personal Truly Exceptionals as well as your three Professional Truly Exceptionals, so they stay right in front of your attention, all day and every day, over the week ahead.

Here's a sample of a recent one-page scheduler of mine

When I complete a task during the day, I record a "V" next to it for "victory." This keeps me cheerful, releases the energy of completion and boosts momentum. Often I make micro-notes next to something I've just accomplished to give me a little more awareness around why it worked. At other times, I'll add a few words about how I'm feeling during a particular time block or an opportunity for optimization. These all go into the weekly story that I write in my journal at the end of the week, as I review it.

Step #8: Execute on + Live the Template

The final step in The Weekly Design System is to take a few moments each morning of the new week to revisit your Truly Exceptionals and your written schedule—time blocks and all—for the day ahead of you. This will promote clarity and activate your ability to say no to distractions, and vote yes to only those pursuits you've promised yourself you'd do. To achieve maximum productivity, performance and life balance, as you steadily scale the summits toward your Lifetime Big 5 target.

252

That's it! The Weekly Design System for consistently exercising the world-class weeks that become the world-class months, then quarters, then years, then decades that produce a world-class life.

The more regularly you use it, the easier the practice will become. And the greater will be the rewards you enjoy.

I know the material here has been robust and challenging. Yet my duty is to offer you the methodology that will help you realize your genius. Congratulations on being the kind of learner and heavyweight leader who embraces granular information in a culture where many only value easy. To watch the complete training video on the process, visit TheEverydayHeroManifesto.com/WeeklyPlanning

Some shorter chapters are ahead, as we near the end of our time together.

One last thing. Some clients wonder if The Weekly Design System stifles spontaneity. Actually, the process will give you more free time to do fun things than you've had in years. As someone once said to me, "Let planning be your springboard so spontaneity can be your splash."

62.

The "Just Because" Code
for Everyday Heroes

A little more of my "poetry," to bulletproof your optimism and fortify your faith in all the blessings and wonders destiny has placed on the path ahead of you …

… Just because your past was painful doesn't mean your future won't be miraculous.

… Just because you didn't do something yesterday doesn't mean you can't achieve it today.

… Just because you couldn't see a solution to a problem a little while ago doesn't mean a solution isn't on the way right now.

… Just because someone breaks a promise made to you doesn't mean you shouldn't keep the promises you make to others.

… Just because someone took more than they gave doesn't mean you shouldn't be a majestic giver. And mightily generous.

… Just because a person is always late doesn't mean that you shouldn't be on time.

… Just because daily reading isn't so popular in a world of cyber-zombies doesn't mean that you shouldn't be a lifelong book lover. And the most knowledgeable person in your field.

... Just because someone you trusted betrayed your belief in them doesn't mean you shouldn't be trustworthy.

... Just because a dream you pursued led to fierce disappointment doesn't mean you shouldn't remain a delighted dreamer. And a fervent possibilitarian.

... Just because someone you love behaves unlovingly doesn't mean they don't deserve your love. (Beneath anger always lies grief and underneath attack always exists sadness.)

... Just because many people are negative and pessimistic doesn't mean that you shouldn't make a right-angle turn from the herd and be a genuine hopefulist, spreading your magic for all the world to see.

... Just because impeccable politeness and meticulous manners are in short supply doesn't mean you shouldn't be of a unique breed—and be the most considerate, sophisticated and dignified person in your community.

... Just because going the extra mile isn't so common anymore doesn't mean that you shouldn't represent uncommon delivery. And exquisite ability. Your integrity demands that you refuse to participate in and send out any form of mediocrity, right?

... Just because you made a mistake doesn't mean the respect people give to you is mistaken.

... Just because some human beings are all about themselves doesn't mean you shouldn't stand for helpfulness, service and kindness, with few limits.

... Just because you have wounds to heal and limits to dissolve doesn't mean you're broken.

... Just because other people are currently better at a skill than you doesn't mean you can't practice your way to dominance of that arena. And then virtuosity in the world.

... Just because you don't have the life your highest self seeks right now doesn't mean destiny will deny you the lovely reality of your highest longings.

... Just because not so many people know how to forgive doesn't mean you shouldn't let go of old grievances and move ahead with all that excites you.

... Just because many around you are too scared to be fully human doesn't mean there's no value in your exemplifying the bigness, lovingness and greatness that are the molecules that make each of us real.

... Just because life is a relatively short ride doesn't mean that you shouldn't prepare to be around for a long time. So you make your magnificent mark.

63.

Death's Just a Hotel Room Upgrade

I have fear within me. Because I am human.

My voice truly shook with terror when I was asked to speak in front of ten people at biology lab in university.

When I meet celebrities, visit with someone new or am questioned intensely by border control agents, I generally get nervous. (I've read that only bandits are calm around that last group.)

As an introvert, I'm uncomfortable at social functions such as weddings, birthday celebrations and—the ultimate torture chamber—dinner parties.

Yes, I've trained myself to speak before large audiences and to relax in intense public situations (as can you). But it's not my sweet spot. I'm simply being honest.

But if there's one thing that has never frightened me at all, it's dying.

I recently had a conversation with a good friend about death.

He was speaking of how he spends a lot of time thinking about his ending. Seems that he worries over how it will happen, what the experience will look like and whether harps will be playing loud classical music on the other side.

For me, I'm actually *looking forward* to dying, if you don't mind me saying.

I must be clear: I love life intensely, immensely, and am having quite a ride.

… I live for my family.

… I adore my craft and the privilege to serve. Tears come to my eyes right now as I write this and reflect on the way my readers treat me. Not sure I deserve it, yet I thank you.

… I feel blessed to have such wonderful pals who make me think, laugh and, at times, eat too much *cacio e pepe*.

… I love the stacks and stacks of books that enchant the rooms of our home, my mountain bike rides, my frequent travels to the places I love, which include Rome and Alba, Mauritius and Puglia, TriBeCa and Franschhoek, Zurich, London, Dubai and Mumbai.

… I am beyond grateful for the leadership speaking tours I've done across the globe, the incredibly great clients I'm blessed to work with, the sublime meals I've enjoyed and the glorious sunrises my aging eyes have been able to enjoy.

All that's cool. Really fun. Exhilarating, often. Yet I don't need any of it. I'm no longer *attached to it*. I *disidentify* with it, meaning that I don't require all of it to prop up my self-worth and give me a sense of true power.

Be in the world yet never of it, right?

I totally get that life's a fleeting voyage. And that it all ends too soon. And that (even with its inevitable tragedies) each day on Earth is a very precious and perfect gift.

Yet I'm not concerned about leaving because I sincerely believe that after our bodies degrade to dust, all that we truly are *continues*.

Our highest, wisest, strongest, undefeatable, noblest, eternal and all-loving selves—our souls—return to the source from which they came. And advance toward infinity.

And I don't think this place that they go back to—or, more

precisely, become more fully immersed in—is a bad place that we should be frightened of entering, with hot fires and nasty rulers of the underworld waving their pitchforks at angels and swearing at saints.

No. Not at all.

I believe that after we die, we simply go back to the light. A state of being that's complete creativity, total truth, epic bliss, limitless love. And a place with really, really great coffee.

Okay. Maybe I'm going too far on the coffee part.

Yet please allow me to offer up this philosophical rant in another way ...

... It's almost like, as we do our earthwalk, we're staying at a three- or maybe a four-star hotel.

Then we die. Nothing tragic happens, really. We actually get upgraded. To a five-star property.

The previous place looked good. But the new place will blow your mind.

Why would you resist the transition? When it's to an even better destination.

64.

Why Aristotle
Slept on the Floor

One of my confidants just happens to be one of the world's bestselling authors.

I'm not talking a few million copies kind of bestselling author. I mean seriously phenomenal sales (yes, as in more than 100 million copies).

One night, as we were having a special dinner together in a tiny town in Europe where he had secluded himself, he shared something that still stays with me.

The writer explained how his rare-air accomplishment brings with it the tendency to stop, accept the current boundaries of his craft and step into a defensive mode to protect his success rather than remaining on the offense to become even more skilled at the work he does. He's achieved more in his field than most people ever will, so there's a strong attraction to rest on his laurels and not do much of anything anymore. He needs for nothing and has little left to prove.

Yet he understands that nothing fails like success and history-makers always protect the passion they had as amateurs. *The thing about a master is that they never think they are a master.* Legends never stop seeking to own their genre and to lead their field and to become so good they operate in a completely different orbit from everyone else. Golf great Bobby Jones, on watching Jack Nicklaus showcase his genius at the Masters, observed: "He plays a game with which I am not familiar."

The main reason to keep pushing for better—even when you're at the top—is not more fame, fortune and adulation. It's to experience even greater personal growth, to befriend even more of your unseen talents and to uplift the caliber of your character by pushing yourself to produce even more jewels while dutifully serving the whispers of your most supreme spiritual self. (Yes, I do very much believe that operating at world-class is a massively spiritual exercise because you get to honor the force that rules the world while you enrich your brothers and sisters on this planet.)

So, guess what my friend did?

He booked a very long stay at a very cheap motel (not hotel). And began to write his next monumental and influential blockbuster.

He forced himself to get away from the luxuries and conveniences of his daily life to get back to basics, return his boots to the ground and make himself uncomfortable. Because struggle is a profound source of originality. And restraint makes us vastly stronger.

This revered (and very wealthy) author lived in a cheap motel room. *For an entire year.* And wrote the best book of his career.

I've read that Aristotle used to sleep on a stone floor every few weeks to stay tough, grounded, nimble and humble.

I've also read that young Spartans would train in cold conditions, wearing nothing more than a tunic and sandals, to ready them for the brutal trials they would face at war. Their mothers would recite as they marched off to battle, "Come back victorious. Or dead on your shield. Otherwise, don't come back at all."

We've become a culture of the too easily bruised, the too terribly delicate and the too readily weakened. We've become a society of snowflakes, complainers and hedonists who wish for only ease, pleasure and luxury, at every turn of each of our hours.

Yet to do towering work that stands the test of time and builds a life that you'll be ever so proud of demands that you place yourself in harsh places. And force yourself to do difficult things. So that the struggle introduces you to your hidden strength. And confidence. And brilliance.

I adore these words of the Stoic philosopher Epictetus: "But neither a bull nor a noble-spirited man comes to be what he is all at once; he must undertake *hard winter training* and prepare himself and not propel himself rashly into what is not appropriate to him."

I do my best to live the message of voluntary austerity that I'm encouraging in this chapter, relentlessly forcing myself to try new things, test new opportunities, challenge my winning formulas, get up even earlier, fast even longer and exercise even harder. Stretching myself and constantly growing is the only route to avoid the obsolescence and apathy that will send you to an early grave.

In Hollywood, they have a term I think about often—"jump the shark"—that is used as a reminder never to take success for granted. I'd like to tell you more about it.

Many years ago, there was a wildly popular TV show called *Happy Days*. The supercool main character (played by Henry Winkler) on this sitcom was a bad boy named Arthur Fonzarelli, known as Fonzie or simply "the Fonz." Millions would tune in to watch each weekly episode and the show became a sensation. (I loved the show and even had a fake black leather jacket like Fonzie's to prove it.)

At the height of the show's success, something happened.

The plotlines started to lose their tightness and the fascination of the stories began to falter. The dialogue became repetitive and dreary and many of the once-imaginative ideas looked tired.

THE EVERYDAY HERO MANIFESTO

My guess is that after many seasons at the pinnacle of network television, some of the hugely well-paid actors got bored, many of the scriptwriters drifted into autopilot, scared to try something inventive that might cause them to fall flat on their faces. The specialness that had once wowed viewers simply left the building.

In one episode, the premise seemed to be calculated purely to attract eyeballs: Fonzie was going to put on a pair of water skis and jump over a shark. Hard to believe, right?

Despite the fact that the Fonz achieved the feat, "jumping the shark" became a term used in entertainment circles when a series has passed its sell-by date. It's used as a cautionary phrase to challenge creatives not to resort to lazy ways of getting attention for their product because they've grown too comfortable to rise to the next level of innovation. And to avoid being so consumed with protecting the success one has generated that you fail to keep growing and taking the risks that will cause you to win even more.

65.

Shatter Your Winning Formula like Miles Davis

Last night I watched a documentary on jazz heavyweight Miles Davis. You would have loved it.

I learned...

... Miles Davis grew up in a rich family, yet was subjected to racial prejudice, which hurt my heart as I learned of it.

... He played with virtuosos such as Charlie Parker and Duke Ellington, modeling their style until he developed the bravery to disrupt the status quo and the resolve to create an entirely new way of playing.

... He loved Ferraris, tailored suits and other attractions of the high life, and developed addictions to alcohol, heroin and cocaine.

... He cared strikingly little about the opinions of others and appeared to be nearly completely true to the man that he was. (Oh, how rare and important this is!)

... From the moment he woke up until the moment he slept, he thought mostly of one thing: music. Nothing else mattered. Really.

Yet what stands out about this giant of the trumpet, who died suddenly of a stroke at the age of seventy-five, is his steadfast unwillingness to repeat his winning formula.

Miles Davis revolutionized the way a jazz record sounded with *Kind of Blue*, with its haunting melodies and ethereal beauty.

Then, as the late sixties brought an emergence of rock and funk, he surprisingly shifted gears, shedding his tailored suits and entering an all-new glam stage (wearing big Jackie O–like sunglasses, tasseled shirts and supple leather pants).

With *Bitches Brew*, an album that guitarist John McLaughlin described as "Picasso in sound," he showcased a revolutionary (and rebellious) style that bordered on psychedelic.

Then came his experiments with electronic music, which produced completely new jazz forms.

In one scene of the documentary, Miles Davis's son revealed that his father never kept any of his old records at home. He just wasn't interested in what he'd done before—only in what was occupying him in the moment. He was far more fascinated by pushing the envelope, exploring fresh frontiers and pursuing the artistic expansion that always lives on the other side of normal, acceptable and commercially viable.

As one of the musicians who played in his band observed: "He didn't want us to play what we knew. He wanted us to play what we *didn't* know."

So he—and they—would always stay at the vanguard of the field they were in. And showcase a breakthrough style that would stay cool, relevant and inspirational well into a lavishly colorful future.

66.

The Antifragile Artist
in the Shiny Purple Suit

Nassim Taleb's "antifragile" concept—which speaks to the ability to become stronger in the face of greater disorder—resonates with both the warrior as well as the poet within me.

In my prayers, meditations and journaling sessions, I practice hard and long to become the kind of creative force and human being that grows more steadfast and courageous as things get more challenging and messy.

To know triumph in the face of turbulence is to receive a breakthrough that is boundless.

Which brings me to a painting outside my writing room at home.

A reader who said my work was helpful gave it to me, so generously. And I am grateful for the gift.

I placed it so that I see it before I start writing in the morning. And once I leave at the end of the day.

To remind me of what real artists do. And how genuine exceptionalists roll.

The image is of Gord Downie, the lead singer of a band called The Tragically Hip, one of the greatest rock bands of all time (even though they are not globally so well known).

I saw them play live four times, including a near-religious experience at the Fillmore in San Francisco and their final concert in their
hometown of Kingston, Canada, with my daughter and my son standing on the chairs next to me, fists raised in the air. Eyes wide open on
an evening to behold. The experience was sort of tragic, too. Allow
me to explain why …

A symbol of mastery that inspires me daily

… Downie was a luminary from an otherworldly realm. His song-writing and singing capacities were magnificent and spirited. And the way he moved when he did his thing was like no other front man I've ever seen. Jagger, even at his best, only came fairly close.

A true rock star at the Fillmore

Gord Downie was a showman, hypnotizing audiences, creating onstage spellcraft and channeling lost legends as few have ever done. People at shows held homemade signs that read "In Gord We Trust." And millions really did.

And then it all changed. As life always does …

… One December, Downie—in Kingston for the Christmas holidays—collapsed while walking on a busy street, falling into a full-blown seizure before stunned onlookers.

After intensive testing, his doctor delivered the news at an over-flowing press conference: the musician had a rare form of brain cancer known as glioblastoma. And the prognosis was that the disease was terminal.

Downie was advised to wind down his affairs, say his goodbyes and never tour again with the band he loved so much.

But Downie was antifragile. And so he continued.

The Hip—as they are affectionately known to their legion of fans—set about on their last series of performances to deliver their love to all those who had supported them for so long. Custom top hats, flowing scarves, dazzling shiny shirts and purple-sequined suits were made for the star to wear on the tour. Emergency crews stood on standby at every show.

Given the illness, the group worried that their lead singer could experience a seizure onstage or that he wouldn't have the energy to finish the shows, due to his exhausting chemotherapy treatments.

And yet here's the extraordinary thing that I feel the need to mention: as the shows continued, Gord Downie grew *stronger*. As the road show visited city after city, his electricity increased, his charisma rose and his wizardry amplified.

The last show, which was broadcast live on national TV and watched by nearly twelve million people, was summed up in a one-line tweet by the Toronto Police Department that said, "Dear world, Please be advised that Canada will be closed tonight at 8:30 PM."

As mentioned, my children and I attended that performance. We cheered and clapped and danced and cried. Everyone in the concert hall knew Downie was dying.

In Montenegro for a leadership event around a year later, a friend sent me a message. As the sun set over the Adriatic and I sat on the terrace of a cabin that used to be part of a fishing village, I read that Gord Downie, the antifragile artist in the shiny purple suit, had passed on. To a better place.

67.

The Keep Your Fire Blazing Theory for a Lifetime of Audacity

It's very early in the morning as I write this piece for you. Darkness envelops our home, a cup of fresh mint tea sits on my wooden writing table next to the stack of papers of the manuscript. "Roads" by Portishead plays. And the vibe feels just right.

You'd love it, if you were sitting here with me.

In the quietude of pre-dawn, I reflect on the furious fire so many good souls had blazing within them to achieve their sacred desires and materialize their heroic longings, before a world of bills to pay, debts to service and obligations to attend to turned the inferno of possibilities into smoldering embers of lost opportunity.

Kindly know that the discomfort of growth is always less than the heartbreak of regret.

Makes me think of the words of Ayn Rand:

> Do not let your fire go out, spark by irreplaceable spark in the hopeless swamps of the not-quite, the not-yet, and the not-at-all. Do not let the hero in your soul perish, in lonely frustration for the life you deserved, but have never been able to reach. The world you desired can be won, it exists, it is real, it is possible, it's yours.

So as you pursue the call on your life to make your dreams real and your excitements true, never allow the feisty zeal that is central to your aliveness to be smothered by the responsibilities of your adulthood.

And in a civilization of human beings sleepwalking through the finest years of their lives, go ahead and fuel the majesty of your audacity. By regularly reaching for what the herd claims to be impossible.

68.

How Heavyweights Work

The way most people work dates back to an ancient era.

The idea that working longer and harder makes you more productive and better is outdated. And profoundly flawed.

It comes from an age when most workers toiled on a factory line. And by putting in more time, they would create more products. Productivity was tied to the number of hours spent moving.

But now we exist in a completely different period. The Factory Age has morphed into the Mastery Economy. As cognitive laborers and creative leaders, you and I are rewarded not for the hours spent on the line but for the richness, impact and experience of magic that our craft delivers to others (yes, you *are* in the business of helping human beings participate in *magic*). The heavyweights who send masterwork into their marketplace are the ones who receive the most money, acclaim, lifestyle freedom and spiritual satisfaction.

Here's the main point I'm trying to offer for anyone in the business of producing indisputable artistry: *Working more mostly produces less.*

Yet it's the rare breed of modern worker who gets this fundamental (and transformational) truth. And who then makes the time to perform incredibly intensely when they create and then recover astonishingly deeply when they are off.

Here's the maxim I want you to meditate on: *Legendary producers are professional resters.*

The people who are able to consistently perform extraordinary work are those who out-focus, out-invent and out-work everyone around them. When they work, they really, really work (versus playing with their devices, chatting with their friends and shopping online for shoes, new shirts and vacations to exotic locations).

And after they've expressed their mastery in a hot burst of gargantuan glory, they go dark.

Yes … they go ghost. Unavailable. Invisible.

They regenerate. They refuel. They replenish. They renew. They read. They walk. They improve their cooking, watch great films and have fun with their family. And they nap (napping is my secret weapon).

This is the seasonal or cyclical way of running a day and then a week and then a month and then your years, where you work with the sweatiest of passion and then pull back and fully recover. So you restore your assets of genius back up to their highest capacity for another excellent round of magnificently creative, focused, inspired work.

Such a way of operating is unusual and counterintuitive, given the way we've been socially programmed to think about productivity. Our culture trains us to feel shame if we're not "hustle and grinding" by working most of the time. But working most of the time leaves you and me exhausted, cranky and empty. It erodes our energy. It drains the sense of exuberance and spirit that's absolutely necessary to do work that towers above that of your peers and makes your honest imprint on history.

I'm just not a fan of the "hustling and grinding" way of being. Because it's unsustainable, over the course of a career (or even a quarter). Overwork is often, I believe, insecurity masquerading as productivity. And public bravado.

273

"There is a time for many words and there is also a time for sleep," wrote Homer in *The Odyssey*.

So remember that the secret to getting more headlining work done is to work *a whole lot less*. Balance periods of peak intensity with cycles of genuine recovery. So that in those hours that you do produce, every ounce of your prowess gets to see the light of day.

69.

The Little Things
Are the Big Things

As I write this fairly short chapter for you, I'm in pain.

Not macro, serious, brutal pain.

No. Thank God.

It's so much more minor.

You see—somehow—last evening, a tiny insect made its way into my bedroom. And so it fed on me (most likely quite joyfully), for much of a long night.

The result: red blotches of swelling where the uninvited critter worked his craft on my unsuspecting body.

As I soaked in my tub this morning, I thought of what the founder of The Body Shop, Anita Roddick, once said: "If you think you're too small to have an impact, try going to bed with a mosquito."

The little things really can have outsized consequences.

Actually, in so many ways, I've discovered the little things are the *big* things.

… Sweating the micro-details on your tour de force for another six months when you think it's pretty much done is what will make you a master (and brings on some seriously great karma for you).

... Eating in a way that ensures micro-wins within your nutritional plan stacks into exponentially good health over time.

... Writing a handwritten thank-you note to the chef of a restaurant that recently delighted you, or to a service provider that over-delivered for you, is a minor act with major gains.

... Making the time to reflect on the strategy that has made your business successful and then building out battle charts to accelerate innovation, value creation and public service isn't the biggest move in the world, yet acting on what you've come up with just might change the world.

... Doing those tiny acts of discipline such as getting up early, being consistently friendly, showing up fully at your workouts and keeping each of your promises can seem like insignificant things, yet *every action has a consequence* and doing those small acts delivers extraordinary leadership and success when extended over your lifetime.

And so ...

Please recall the one-line brain tattoo that I've been teaching for the past few decades and reinforcing gently throughout this book because it's so essential to your everyday heroism: *Small, daily, seemingly insignificant improvements, when done consistently over time, lead to stunning results.*

And then make sure you close all windows and doors before you sleep.

70.

Become a Creative Athlete

Don't just get fit to look really good. Get strong to lift the world.

Get physically strong to have greater concentration. To extend your stamina when you sit down to create. To toughen your body so you maximize your ability to generate the big ideas that solve enormous problems.

Exercise regularly so you become a better artist. Work out harder so you become a better leader. And stay on that treadmill longer so you can roll like a movement-maker.

I've found in my own life that there's a direct and profound relationship between the grade of my Healthset and the quality of my craft.

When I'm in superb condition, by training hard, eating well, fasting often, hydrating properly and resting intelligently, I produce my top work. My brain just works brighter, I feel happier (your moods dramatically affect your performance), I can sit at my writing table for many more hours, immersed in flow state, and I have access to a whole lot more willpower (so I don't feel like checking my social media feeds to escape from having to write a technically demanding section that I've been resisting).

Stepping up your physical game will make you more money (because you're able to increase your productivity), help you remain more patient, peaceful and loving when you're in the presence of your family (thanks to the enhanced neurochemistry exercise turns on), and grow your sense of awe, wonder and aliveness.

So my loving yet firm encouragement is to get super-fit so you push outright poetry into the universe. To see how far you can go. And to make other people's lives a little (or a lot) better by the stardust that you've shared, while you optimize your own experience of living in the process.

Yes, become a creative athlete. Not just for leaner abs and tighter glutes. But for the building of a better civilization.

71.

How SuperProducers Do It

In one of the most fascinating studies ever performed in the field of social psychology, eight men in their seventies were brought to a converted monastery that researchers had carefully set up to look exactly as things would have looked *twenty-two years earlier*.

At the outset of the experiment, as the men entered the building, some were hunched over, while others used canes. Music of a bygone era played, magazines and books from that earlier time sat on the shelves, and artifacts from that previous age had been neatly organized so that it actually seemed that the participants had walked into a time warp.

The leader of the study, maverick Harvard professor Ellen Langer, now heralded as "the mother of positive psychology," instructed the men to think, feel, speak and act as if they were their younger selves of twenty-two years before. They were told to *inhabit* that previous period as if they were really back there.

After five days at the monastery, a series of biomarkers of age were tested. Remarkably, the men looked younger, were physically more supple, showed improved manual dexterity and even had better eyesight. As they waited for the van that would return them to their homes, they participated in an intense game of touch football, shouting and hollering like teenagers.

In studying the outcome of this striking trial, Langer concluded that the illusion that had been created as the participants stepped into their younger selves had caused a rewiring of their perceptions and a reworking of their self-identities. Rather than believing the cultural biases (and societal brainwashing) of how people in their seventies should perform, they shattered that story and grew younger. Because they saw themselves differently.

To me this is a life-changing example of how re-ordering your self-identity will transform your capacity to express your mastery. And a fantastic model on how your personal story about your ability will determine how well you manifest your potential. Human beings never behave in a way that is inconsistent with their perception of who they are. They just don't.

... If you don't see yourself as the kind of person who has what it takes to accomplish world-class results, you won't even start to do the work required to achieve world-class results. What would be the point?

... If you don't think you have it in you to execute on your vision-ary venture, you won't seek the mentoring, invest in the learning and take all the steps needed to realize your fantasy because—in your mind and heart—a negative ending has already been scripted.

... If you don't believe you have the power to shape our world and influence your fate, you won't protect the environment, treat strangers well and help the less fortunate because you've installed a predetermined conclusion that you don't really matter. And the stars rule your destiny.

This way of operating—and this is really important to know—creates a self-fulfilling prophecy.

Your perception of your capacity actively creates your reality. Your false psychological, emotional, physical and spiritual programs are the very roadblocks that prevent you from entering the highway toward your grandest desires. Any part-time faith in your individual greatness causes the very part-time results that make you feel even less confident. Which brings me to how superproducers do what they do.

While we think we see reality each day, what we are really viewing is our *perception* of reality. We *process* all that's outside us—all events, conditions and experiences—through our own unique filter. Our own personal lens. A "stained glass window" of sorts, to use mythologist Joseph Campbell's term.

This filter has been constructed, over the course of your life, by what I call in my mentoring methodology "The 5 Creative Tools." Refine and then optimize these and you'll completely re-engineer your personal narrative on how life works and your ability to produce amazing results within it. Remake and refine your private story and you'll begin to perceive a whole new world, the kind that members of the majority almost never see, keeping them stuck in pessimism, scarcity and ongoing insecurity—rarely catching glimpses of the ocean of possibility and opportunity that is right in front of their eyes.

Upgrade your self-identity consistently and your behavior will transform to match your new understanding about what's possible for you to create, achieve and become. Continue operating like this on a daily basis and you're absolutely guaranteed to generate a positive feedback loop where your positive behavior keeps causing the excellent results that feed your new healthier identity, which then leads to even more of the positive behavior.

This is the transcendent process that *any* human being can follow—no matter their age, nationality, economic background or education—to radically transmute their productivity, prosperity, happiness and impact.

Here's the learning framework that I usually only teach to the clients in my online coaching program *The Circle of Legends*, which I'm excited to now share with you:

HOW SUPERPRODUCERS DO IT

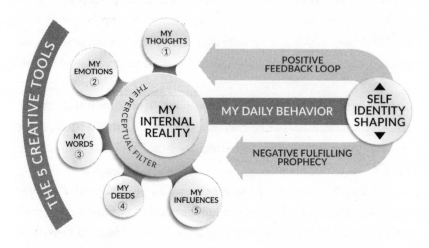

As you can see, The 5 Creative Tools that you need to deploy in order to restructure a completely new personal story that will elegantly rework your personal identity are these: your thoughts, your emotions, your words, your deeds and your influences. These are the forces that have, over time, created the filter through which you process the world, forming your own unique explanation of how the game works and your own role within it. Again, change your filter on reality and you'll actually change your reality.

As you improve the quality of each of these five tools, the way you perceive yourself will rise to match the improvement. And as you rescript and reprogram the way you see yourself, the quality of your success, joy and internal peacefulness will automatically rise with you.

As you can see by carefully looking at the visual model, the pathway to becoming a superproducer (and heroic human being who expresses the fullness of your gifts, talents and virtues) starts by purifying the five forces that create your inner reality and shape the way you process the world outside of you.

Keep refining your internal life and your behavior will improve to match your enhanced self-identity and advanced perceptions. Your better behavior then sets up a positive feedback loop by giving you the positive results that confirm you now are the kind of person who can achieve world-class results and an existence of great beauty. This, in turn, makes your thoughts, emotions, words, deeds and selection of your influences even better. A positive feedback loop that creates an exceptionally valuable upward spiral of success, that when applied over long periods of time, stacks into *explosive* gains.

Or ...

... If your 5 Creative Tools are mediocre, they will install a negative perceptual filter that, as you understand reality through it, will set up a negative self-identity that will then produce the negative daily behaviors that match it, thereby creating a *negative* self-fulfilling prophecy. Because your inner life and inferior way of interacting with reality will reinforce that your negative way of seeing the world is accurate. Even though it's not.

So, today, my vast encouragement is for you to take a good hard look at the caliber of your 5 Creative Tools. Commit to cleaning up your thinking, elevating your emotions, polishing your words, bringing higher mastery to your deeds and making certain that the influences you surround yourself with are uplifting, superb and aligned with the excellent standards you seek to operate at.

And then go out into our world and remain steadfast on your process of becoming the kind of superproducer and utterly awesome person you and I know you deserve to be.

72.

Escape Post-Moonwalk Astronaut Affliction

Apollo 11 astronaut Buzz Aldrin, part of the first space crew to land on the moon, was asked what it was like to be there. His poetic response? "Magnificent desolation."

Yet as the years passed, this man, who walked on the lunar surface for about three hours, struggled with depression and alcoholism. He was filled with a sense of aimlessness and the inability to find an undertaking that would excite his enthusiasms after his life-altering experience.

How does one follow up on the accomplishment of reaching the moon?

Aldrin wrote in his memoir, *Magnificent Desolation*, that after the lunar landing "there was no goal, no sense of calling, no project worth pouring myself into."

And so ...

... As you make your ascent into higher flights of exceptionalism and the loftier reaches of your finest abilities, beware of the phenomenon of "Post-Moonwalk Astronaut Affliction." This is the tendency for any elite performer to feel a malaise or endure a state of apathy after achieving the targets they have always dreamed of achieving.

You've done all you set out to do. Likely, you've realized brave goals no one you know has been able to materialize. You now have the reputation, career, wealth and lifestyle of your richest imaginings and most luxurious enthusiasms. You've made it. You're a standout and a headliner and a genuine heavyweight on the planet. World-class has become your new normal. Now what? Like Buzz Aldrin, you wonder how you can top this. This fills you with emptiness. And existential angst.

The solution? Simple. Never, ever settle. Never stop setting and then moving toward your next-level goals and more exhilarating challenges. So you constantly explore hidden and unseen creative heavens. So you continually bask in the bright light of uncharted universes. So that you regularly embark on exhilarating adventures.

And heroically get introduced to previously undiscovered sides of your most amazing self. Because life's greatest sadness is never getting to know all you truly are.

73.

Resilience Lessons from the Human Who Lost His Face

Leadership and courage are less about being born into boldness and more about what you do when you're frightened.

The people we consider saviors, guardians and protectors are mostly good, ordinary people who, in moments of adversity, threat or danger, found strength they didn't know they had. Think of Mahatma Gandhi and Amelia Earhart. Alan Turing, Helen Keller, Emmeline Pankhurst and Galileo.

We all have untapped valor within us. *You absolutely are much stronger than you know.*

Which brings me to Niki Lauda, the former Formula One racing world champion. And what he experienced on August 1, 1976.

It was early in the race at the German Grand Prix at Nürburgring. As Lauda made a turn at a fantastically high speed, he lost control and hit a wall, his Ferrari exploding into flames.

Lauda was trapped in his car for *forty-three seconds*, at temperatures that neared *425 degrees Celsius*.

His body was horrifically burned. One onlooker reported that it appeared as if his face was melting off his head. *His face was melting off his head.*

"Another ten seconds and I would have died," admitted Lauda.

At the hospital, things looked so bad that a priest was called in to deliver last rites. When Lauda's wife arrived and saw her husband's condition, she fainted.

The racing legend later explained to a reporter:

> When I came into the hospital you feel like you are very tired, and you would like to go to sleep. But you know it's not just sleeping. It's something else. And you just fight with your brain. You hear noises and you hear voices, and you just try to listen to what they are saying and you try to keep your brain working to get the body ready to fight against illness. I did that and that way I survived.

In an astonishing display of fighting spirit, *only forty days later* Lauda—with bandages still covering his damaged scalp—forced his racing helmet over his head and proceeded to compete at the Italian Grand Prix as startled onlookers gasped at his display of fortitude and competitive spirit.

Spending time with Formula One legend Niki Lauda at the Montreal Grand Prix

287

"While I can walk and drive, why lie in a clinic?" he said. "This is my world."

He placed fourth that day.

After retiring from the sport, Lauda went on to become an aviation entrepreneur and a successful businessman, rarely appearing in public without his famous red cap that covered his fierce scars. "I have a reason to look ugly. Most people don't," he stated with a mischievous grin, adding: "The cap is my protection from stupid people looking at me stupidly."

Your takeaways from this example of limitless unconquerability:

Takeaway #1: Own Your Toughness

Resilience and extreme grit are not innate qualities. No. They are character traits that get forged in the fire of dangerous conditions. Why condemn difficulty when it is the very medicine and supplementation that will make you stronger? Befriend it for what it is: a necessary condition that will promote your evolution.

So-called "problems" are actually platforms required for the prodigious power sleeping within you to awaken and express itself.

Takeaway #2: Get Back into the Car—Fast

Lauda admitted he was scared to race again.

To get back into the seat roughly six weeks after nearly meeting the Grim Reaper seemed, to most spectators, an act of insanity.

But Lauda knew that the longer he waited, the more intense would be his fear. And so, he felt the pain, dealt with the dread and got back into the seat. It's the same for you and me: when we face a trial or a tragedy or even a catastrophe, it is our responsibility, if we wish to have integrity, to stand up and keep on going, as quickly as possible.

Because the place where failure happens can also be the space where courage unfolds. And life slows down for no one.

Takeaway #3: Never Stop Accelerating

Lauda kept on racing—even after he left the track.

After retiring from Formula One, he started two airlines. He wrote a book. He continued his winning streak.

You see, for the rare-air producer, there is no finish line. Advanced performers love winning so much that retirement and complacency are seen as dances with death. *Such souls have practiced being spectacular so often that unspectacularity has no place within their operating system.*

The real reward of high-octane productivity is the realization of your genius. And what the journey to even loftier summits of exceptionalism pushes you to own.

Like Niki Lauda, you must never coast. You owe it to your grandest nature never to rest on your laurels. Do not slow down. Refuse to get sloppy. Resist basing your self-identity on the trophies you won many years ago. You are so much greater than this.

This brings to mind something the famed psychologist Abraham Maslow observed: "One's only rival is one's own potentialities. One's only failure is failing to live up to one's own possibilities. In this sense, every person can be as royalty. And therefore must be treated like royalty."

And so, should you wish to surrender—when the conditions get tough—remember the man who lost his face. Then carry on. With high speed.

74.

Charles Darwin and
the Extreme Agility Advantage

Charles Darwin was a cool cat.

... He studied barnacles for eight years, from 1846 to 1854. One of the primary practices of mastery is peerless amounts of patience, isn't it?

... He circumnavigated the globe on HMS *Beagle,* where he was offered the chance to visit places such as Patagonia, Tahiti and New Zealand, and study everything from exotic rock formations to seldom-seen wildlife.

... He produced a 770-page diary, wrote 1,750 pages of field notes and made distinct catalogs reporting his granular findings.

And then, after all his thinking, training and experimenting, he arrived at the Theory of Evolution.

As I understand it, at the root of the whole explanation of how a species evolves is his concept of "survival of the fittest."

Let's go deeper, because I think it will help you navigate the volatile era we currently live in.

When I was studying biology in my university days, before entering law school, I learned about the genetic mutations that happen in all living creatures.

When a mutation creates some kind of advantage that helps a being thrive in a new environment, that new form survives. It propagates. And then, as it continues to win, it dominates. This process is called natural selection.

... Penguins—although they are birds that cannot fly—have endured because they are superb swimmers. And because in Antarctica there are no predators on land.

... Giraffes developed long necks to eat food high in trees, causing them to thrive in hard conditions, as their competitors died out.

... Humans, who could stand upright, had the advantage of being able to forage for food and bring it back to base camp. So we're still around.

The members of a species that had qualities that allowed them to not only survive but also to prosper gained superiority in constantly shifting conditions.

You and I live in a time of cataclysmic change. Our environment is shifting radically in the creative sectors, commerce, technology, athletics, the sciences and life in general.

And so ... kindly know ...

... The leader who is prescient enough to see around corners, who can guide their agile organization to add hypnotic value and who is ahead of their time will rule the field.

... The worker who loves to learn, develops novel skills and exemplifies expertise will be the one who gets promoted and applauded, even in—especially within—a difficult economy.

... The creative maker who refuses to do things the way they have always done them and passionately plays out on the razor's edge of originality will stay hot, while peers grow cold.

... The human being who develops the quality of adapting swiftly, outgrowing themselves daily and seeking the joy amid uncertainty will assume tribal dominance.

It's the natural selection that Darwin taught us.

Nature really will select out those who fail to be nimble, curious, hardworking, resourceful and masterful. They cannot survive. Because they are weak. And refuse to, or cannot, adapt to the changed environment.

The lesson? When upheavals come, don't resist the glorious opportunities for growth. Or you'll end up like the dinosaurs, stuffed and sitting pretty in a museum frequented by schoolkids carrying superhero lunchboxes.

75.

The Free Money Model
for Advanced Prosperity

This chapter is very relevant for those seeking a life of richer prosperity, abundance and lifestyle freedom. Consider the visual paradigm below. I understand it may initially seem somewhat metaphysical, yet I can assure you it is exceedingly tactical.

THE FREE MONEY MODEL

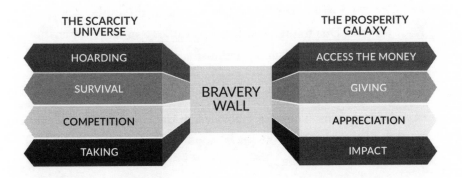

The left-hand column describes the modes used by the majority, the central habits that keep too many fine people stifled in scarcity. And financial insecurity.

Let's look at the first one: most of the population hoards what they have, clinging to whatever they own (or simply possess through debt-driven buying) like a little kid holding tightly to their favorite nap-time blanket.

But holding too rigidly—spiritually speaking—to what you have prevents the universe from sending you more. Because your insecurity sends a message to the force that runs the world that you're ungrateful for all you have. And because you're in such fear, there's simply no room for the energy of prosperity and that which is meant for you to find its way into your reality.

My cheerful suggestion is to let your things be your servant, never your master. We are born with nothing and we exit with nothing. Between those two states we are *mere caretakers* of whatever we are blessed to enjoy through the fruits of our labor, along with Fortune's goodwill. Hold what you have with a very loose grip. Don't let material goods form the basis of your identity (or your self-worth). Ironically, when you develop the power to stay cool—even if you were to lose everything—life celebrates your sentiments of abundance by sending you even more.

Moving to the next pitfall that shackles many members of the majority, a lot of human beings are caught in the limbic hijack of basic survival. Due to their fear (born of earlier trauma), they are not accessing the wiser reasoning within the prefrontal cortex of their human brain. Instead, they have unconsciously closed access to this advanced intelligence and are operating from the reptilian brain of the limbic system. They are grounded in the fight, flight or freeze response—unable to see the sea of opportunity for producing prosperity that exists all around them. Their fear also shuts the doorway into their heart, so they are blocked from unity with their natural creativity, largest wisdom and native jubilance.

Money is a psychological and emotional (and, yes, even spiritual) story. Many people run a daily fable that financial wealth is the domain of cheats, liars and thieves. And that economic riches only come to lucky winners or those blessed with gifts that "regular people" don't have. This very fairy tale actually creates their reality because, as you now know, your daily behavior always reflects your deepest beliefs. And if your core philosophy is that you're not the kind of person who can enjoy freedom with respect to money, you will not follow the fundamental habits and practices that are certain to materialize economic wealth. A philosophy of lack is often accompanied by the expectation that one's hand be held and that aid be given. Because such people have been seduced by the idea that they don't have the power to manifest their visions of success with money.

Yet look at the richest people on the planet. Many of them grew up poor. They started with nothing but a breakthrough idea. An insight that would deliver astounding benefit to humanity and challenge the traditional way things were done in their field. Then—rather than retreating when things got tough—they persisted. These creative heroes outworked everyone around them. When problems surfaced, they did not shrink from their ideals. When jealous critics and angry cynics tried to troll them, they did not shirk their responsibility. To do their mighty mission.

Still looking at the left-hand column of *The Free Money Model*, you can see that—for human beings stuck in The Scarcity Universe—competition is everywhere. Those who inhabit this orbit see the world as a limited rather than an infinite place. Business (and life itself) is a zero-sum game: for one to win, another must lose. Terror lives in their hearts that there's not enough for everyone to have exactly what they desire. This is a belief based not on reality but on a flawed psychology and emotionality, which remains unresolved in those who spend their days in this particular realm.

And, finally, as you can see from the teaching framework, in a perceived world of such scarce resources that must be fought for and then ferociously stockpiled like ancient hunters on the savannah, those of this group are often very much takers.

... They take more from the organizations they work for than they give. (Someone who isn't at least delivering helpfulness in proportion to what they're being paid for is stealing from that company, aren't they?)

... They rob the brightest ideas of others because they have little ownership of their personal powers and have disowned their primal originality.

... They take handouts and benefits that they haven't truly earned and show up as victims because they've neglected their gifts and disbelieve in their inherent agency to shape things outside of them.

Okay. Now let us look at the right-hand column of the paradigm, which—as you study it carefully—you'll see is *very* different. You absolutely can enter this alternate galaxy by moving through your fear and crossing "The Bravery Wall," doing the opposite of those who populate The Scarcity Universe. Doing the opposite of what most people do is almost always the best strategy for victory, by the way.

Among the billionaires I've been mentoring for over a quarter of a century and the entrepreneurial titans I advise, here's how almost every single one of them thinks, feels and acts:

... They viscerally understand that all the money they want is already in existence. It's out there, waiting for their warm embrace. They believe that they simply need to unlock the hidden value within their marketplaces that will allow them to *access* all the riches they seek. And these possibilitarians are deep believers in the boundlessness of *everything* in life. If they lose a business deal, they remain tranquil as they trust an even better one will appear when the time is right. Should they lose a prized possession, they really don't care too much. They know that nature always unfolds for one's favor. And they abide by the spiritual law that *once you reach a place of inner freedom and everyday heroism, where you're unafraid to lose everything, you will not be scared of anything.*

… They get that giving electrifies the receiving process. Rather than drowning in the frightened energy of acute survival, they are serene and in tune with the truth that our galaxy is a palace of infinite opportunity that—excellently, confidently and ethically seized—will provide unbridled fortunes of prosperity. There's no limit to the stars in the sky, the ideas a human mind can imagine or the treasures you can experience. And so they eagerly give the gifts of their labor and the wonders of their spirit as *freely* and spectacularly as they possibly can, which causes them to enter a secret sphere where money flows *easily*. And where miracles—sent in reply to their benevolence—are real. And surprisingly frequent, because the rewards of karma are real. And the universe has a most fair accounting system.

… They understand that what you are grateful for grows. And all you appreciate expands within your consciousness. Start celebrating all that you have been granted, however small or large—from food on your family's table to a job that allows you to make a difference, from good books you are able to read to those friends who lift your state—and what you applaud will be magnified. So even more of it will flow naturally into your days.

… They are possessed by service and obsessed with impact. And because they enrich the lives of so many, a loving reality responds with plenty.

As we round out this chapter together, I'll mention the words of metaphysician Catherine Ponder, whose book *The Dynamic Laws of Prosperity* I often recommend to my clients to scale their fortunes with integrity:

> The shocking truth about prosperity is that it is shockingly right instead of shockingly wrong for you to be prosperous. Please note that

the word "rich" means having an abundance of good or living a fuller, more satisfying life. Indeed, you are prosperous to the degree that you are experiencing peace, health, happiness and plenty in your world. There are honorable methods that can carry you quickly toward that goal. It is easier to accomplish than you may now think.

Inspiring, right?

76

Put Down Your Phone
and Talk to a Person

Earlier this morning I visited a coffee shop.

I'd just finished an intense spin class and was still a little sweaty. Forgive me.

I had a head full of new ideas, a heart set to do *strong* work (after a nice hot shower) and a spirit animated to make the world a tiny bit better via my own minor contribution.

As I stood in line, I dreamed up an exciting concept for a new online course. After I collected my coffee, I headed to the nearest table so I could download the insights on my phone.

As I did so, I noticed a man seated on a long bench. His beard was grizzled, his hair ruffled, and he sported one of those plaid work shirts that farmers wear. And—uniquely—he had a leather briefcase with gold-colored hinges resting on the table in front of him.

Interesting. And so I said, "Good morning."

He could not have been more gracious.

He smiled. We spoke. He revealed that he grew up in Connecticut, in an eight-house town. By the Atlantic Ocean. He spoke of his family, shared some of his disappointments and made me laugh with a few of his vivid stories.

I told him that I, too, grew up in a tiny town. And that I, too, was raised close to the sea.

I confessed that I longed to live in a cottage on a clifftop over-looking the water and lead a simpler, more monastic and far more spartan existence. The lifestyle of an artist. The life of a blue-collar creative laborer.

We talked for another few minutes—about the wonderful people who live at the ocean's edge, the joys of fresh lobster and the need for more respect, kindness, caring and love in our world.

Initially, I'm embarrassed to say, I thought my new friend was a vagrant—in the café to stay warm from the cold. I now realized he was a king of sorts. Wise. Gentle. And sophisticated. In an eccentric sort of way.

My sense now is that he was a prosperous fisherman—perhaps the owner of a seafood company—who was visiting the city for a meeting with a lawyer. Not sure, really.

All I know is that I must never judge someone by how they look. That I need to put down my phone, even more often.

And talk to more people. Who make me better.

77.

The Shortest Chapter
in the History of Productivity

Stop rehearsing your limitations. Start exporting your magic. You've been granted the chance of a lifetime!

Alternate chapter content: Dream big. Start small. Act now.

(Please. And thank you.)

78.

Business Is a Beautiful War

I hesitated before writing this passage.

I very much want this book to inspire you to achieve amazing things, to move you to become your highest and to cause you to perform at the peak of your powers. While you live happily.

And yet I also am determined to do all I can to guard your safety. By continuing to speak honestly. Even if you don't like what I say.

So I need to write this: *Business can be a joyride. And it can also be a blood sport.*

When things are good, you get to pursue your creative cause, realize more of your genius, spread your movement and build a finer future.

And when conditions get tough (and they will) ...

... Partners you trust will commit treachery.

... Teammates you valued, encouraged and treated exceedingly well will let you down deeply.

... Suppliers you supported will take advantage of you.

... Jealous competitors and ruthless copyists will steal from you.

So while I do believe that you need to fortify your innocence, insulate your hope and nourish your optimism so you stay positive and strong, to survive—and flourish—you really must also do whatever it takes to battleproof yourself from harm and hurt. Our world is magnificent. And it's cruel.

Remember that old movie *Million Dollar Baby*?

What did the coach continually tell the boxer he was training?

… Never let your guard down.

… Never assume that all will go according to your plan.

… *Always protect yourself.*

So maintain your belief in the goodness of people. For sure. Most people I've met over all these years I've conducted business have been ever so honest, decent and caring.

Definitely do expect fantastic events to unfold in your future. Because, trust me, they will.

Yet also be cautious, in careful defense of your self-interests.

"Trust yet verify" is the phrase that comes to mind.

As does: "Pray to Allah. Yet tie your camel."

Because business is a beautiful war. And winning celebrates the strongest generals.

79.

Be Serious When You're Serious

A well-intentioned and polite follower on social media sent me a direct message the other day, saying: "Hi Robin. You always seem so serious. Don't you ever have any fun? Don't you ever chill?"

Made me smile.

My reply? *"I'm serious when it's serious.* And when it's not, I have a ton of fun."

When I show up, I really do come to play. I completely bring it on versus mail it in. If I'm not increasing my expertise and upgrading my craft—daily—I'm on the decline toward oblivion. With one foot in the graveyard of has-beens and also-rans. The minute I begin to think I'm a master really is the moment of descent into irrelevance and obsolescence. When I'm writing a new book, handcrafting a message for my mailing list, preparing a keynote or shooting a video for my members in *The Circle of Legends* online mentoring program, I'm serious. Because I'm a professional. (And I hope to be doing what I do for a long time.)

And because ...

... generating absolutely first-class output for my clients and followers *truly* means the world to me.

... practicing my craft and honoring my trade in a way that represents the values I do my best to live by is part of what I understand integrity to be.

... blocking out distractions, limiting my movements and getting down to forging the labor that brings intellectual, emotional and spiritual salvation to my earthwalk is mission-critical to me.

When I work, I work swiftly, intensely and with a focus that is far beyond fierce. I hold myself to the highest of standards and aim for the inspiration of a man haunted by the ghosts of geniuses that history has long since forgotten. Makes me think of what playwright George Bernard Shaw wrote:

> I want to be thoroughly used up when I die, for the harder I work the more I live. I rejoice in life for life's own sake. Life is no "brief candle" to me. It is sort of a splendid torch which I have a hold on for the moment, and I want to make it burn as brightly as possible before handing it over to future generations.

And then, once I'm finished (and fully spent, leaving little on the table), I shift into completely *unserious*.

I'll go for a drive with my exceptionally wise daughter or sit in the sunshine chatting with my amazingly optimistic son.

Or I'll work on improving my *bucatini al limone* (the water the pasta is cooked in must blend with the olive oil, lemon juice, mint leaves, pecorino cheese and *bucatini* with perfect calibration for the "cream" to be just right), or dip into my library to read a book I've purchased yet never read, or head to the gym for a very good spin or watch a film that will provide some good entertainment (and relief for my tiredness).

Because like I said before, if you take yourself too seriously, no one will take you seriously.

Seriously.

80

The 4 Major Communication Practices of Movement-Makers

Whether you script screenplays, write code, work at a bakery, lead a company, teach yoga or manage a salesforce, you're in the business of building a base of fanatical followers who will evangelize your product. And become fervent ambassadors for your personal brand.

This makes you *a movement-maker*.

Know and trust that the more exuberantly, masterfully and consistently you grow your movement, the more gains you'll see in your income, influence, impact and spiritual fulfillment.

The more people you enroll in your mighty mission and the more lives you serve, the more good things will unfold in your future. Often by apparent coincidence.

The more humans you help, the more Fortune will show up to help you, yes?

The greatest movement-makers of all time have one thing in common: *They were fantastic communicators.* Through their words and ways of operating, they were able to persuade their people to follow them up to the mountaintop.

"Don't ever diminish the power of words. Words move hearts and hearts move limbs," said scholar Hamza Yusuf.

I've wanted to share my best ideas on how extraordinary leaders and the heavyweights of humanity communicate with a wider audience for a long time. So I'm really happy to create this chapter for you. Fully applying the knowledge you are about to acquire in this section alone will yield value in multiples of your investment on this book. So turn up your attention. And fasten your seatbelt.

The learning model below deconstructs the four key elements of becoming a genius-grade communicator:

THE 4 MAJOR COMMUNICATION PRACTICES OF MOVEMENT-MAKERS

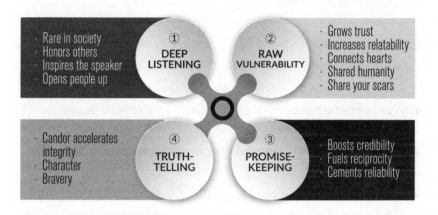

Practice #1: Deep Listening

First, appreciate that the communicator who listens the best is the leader who learns the most. If you're doing all the talking, you're not doing any growing.

Second, the person asking the questions is the one in control of the conversation. Get great at deploying brilliant questions, with the utmost of sincerity (manipulation degrades credibility, of course).

Third, increasing the volume of your listening is one of the finest acts I know of to show another human being overwhelming respect, especially in this civilization of non-stop chatterboxes who adore the sound of their own voice. I kid you not: training yourself to listen from a place of deep interest, matched with a blazing wish to understand the talker, is a powerful means to make anyone fall in love with your mission, your movement and you as a person.

Being flawlessly present and genuinely engaged (instead of checking messages, thinking about what you'll eat for dinner, or rehearsing your answer) exponentially makes the other feel important, connected and *safe* with you. All this accelerates trust massively. And trust is the bedrock of any great relationship, whether at work or within your private life.

Practice #2: Raw Vulnerability

This one's another entirely rare trait, which means that once you implement it daily, to the point of automaticity, you'll differentiate yourself from *everyone* in your field.

When you tear off the social mask that most human beings wear to look cool, popular and avoid rejection (oh, how many gorgeous opportunities are lost because we're too cool to take a risk and too insecure to look silly!), others become highly attracted to you. Your being real and exercising the bravery to "do you" gives everyone around you permission to also be real. Create a culture of human beings who feel it's fine to be their true selves as they work together around an emotionally compelling crusade and you'll activate the alchemy that makes world-changing movements.

Pretending to be someone you're not, just to fit in and be liked, also consumes huge amounts of creative, productive and emotional energy that is quickly returned to boost your performance and influence once you have the wisdom and guts to be yourself.

Practice #3: Promise-Keeping

So simple. So *transformational*. So unusual, these days. Try very hard not to make even one promise that you cannot keep, to be the kind of creative leader, exceptional performer and outstanding human being who follows through on each promise you offer, whether it's to deliver spellbinding quality on a project (before a certain date), send the book you told a top client you'd send them at a lunch meeting, start the running group you told your friends you'd set up, or have a family dinner at least three nights a week as you vowed you would.

Each promise you keep increases the trustworthiness you have in the mind and heart of the person on the other side of the promise. Do what you say you will do, without fail, and you'll soon become a hero in the eyes of all who know you. The esteem, loyalty and admiration they have for you will soar. For sure.

Even more important than the consistent keeping of the promises you make to others are the self-promises you set and then keep for yourself. Practice delivering on these and you'll experience *explosive* gains in your willpower, confidence and talent to get giant things done. You'll also grow beautifully in the honor and self-respect that then turns into the self-love that causes you to stand steadfast against any obstacles that threaten to stop the making of your mesmerizing movement.

Practice #4: Truth-Telling

Any lies you make are being witnessed by the sovereign self that is your essential nature. Your best dimension sees any dishonesty that your weakest, egoic side feels the need to participate in.

Every mistruth stains your character and all breaches of integrity scar your soul. Each breach of your sterling power through the speaking of that which is not true not only dissolves the faith another person has invested in you, it harms your conscience and steadily remakes you into a human being who has zero intimacy with your own values, virtues and ability to realize a meaningful mission that somehow uplifts society while owning more of your hidden potential.

By speaking your truth, even when your voice is trembling and your hands are shaking, you'll multiply your dignity and amplify your credibility and advance gloriously in the specialness that your destiny has written into your future.

———

I wish to share a final idea to help you breathe life into your most consuming visions and fill your most arresting ambitions with the electricity that will translate them into experience...

... It's far more important to seek to become a movement-maker not because you want the ego stroking that becoming the leader of a movement brings with it but because you have an uncommonly clean dream for a vastly brighter world. People who change the course of history rarely have the interest of making history. The ones who make a mark on our civilization cared less about being famous and powerful and more about being useful.

And making things better for us all.

81.

That Time I Learned How to Surrender

We've lived in the same home for a very long time.

As a writer, leadership adviser and professional speaker, it was essential to me to find a house that was in an extremely quiet place. With un-nosy neighbors. And woods fairly close by. It needed to be a place that would make my beloved family happy, where I could work my craft optimistically, and a space where I could retreat from the intensity that my public life can sometimes be.

I remember reading a piece in the *Financial Times* about the legendary singer of The Who, Roger Daltrey. He spoke of his life touring and then of his longing—once a tour was done—to see his garden and trout farm in East Sussex, England. Daltrey called that simpler, slower and more isolated existence—away from the intoxicating crowds and jaw-dropping stadiums—his "little life."

I, too, found a spot for my little life. At our home ...

... when I first purchased it.

And yet, as the city we live in has expanded, here's what has happened:

... New housing developments have gone up, which has led to a lot more traffic, noise and density.

... The nearby forest preserve where I used to mountain bike almost daily is now filled with tourists, discarded plastic bottles and unattractive cardboard coffee cups. (An off-leash dog almost chewed my leg off last week.)

... The compact airport that seemed so far away many years ago has now expanded so that I have small planes buzzing over the tulip garden in our backyard.

Sure, I could move. I get that and have thought of this and have been ready, at times recently, to do just that.

Yet, here's the thing: this is our *home*. My kids have grown up here. I've written many books here. Most of my family's greatest moments have happened here.

And, to be honest, my heart still *adores* this place. It has the patina of such happiness, creativity and soul.

So, earlier today, as I rode through the woods—past the plastic bottles and alongside the discarded coffee cups—I realized something special.

The changed outer conditions around my home were heaven-sent angels to activate the weaker parts of me. So I could become more aware of them and process through them and work with them, so I could then release them. Please recall: to heal a wound you first need to feel the wound. *Dragons undealt with can never be defeated.*

Fortune was inviting me to *use* what it was sending me for my elevation rather than resisting the opportunity, hoping things would return to the way they were.

I was being requested by my higher power to rise in the agility with which I met change. And to purify my character to meet the new conditions more courageously, easily and serenely. To adapt. To evolve into a more powerful human being who was even less dependent on worldly circumstances for his positivity, peacefulness and liberty.

Actually, as I reflected more deeply on the astonishing gift that life had delivered to me, I understood that I was being encouraged to learn the highest of all spiritual lessons …

… to let go.

… to detach.

… to welcome *whatever* comes.

… to surrender and embrace the intelligent unfolding of life.

To accept *all* experiences as blessings designed to realize my promise.

Of course, I do know that as I continue to do all of this—trusting that Nature Knows What She's Doing and using the novel scenario to ascend personally rather than blame, complain and condemn—all the noises and garbage and irritations will probably vanish. They just will. Because that's how this game works. At least for me. (Maybe the owner of the very mean dog will even invest in a really good leash.)

Roll with instead of fighting the lessons life is sending you and everything starts to work better for you.

Fighting change is asking for trouble. Resisting your new normal is a recipe for misery. At least that's what I've found as I've lived out a life, over all these years in earthschool.

Reminds me of something Glen Matlock, the former bass player of the Sex Pistols (who was replaced by Sid Vicious), mused: "Things move on. The way of the universe is to default to a state of flux."

Given this truth, why cling to the past when what's happening is even greater (even though it may not look or feel like it—yet)?

82

You Never Know Who Is Standing in Front of You

Treat everyone who crosses your path with decency, respect and clear honesty. It's not only the right thing to do, it's the wisest thing to do. Because you never know who is standing in front of you.

... I've been seated next to a passenger on an airplane who turned out to be the brother of a top client.

... I've had people who've attended my seminars standing behind me in a grocery line (studying what I was purchasing as I placed it onto the checkout belt, like an eagle scanning its prey).

... I've been in a restaurant, in a foreign country, with the CEO of the organization that had invited me to speak sitting at a table right behind me.

Which brings me to another story ...

There's an enormously popular bar in Dublin that's frequented by the locals.

One evening, a table of three young men were drinking their Guinness, carrying on playfully and having the time of their lives.

The phone rang. The manager of the establishment picked it up. And learned that U2 frontman Bono would be arriving shortly to enjoy a drink. The caller requested that a table be reserved for the iconic rock star.

With swift movement, the manager headed over to the table where the loud men were sitting.

"Bono's coming by. Would you guys mind giving up your table?"

"Bono? For him, we'd do anything," replied one of the friends, as they rose to find another part of the bar to continue their boisterous conversation.

Thirty minutes later, Bono swaggered into the room, wearing eclectic sunglasses and carrying the air of someone used to being stared at. With him was a quiet man in a black leather jacket.

The two took up the reserved table and enjoyed a drink, pretty much keeping to themselves.

On seeing Bono, the three young men darted over to the table.

"Hey Bono, we're huge fans. Could we have a photo with you?" asked one excitedly.

"No problem," said the musician.

Another of the friends looked at the low-key man in the leather jacket.

"Hey mate, would you mind taking a picture of us with Bono?"

"Sure, I'd be happy to," came the polite reply.

A little later, Bono and his friend left the place. The manager rushed over to the friends, who were still enjoying themselves immensely.

"You blokes are numbskulls. I can't believe what you did!"

"What did we do?" wondered one of the young fellows sheepishly.

"Don't you know who that was with Bono?"

"No," the friends said in unison.

"That man in the leather jacket, the one you asked to take the photo, was Bruce Springsteen."

83.

The GCA Index for A-Lister Performance

As we near the end of our time together, I'd like to offer you a learning framework that will unite a number of the core principles of my philosophy for peerless productivity, expert performance and a life of beautiful impact:

THE GCA INDEX

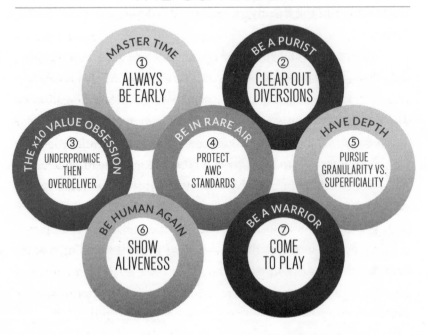

In this age of dramatic distraction and deep change, I invite you to consider the seven Gargantuan Competitive Advantages (GCAs) that, when implemented with regularity, will make you unbeatable in your field.

Before I run you through these, I invite you to note two overarching themes at play on our planet today:

Theme #1: The Mass Mediocritization of Humanity

I'm not judging. I'm simply reporting: the majority of people on the planet today are allowing large amounts of mediocrity to overwhelm their lives. Watch how they work, what they think, the words they deploy, the food they eat, the habits they apply and the way they behave, and it's clear they have given away their sovereign power to represent mastery to false beliefs, past hurts, current challenges, daily disturbances and inexcusable excuses. These good souls are built for greatness, yet have resigned themselves to average.

Theme #2: The Collective Deprofessionalization of Business

When was the last time you visited a store or dined at a restaurant or entered a coffee shop and saw a worker operating as a virtuoso, fully engaged as a maestro, wildly skilled and inspiringly knowledgeable? What's far more common now are people who are paid to be delivering a service playing with their devices, dreaming about their lunches, fooling around with their coworkers and essentially looking for ways not to have to do too much of anything while masquerading as hardworking (and caring). Too many potentially awesome producers show up late, make many mistakes, are not really present, show poor manners, offer little help and act like they are doing you a gigantic favor by interacting with you—instead of understanding that it's because of the business that you and their other customers choose to give them that they even have a job. And that excellent performance is a gateway into greater self-esteem, personal joy and spiritual strength.

With this context in place, let us study the seven GCAs that—immaculately executed on—will allow you to make quantum leaps as the kind of A-List producer who dominates their domain, discovers the fullness of their capacities and experiences a life they are proud of at the end.

Yes, these GCAs are simple. *Because success lies in a masterful consistency around the fundamentals.*

GCA #1: Always Be Early

I do believe it to be true that if you're not early, you're late. And that it's smarter to show up for a meeting a whole hour in advance than even one minute behind. When I have lunch with a business legend, they usually are already seated at the table when I arrive, generally reading a book. Or writing notes in their creativity journal.

GCA #2: Clear Out Diversions

It's easy to become the victim of too many activities and too many possessions. I've been encouraging you—in much of our journey together on these pages—to simplify your life. To become a purist (and a minimalist). To build your days and lead your life around only a few major pursuits. So your gifts and talents remain concentrated around your priorities instead of scattered around many trivialities.

GCA #3: Underpromise Then Overdeliver

The 10x Value Obsession is a concept from my advisory work that speaks to the process of ensuring that, at every touchpoint with a customer, you deliver ten times more value than they have any right to expect; from the initial approach to well after the sale, you stun and dazzle and wow your user with goodness. Keep stacking on the rewards, every step of the way, until it becomes an outright hurricane of magic that changes your customer's life forever. Do this impeccably on an ongoing basis and the entire marketplace will most certainly beat a path to your door. And you will ascend into a competition-free territory, no matter the state of the general economy.

GCA #4: Protect Absolutely World-Class Standards

The standards you hold your life to are profound indicators of the levels of success, influence and everyday heroism you'll reach. Here's a valuable rule to play with: *We get in life not what we wish for but that which we settle on.* In all that you do, hold yourself to the highest of ideals and codes of performance. Never do anything that demeans the person of ironclad excellence, unchangeable nobility and unmessable-with-integrity that you've promised your finest self you'll become.

GCA #5: Pursue Granularity versus Superficiality

This is a big one in a culture gone ultra-light. So many human beings no longer go deep—in their thinking, in the way they analyze situations, in the quality of their preparation, in the caliber of their daily rituals, in the rigor they apply to their craft, and in the overall unfolding of their lives. To adopt a granular approach is to be a heavyweight operator who exercises thoughtfulness, patience, meticulousness, pride and mastery in your activities—dramatically differentiating you from others in your field. Do work that is *substantial*. And be a person of *substance*. Going granular means rejecting all sloppiness and resisting any hint of laziness by doing your job and rolling through your personal life in a near-flawless, immensely skilled, yet wonderfully soulful way. What an advantage.

GCA #6: Show Aliveness

I recall standing at the counter of a café in Boulder, Colorado. I provided my order and thanked the barista. He was there yet he just wasn't really there, if you know what I mean. Very much in cyber-zombie mode. Zero presence. In a trance. His mind seemed to still be at home and his heart and soul were likely on some sunny Caribbean vacation. Only his body was in the shop. Going through the motions with little passion. Oh, what an important word is "presence" in our age of endless technological interruption. The biggest gift you can give a customer, as well as any human, is the wholeness of your attention. The largest present you can give a loved one is the treasure of your aliveness—being completely there when you are with them. Listening gloriously. Being sincere and interested. And engaging with them totally. Rare these days. And yet essential to a world-class life that soars with happiness, impact and contribution.

GCA #7: Come to Play

The moment you get to work, it's showtime. You are in show business and when you start to work each morning, you've stepped onto a stage. You're only as good as your last performance. And everything you do either brings you nearer to greatness or closer to ordinary. One mediocre result is the beginning of accepting average. So when you do your job, come to play. Operate above your pay grade. And punch above your weight class. Anything less is destructive to your primal genius.

———

Okay. There you go—seven best practices that, when regularly applied, will cause you to experience breakthrough wins. And gargantuan advantages as an A-Lister. I invite you to accelerate your training around them.

Beginning this precious day.

84.

Steve Jobs's Last 6 Words

The final words of Steve Jobs, according to his sister, were these:

"Oh wow. Oh wow. Oh wow."

When I read them the other day, I was moved. And reminded of the striking fragility of life.

I believe you have a call on your life to make humanity better. Yes, you do.

No excuses. No escapes. No postponements.

… I know you have sleeping potential within that you've never unleashed, as well as luminous promise that is begging to be explored.

… I believe that your fears can be fodder for even greater success, so you must not lose your nerve when problems appear.

… I am certain that your past has no power over your future unless you decide to let it.

… I feel highly confident that your life can rise into the realm of the sublime, if you begin to make a few simple new choices and then follow through with triumphantly consistent commitment.

I hope you find some quiet time in this culture of intoxicating noise to reconnect with the signal, to revisit your childhood desires, to re-access forgotten entry points into your merits, to sit sagely in the indisputable wisdom that even the longest life is a pretty quick ride.

And that before you know it, you'll be ashes and dust. The road trip you and I are on goes by in a blink, you know?

You owe this reflection to yourself—and those who depend on you, appreciate you and hold love within their hearts for you.

Today is a bonus of sorts, overflowing with prized bounty, worth celebrating. It's a gift of pure opportunity. To consider the ideals you've never envisioned and *to take risks you've not taken.* To give the compassion you know should be given. And to take a valiant stand for an exalted way of thinking, feeling, doing and being.

Our civilization needs more civility. And dignity. And braveness. We really do need you at your finest. We all want you to fly. So that when you reach your end, you exclaim, "Oh wow. Oh wow. Oh wow."

85.

When Things Seem Hard, Trust Your Strength

I was on a mountain bike ride through the woods just before I wrote you this.

I was reflecting on the truth that, as humans, we often feel weak and regularly forget all our strength.

So, in a sweaty burst of hot inspiration, I pulled off the trail. Put down my bike and, as the sun set, sat in the grass—and captured these words on my device. Here is the scene:

Here's what I most wish to share with you:

*When things seem hard, we have been granted the chance to trust
    our strength.*
*When confusion sets in, a window is opened for us to enter higher
    clarity.*
When we question everything, we are truly growing.
*When we feel completely alone, we are most connected to the shared
    experience of everyone.*
And therefore we are united.

In tumult and storms, remember all you've been through.

The violent waves will eventually become very still waters.
The discomfort of transformation will return the bliss of new wisdom.
And power that is cleaner.

… You are stronger than you know,

… braver than you can admit,

*… and more capable of navigating anything life can throw at you
    than your intellect can ever teach you.*

You are as powerful as the rain.
You are as unconquerable as the tide.
You are as good as the harvest.
You are as bright as the heavens
that carefully guide your way.

When scared, ask: What would heroism do?
When worried, wonder: How would confidence behave?

When angry, question: Where can understanding be given?
When hurting, go where optimism lives.
When insecure, follow where self-love leads.

All is unfolding for your benefit. Nothing is against your happiness.
Your tests will yield triumphs.
Your good deeds will produce noble success.

Great rewards are on the way.
Trust in your process.
Don't lose your nerve.
Compare your journey to none other.
You are flawlessly protected.
And richly guided.

By the force that rules the world.

86.

You Can't Inspire
If You're De-inspired

The celebrated leaders, revered revolutionaries and world-builders of history all came from a place of unusual inspiration.

Their genius was less in their ability to execute on the dream and more in their capacity to imagine the dream—and then electrify followers who proceeded to make the vision real.

Yet here's the main insight to play with ...

... You can't inspire others if you are feeling uninspired.

I know that seems like an obvious statement. And I'm sorry if it seems trite. Yet I don't think it is.

I don't believe in titles much. If you've read *The Leader Who Had No Title*, you already know this. Yet if there's one I'd want to wear on a badge on my lapel (or black T-shirt), it would be this: CIO—Chief Inspiration Officer.

The job of a world-class leader and expert performer is to galvanize their teammates around a singular purpose that excites them to step into their peak performance and highest prowess. So they become bigger than they were before they met you.

The calling of the servant hero (and outright legend) is to capture the minds, hearts and souls of those who have faith in them. And then push them to realize amazing feats while distributing astounding benefits to those they serve.

Yet you really can't uplift others if your own creative energy and productive enthusiasm have been downgraded.

I take my personal inspiration very, very seriously. It's a core tool of my trade.

I generally avoid most news, people who make me feel bad and dark physical places that are devoid of wonder.

Instead, I seek out that which lifts my hope, boosts my art, grows my game and fuels the inner fire that stokes my sport.

... I'll leave for a week to stay in a sparse cabin in some impossible-to-find village by the sea. Just because I need a shot in the arm. To finish a key project. A new place brings with it fresh energy.

Here's a pic from a recent trip:

At the writing sanctuary by the ocean

... Or I'll reach out to someone I admire just to have a conversation that sets me aflight. And restores my fury to reach closer to mastery.

... I'll pick up a book that excites my spirit.

... I'll go for a run rather than spend time online, meditate instead of medicating myself with some sensational television show or go sunbathe in my garden while country music plays.

... I'll open my journal and do a diagram, mapping out my intentions (intentions are creative, remember?) for my next twenty-four months that might look like this:

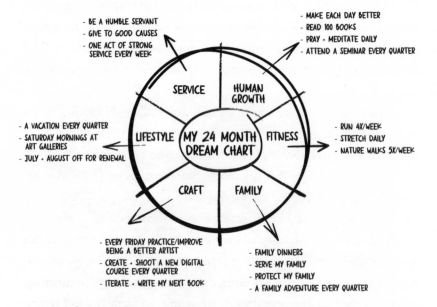

... I'll call my parents, asking my father about his life lessons and seeking his guidance, and listening to my mother's wisdom before getting her recipe for a favorite childhood meal that I'm attempting to replicate (I'm working on her awesome vegetable soup these days).

... I'll go for an extended walk through my home city, discovering new neighborhoods, taking photos of interesting sights and initiating quick conversations with fascinating people.

... I'll watch a film that reminds me that legendary is not for the faint of heart and all possibilitarians have it hard before they have it easy. (Actually, it never really gets easy: the danger just becomes more familiar, so it's easier to navigate and you don't give up so quickly.)

I do all these things to fuel the fumes of my will to excel. To reactivate my most pristine and supreme productivity. To hypnotize myself away from doing what's busy, trivial and pleasurable and to refocus on my duty to be of assistance to society. So I do not remain too long on empty. So the innocence of my aliveness remains highly alive (within a population of too many dead people walking).

Now, I don't mean to suggest that I'm *always* inspired. This is *not* true. Some think that I'm *always* overflowing with elation, energy and the drive to get my deliverables done. Nope. I'm human. So I have moods, natural rhythms and personal seasons (sometimes in a single day!).

As an artistic laborer, I've learned to trust these alternating cycles of inspiration and demotivation, realizing that my higher power is leading me at every step. When it's in my best interest to produce high-quality work and sing my song, the drive to do so just shows up. Yes, often at 5 AM. Not sure why. It just does.

As a creative worker, I trust the seasons. I truly do.

And when I'm de-inspired and have zero game, I see it as the Muse leading me into an off-season. And my better instincts welcome me to take a break (whether that means taking the morning off, the day off or the entire week off—or even longer—so I return ablaze with exuberance and imagination; I dream of taking a year-long sabbatical in a far-off land sometime soon).

I know artists such as Ernest Hemingway and Stephen King work with daily consistency. I very much understand Pulitzer Prize winner W. H. Auden's statement: "Routine, in an intelligent man, is a sign of ambition."

E. B. White's line about "a writer who waits for ideal conditions under which to work will die without putting a word on paper" makes eminent sense. It just doesn't quite work like that for me.

Here's my reality: the Muse doesn't visit me every morning or tuck me in every night, with a fairy tale and a sweet kiss. Some days complete paragraphs download with such miraculous spontaneity that I struggle to capture them. And on other days I simply stare at the wall. And count cobwebs in the corners.

And guess what? I've come to understand that this is all just fine. It's my personal process. To resist it is to demean it. The universe is leading me and it's to my advantage to work with it, versus fight it.

I guess what I'm saying is that I rarely force my creativity. When I do, what I make is mediocre at best. So why even bother? When I'll have to do it all over?

And even when I'm in one of the fiery cycles of consistent daily productivity, if I sit down to write nice and early one morning and nothing comes (or purely average work appears), I stop. I'll go for a walk or have lunch with a pal, trusting that there's always tomorrow.

Inspiration. How I adore this word! It's so essential to protect it, so you do work that makes a difference.

The word itself is derived from the Latin root *inspirare*, you know? It actually means "to be breathed into" ...

... by the intelligence that grants good fortune.

... by the current that makes dreams real.

... by the deities of dramatic accomplishment, towering achievement and impact that knows no bounds.

My wish at this moment as I write this for you? That you manage your inspiration well. And then push it proudly to a public aching to experience more of it.

And yes, when you work and live in this style, you will be called a freak, considered a weirdo and classified as strange, in a culture where many members of the majority have lost their fire and discarded their awe.

"And those who were seen dancing were thought to be insane by those who could not hear the music," wrote Nietzsche.

May you and I engrave these words upon our minds, hearts and souls.

87

The Six Months Left to Live Question

A fire blazes as I work. The crackling of the logs fills the room I'm writing in. "Standing Outside a Broken Phone Booth with Money in My Hand" by the Primitive Radio Gods plays. I know it's an ancient song. Yet it lifts my vibe. And makes me feel a little sad.

Which makes me wonder ...

Just imagine. For only a second. That you had merely six months left to live.

... Six short months to do all those things you'd promised yourself you'd do.

... Six months to visit the Taj Mahal and listen to Beethoven's "Moonlight" Sonata and see the *Mona Lisa* (so much smaller in person, right?) and explore the Great Pyramid of Giza.

... Six months to write letters of forgiveness to those who wronged you (or letters of apology to those whom you've hurt) and letters of unembarrassed and unconditional love to those who cherished you. And only saw the light within you.

If you had just six months left to live, what would you simply *stop* doing?

Maybe you'd list items like ...

... refusing to overidentify yourself with your work.

... being busy being busy with digital distractions.

... spending too much time with entertainment and not enough time on your education.

... getting angry over needless things and irritated by trifling matters like noisy neighbors, terrible drivers and frustrating family members.

... putting yourself down by listening to the voices of criticism and self-loathing in your head.

... beating yourself up for your misdeeds, forgetting that you did the best you knew how to do.

... constantly rehearsing the past so one disappointing experience gets relived a million times in your mind.

————

And what things would you have the weighty wisdom and charismatic strength to begin doing?

... like writing of and thereby re-experiencing the most spectacular meals you've ever had and reflecting on the majestic moments you've been blessed to enjoy.

... like bellowing a loud "I love you" to all the people whom you've never felt safe enough to say this to (but who need to hear the extent of your love for them before you return to the great wide-open space from which you came).

... like taking that trip of a lifetime or planting a special rose garden that your friends will remember you by.

... like eating more pizza, gulping more pasta and savoring more ice cream.

... like dancing naked under a full moon, reading the poetry you were too busy to read and going to the art galleries that you said you'd visit someday. When you had more time and less to do.

... like returning to your childhood home, walking the streets you walked as a kid with a pure heart and an unmarked history—radiating good cheer, high hope and an innocence I wish we all enjoyed more of.

... like taking a nap on a Sunday afternoon, asking for the best table at your favorite restaurant, and singing as you enter your usual café.

... like smiling at strangers (and holding the grin longer than is socially acceptable) and walking barefoot in a daisy-filled park.

... like being with family, mostly. And taking long walks in a sacred forest while the rain falls or the sun sets, sending golden sparkles through the trees.

... like treating everyone you meet like you might never get to see them again. Because a human life is so delicate. And someone can die completely unexpectedly.

What is it that you would do? With only six months of life left to live?

This is the question I ask of you. So you live all that remains of your important and excellent life heroically.

88.

Fame and Fortune for a Line on Your Tombstone?

Sorry to keep raising the idea of death as we reach the short roads of our journey together.

And yet part of me isn't sorry …

… because thinking about death refocuses our priorities, recalibrates our thinking, animates our emotions and re-orders our routines.

Considering my own death isn't something depressing. Not at all. It's actually *inspiring*.

Building greater awareness and intimacy with the fact my days are numbered—no matter how long Nature allows me to live—injects an exuberance, appreciation and sense of urgency into me to represent my best within each of my days.

Connecting to my mortality is a potent way to stay centered around all that's most essential to conducting a thoughtful, creative, valuable and jubilant life.

This morning I read the following piece from a book I love called *On the Shortness of Life*, by the Stoic philosopher Seneca, who lived in Rome and served as a key adviser to the emperor Nero.

In the passage I read, he writes:

So, when you see a man repeatedly wearing the robe of office or one whose name is often spoken in the Forum, do not envy him: these things are won at the cost of life. In order that one year be dated from their names they waste all of their own years.

To me, this statement speaks to the imperative of realizing that many men and women who spend the greatest hours of their finest days chasing fame, fortune and applause do so at the cost of experiencing the real joys, adventures and gems life has to offer.

These people race through their days scaling toward an apex of success that counts for little at the end.

They do it all just to have a year on the calendar named after them.

Seneca is encouraging us to question and then challenge this insubstantial and regret-filled style of experiencing a human incarnation.

He adds: "Some men, after they have crawled through a thousand indignities to the supreme dignity, have been assailed by the gloomy thought that all their labors were but for the sake of an epitaph."

Love it.

Such beings invested themselves in running after things that, once death is near, they realize were merely for a single line on their tombstone.

Not really worth it, is it?

89.

Resist the Titan's Decline

Once you've arrived at total craft mastery, and become a headliner in your field, while making a life of wonder, sophistication, virtue and generous public service, the learning paradigm in this chapter will walk you through the process of the decay that can silently and subtly infect (and then devastate) your crowning accomplishment. Understanding it will help you avoid it. Because with better awareness you'll be armed to make the better choices that will lead to better results.

There is some truth to Silicon Valley legend Andy Grove's statement: "Success breeds complacency. Complacency breeds failure. *Only the paranoid survive.*"

Most of the business and sports goliaths I work with have what I describe as an "optimistic paranoia," in that while they are grateful for what they've earned and hopeful the rare-air achievements will continue, they also—*at the same time*—hold in their minds the idea that they could be knocked off the throne any day, if they take their eyes off the game. They very clearly understand that superstardom is *ephemeral.*

Before we study the model, please consider the term from physics known as "entropy," which describes the natural disorder and gradual decline that *all* systems face. Entropy explains why once-successful people descend into irrelevance and once-revered companies become washed up. To ensure elite performance and maximum impact, you absolutely need to be monomaniacally vigilant against all your hard-won accomplishments being degraded by the natural forces you face as a creative producer and exceptional leader. Success that doesn't last isn't very successful, is it? "Whom the gods wish to destroy they first call promising," wrote literary pundit Cyril Connolly.

Okay. So we begin with you at the apex, a true industry titan. At world-class. Bravo. Very few ever reach the pinnacle of their domain. Yet at the summit is the place you are most vulnerable. Most of the climbers who die on Mount Everest don't perish on the way up to the peak—they succumb to death *after* they've stood on the highpoint of the mountain. These voyagers fall into the sharp trap of thinking that because they made it to the zenith their safety is guaranteed. They forget that it's at the top that the real dangers show up—risks like running out of oxygen, making a mistake due to exhaustion or miscalculating the time it will take to descend.

The same holds true for any human being or organization: *At the peak is where you must be most careful. Complacency will get you killed.*

Most success goes bad shortly after the height of success appears. World-class has an incredibly short shelf life. The pivot? To really understand why greatness is so delicate and then move quickly to install an "Architecture of Endurability" so that your mastery and domain dominance actively *increase*, even as your influence and impact accelerate.

As you can see from looking at the model in this chapter, the first pressure you'll face after your rise to the apex of your field is that of arrogance. All the victories you've experienced can generate a tendency to think you know all the answers, are always right and cannot be defeated. One of my organizational clients used to be, arguably, the most celebrated tech company on the planet. An executive told me, candidly, that he knew things were going to go downhill when the founder stopped listening to his leadership team at meetings because he fell into the trap of thinking only he could foresee the future. Because he had predicted it in the past. He turned out to be wrong. The company is now a rarely discussed also-ran.

THE TITAN'S DECLINE

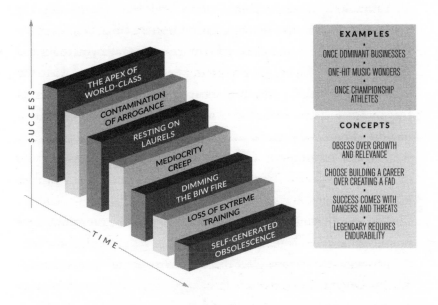

The antidote to arrogance is humility. Practice "The Anti-Irrelevance Rule": as you rise in domain dominance, fight even harder to avoid the pull of becoming smug, prideful and conceited. Keep your feet on the ground, stay focused on your mission-plan and the human beings you are blessed to serve and never forget that you're always a single misstep away from falling off the mountain if you get too cocky. "The greater the artist, the greater the doubt. Perfect confidence is granted to the less talented as a consolation prize," wrote Robert Hughes.

Should a mentality of arrogance contaminate your focus and way of operating, the next stage of the decomposition process, as you can see from the learning framework, is an inclination to repeat the same winning formula that brought about your greatness. You get hooked into becoming protective over what you have instead of being productive, inventive and courageous so you deliver even more of your genuine magic to the marketplace.

In ancient Greece, a wreath made from the leaves of the aromatically scented *Laurus Nobilis* tree was placed on the head of a winning athlete to celebrate their triumph. Over time, the phrase "Do not rest on your laurels" emerged as cautionary advice to victors to avoid any decline into ordinary. I strongly encourage you to ensure that your finest work is always ahead of you rather than taking the easy road and making your current work a mere forgery of the success that made you great. Otherwise, you're certain to become a one-hit wonder.

The next pressure you'll face when you're at the top of your game is "Mediocrity Creep." The metaphor to guide us here is the Broken Windows Theory. In a suburb of a well-known city, a few neighbors allowed broken windows on a few houses to remain unrepaired. This simple and seemingly innocuous lack of care set in motion airborne particles of apathy and neglect that began to pollute the entire community. Other neighbors started leaving garbage on their properties, as mediocrity began to be acceptable. Front lawns were then left unmown and gardens were left for the weeds. This steady creep of low standards infecting this once-splendid neighborhood led to staggering increases in crime. Gangs took over and violence was everywhere. Apply the Broken Windows Theory to your mastery, productivity and life—as well as to any organization that you lead. And know that if you're not *extremely* vigilant, mediocrity can quietly take over. Without you even noticing it.

The next state that follows in the fall of a person or an empire is loss of the enthusiasm to win, what I call "Dimming the Best in World Fire." One of the core traits of a legendary champion is that they simply cannot stand the idea that a time will come when they will not be the champion. The very thought of losing the title terrifies them.

With the decrease of the once-scorching fire to be Best in World, next on *The Titan's Decline* is the loss of the commitment to train extremely hard, like a heavyweight. The performer's cheerfulness gets corroded and their dedication to improve their knowledge and skill degrades. They lose their creativity, and their energy to out-practice everyone around them evaporates. You can see this happen with some Hollywood superstars, for example. All the years of pushing their talents to the razor's edge of their limits, accepting one demanding movie role after another, causes their genius to become exhausted. Sometimes they've also built up a lifestyle of excess with the corresponding high expenses that come with it because they think a limitless supply of money has been guaranteed by their future. All this tension wears them down. So they begin to accept parts that require no mastery, just for the money. And to get a chance for some recovery. This is the beginning of the end. The superstar soon becomes a caricature of their once-glorious self.

All this—of course—leads to irrelevance. And obsolescence. A place you must do everything in your power to avoid. As I am sure you will.

You and your team can do a Titan's Decline Analysis so that you can first spot all weaknesses and then set up the necessary protections by using the worksheet I use with my clients. You'll find it at TheEverydayHeroManifesto.com/TitansDeclineWorksheet

90.

The Necessity of
Artistic Unpopularity

October 3, 1992, was a big day for musician Sinéad O'Connor.

Stunningly famous after a string of runaway hits like "Nothing Compares 2U," she was performing on *Saturday Night Live*.

Yet rather than safely singing her planned song, she turned the appearance on its head. And made it into a ferocious political statement against child mistreatment.

After replacing the original words in Bob Marley's protest song "War" with "child abuse," O'Connor— with fury on her face and a voice that was raging with rebellion—lifted a photo of Pope John Paul II, screamed, "Fight the real enemy," and ripped it in half. It was a scathing indictment of the harm the singer alleged had been perpetrated on children by members of the clergy in her native Ireland.

The behavior caused her fame to collapse. And her career to nosedive.

Many years later, she revealed her motives: "An artist's job is sometimes not to be popular. An artist's job sometimes is just to create conversation where conversation is needed."

The nature of doing work that is profound, transformational and special means it captivates those who understand it and enrages those who don't get it. If your masterwork *doesn't* upset, provoke, anger and trigger the majority of citizens in society, perhaps it really isn't masterwork. It's just ordinary labor.

Your job—as an everyday hero and artistic leader within your domain—is to have enough faith in your abilities and valor in your heart to do that which you know you must do to honor the honesty of your most original self. To offer the poetry, music and magnificence of your spirit that is your absolute truth—even if you get hated when you push it.

So—please—bring your gifts to our world. We really, really, really do need them as never before. And do so *now*. Even if you're loathed.

91.

The Troll Deconstruction

The learning framework that is at the core of this chapter is one of the most widely embraced models in my mentoring methodology, so I wanted to make sure you have it. It will help you block out the hostile voices and the vicious chatter of those critics who will try to stop you from delivering your talents to humanity. You can listen to your condemners or you can passionately press forward. You don't get to do both, right?

Trolls are those bottom-feeders who put down your heartfelt work and demean the sincere magic that you put into the world with your good name stamped upon it. The first step in deconstructing trolls—and taking away any power they might have over you—is, as you can see by looking at the blueprint: *Haters are love teachers in disguise.*

They are. Really.

Anyone who provokes your insecurity and incites that part of you that doubts your mastery is a helper. Their mean behavior brings up your weakness. So you can notice it and then process through it into healing. Wonderful. Thank them. For they've made you healthier, purer and better. They've served your ascent toward your inherent greatness.

The second element of the decode is this: *Beneath attack is pain.* The campaign of a critic is fueled by their own lack of self-love and personal appreciation. Naysayers are mostly disappointed souls who didn't do what you've done, so it makes them feel better lashing out at you. Misery always seeks company. People treat others the way they treat themselves, and human beings experiencing a lot of hurt often hurt other human beings.

THE TROLL DECONSTRUCTION

1
HATERS ARE
LOVE TEACHERS
IN DISGUISE

2
BENEATH
ATTACK IS PAIN

3
LIGHT ATTRACTS
MOTHS AS WELL
AS ANGELS

4
PEOPLE IN A
GREAT PLACE
DON'T TEAR
OTHERS DOWN

5
HATERS ARE
DAMAGED
DREAMERS

6
POWERFUL WORK
GENERATES
EXTREME
REACTIONS

7
TO UNDERSTAND
MAGIC ONE MUST
HAVE THE EYES
TO SEE MAGIC

8
RIDICULE IS A
SYMPTOM OF
INFLUENCE

9
BRAVE PROJECTS
TERRIFY
THE INSECURE
STATUS QUO

345

Then comes the third point: *Light attracts moths as well as angels.* Shining your primal genius into your field and straight across our little planet will cause those who salute your virtuosity to come toward you. But please know that standing in the fullness of your creative glory will also bring out jealous trolls. Like moths to a flame.

Element number four is this: *People in a great place don't tear others down.* Those who are happy, pursuing their mighty ambitions and in a really good place in their lives don't have the inclination, energy or time to hunt down, attack and condemn visionary leaders. The idle and unfulfilled life truly is the devil's workshop. Bored and jealous people will want to troll you as you live your promise because it makes them feel better about their own betrayed potential.

Next, we get to the fifth essential principle for deconstructing the behavior of trolls, so their arrows do not minimize your poetry and stunt your skillfulness: *Haters are damaged dreamers.* Every single human alive today has such talent within them. Yes, most of us have disowned this wealth, as it's too hard and scary to express. But that doesn't mean it's not still there. As children, we designed such daring dreams. Yet due to the negative messaging of those we trusted and the rejection and defeats we've faced as we've leaned into life, the majority have closed their minds and hearts to their powers. And put up walls so they don't experience more grief. It's much easier to sit back in an easy chair and shower bile on someone actively in the game than to look in the mirror, take personal responsibility for your condition and do the growth needed to stand up again.

"For some to love you, some must loathe you," said the billionaire author of *Harry Potter*, J. K. Rowling. Element six of *The Troll Deconstruction* says: *Powerful work generates extreme reactions.* If you do your job well—producing masterwork that shatters the way things have been done and takes the field by storm by destroying tradition—critics will hate all over you. Because it isn't what *they* consider great art. And since they don't have the bravery to open themselves to your innovation, they'll tear you down. Makes them feel safer. Helps them remain secure in their limited and static understanding of the way things are supposed to look while protecting their status as so-called "experts" in the domain. Just know that the more brilliant your product and the more revolutionary your artistry, the more extreme will be the reaction. And that criticism and attack are a coward's paradise.

Element seven of *The Troll Deconstruction* is: *To understand magic one must have the eyes to see magic.* Just think about amateur art lovers. They don't really know much about the arena. They haven't seen the paintings of the great masters and been schooled in what it takes and what they've done. All they see is a blue vase or a woman called Mona. So they usually say, "Is that it? It looks so simple." And then, "I could have done that."

Hmmm. Really? Makes me think about Bob Dylan's line: "Don't criticize what you don't understand." Good, right?

It usually takes decades of daily practice and continuous training to make something look simple. Because true artistry is so much more about what the producer decides not to put into the product than what they put in. That's where the real genius lies. When you really, really, really know your craft, you can totally hone in on what's most important, leaving out all triviality. And superficiality.

This is why it's an excellent idea not to listen to the opinion of someone who is not even in the business of doing what you're doing. They really don't know what it takes. And don't have the acumen to understand what you've done. Because they don't know anything. (Even though they think they do.)

Element eight is straightforward: *Ridicule is a symptom of influence.* You know you're releasing genius into the world when you're being laughed at. Trust you're not only on the right track but sending out genuine masterwork when the trolls mock, condemn and ridicule you. Nice job. You win.

Last one. *Brave projects terrify the insecure status quo.* Yes, brave, beautiful, towering work that will stand the test of the centuries requires that you pull the rug out from under the truths that mainstream society believes to be true. As a matter of fact, product that is truly masterful is so ahead of its time that it takes a ton of time for it to catch on. And for its expertise to be understood. Vincent van Gogh sold only *one* painting in his lifetime: *The Red Vineyard at Arles.* The masterpiece was purchased for four hundred francs in Belgium, seven months before he committed suicide.

Don't let a lack of public success stop you. Your nobility and quest for amazingness beg that you persist.

No matter how many trolls come out to play.

92.

That Time I Met Muhammad Ali

I look out at the glamorous colors of autumn from my writing room at home. The white noise machine that I purchased to block out all nuisance is on. So I have the sound of a gurgling brook to keep me company as I write of this personal story that still makes me smile.

I was fifteen. John Lennon had just been assassinated. His melodic and moving song "Imagine" was being played on the radio constantly. It was Christmas time. In Los Angeles.

I'm not from LA. But my parents thought it would be a good place to be. For a vacation. That year.

They rented a Chrysler K-car. They don't make those cars anymore. I think this is a good thing. My brother and I were embarrassed to be in it. It sure was no Corvette (by far my favorite car at that time; a poster of the '63 split-window model was fixed onto my bedroom wall with tape).

Each day of that trip, Mom would pick up sandwiches and oranges from the grocery store near the motel where we stayed.

And we would explore the city.

We walked Sunset Boulevard. We went to the Hollywood Walk of Fame. We drove through Beverly Hills. In our Chrysler K-car.

And that's where it happened ...

... I was the one who spotted it first. A brown, shiny, gleaming

Rolls-Royce convertible, making its way down the avenue. With other people honking their horns. As they drove by and recognized the driver. *Muhammad Ali.*

I hit my brother in the arm. He was twelve at the time.

"That's Ali!" I roared. "In that car!"

Mom has extrasensory perception. She's always had it, as long as I've known her. She can hear squirrels running in a forest within a neighboring nation. Can see spiders making spiderwebs in nearby galaxies. Nothing ever got past her. If you know what I mean.

"Muhammad Ali? Where?" she asked, immediately.

"He just drove by. In that Rolls-Royce," I said excitedly, pointing to the passing car.

My mother leapt into action like a superhero set to save a burning city. She asked Dad to pull a dramatic U-turn. Across the busy street. In our Chrysler K-car. In active pursuit of the former heavyweight boxing champion. Of the world.

Once on the same side of the road as Mr. Ali, our little car accelerated. To catch up to the Rolls-Royce that was simply cruising along. On that marvelously sunny day.

My brother and I slunk down in the backseat. Mom pressed my father to go faster. Because the legend was still in sight.

I kid you not as to what happened next.

We drove up alongside Muhammad Ali. *Right next to him.* One of his children was on the passenger side and an elderly gentleman that looked like his father sat in the back, on the luxurious white leather seat.

Mom rolled down her window. "Mr. Ali. Hello! Hello!"

Disbelief washed over his face. My brother and I prayed for forgiveness from The Gods of Excruciating Embarrassment.

"Could we please have a photo with you?" she continued, elegantly as always.

The Rolls slowed down. Muhammad Ali pointed to the side of

the road and maneuvered his car toward a place where we could park. In front of sprawling mansions with wondrous gardens filled with carefully cultivated flowers.

We followed. And rolled up behind him. In our beige rental car.

What happened next really is now mythical within the history of our family ...

... Mr. Ali most graciously posed for pictures with me, my mother and my brother. He could not have been more polite and was unfathomably humble for a man of such fame, even as his gigantic hand engulfed mine when we greeted one another.

He was unhurried. Gentle. And full of kindness.

Then—get this—seeing that Dad was taking all the photos, he suggested that I take one of him and my father, together.

Once done, he wished us a delightful vacation and drove off. Into the golden sunshine of Beverly Hills. In his brown, shining Rolls-Royce.

We talked about that encounter for the rest of the vacation. Over cucumber sandwiches and more oranges. Speaking of our meeting with a hero. And celebrating his decency to a simple, unknown family.

Once home, a patient of Dad's made one of the photos into a clock that sat in our wood-paneled TV room. (Yes, a clock.)

Every year, around Christmas time, we'd remember the meeting. With our favorite boxer. Mr. Ali. And we would perform a dinnertime prayer. In thankfulness for the human who reminded us what heavyweight humility looks like.

93.

Don't Worry about Your Legacy

I wrote a book ages ago called *Who Will Cry When You Die?*

It was a work about living a life that people will talk about years after your end. It was an instruction manual for making your name matter and leaving a mark on the world.

I was thirty-four years old when I wrote it. Now, with the swift passage of too much time, I wish I'd picked a better title. Seriously.

Talk of legacy is popular these days. Pundits prescribe that we should do the deeds and perform the acts that will cause our families and communities to honor us as heroes and maybe even have monuments erected to appreciate us once we're gone.

I understand the sentiment and used to live my life in a way that would ensure that I'd be remembered fondly—by many—long after my death.

Not anymore.

I'm not buying what the notion of legacy is selling. It no longer makes sense to me, as a much older man.

I've started shopping at a different store, if you get what I mean.

Who cares what people say about you after you've passed? You'll be food for worms and pushing up daffodils, six feet under. Or a tiny pile of ashes in a tarnished tin urn sitting on top of someone's dirty fireplace. Next to pictures of them with their Little League trophies.

As far as I can tell, what matters most isn't how you'll be remembered by those you leave behind *but how you decide to live while you get to be alive.*

... Were you cheerful during the good days and graceful in defeat?

... Were you considerate to all around you and forgiving of those who hurt you?

... Did you treat your profession with the respect it deserved and do your duty to represent supremacy in each of your enterprises?

... Did you have the conviction to be yourself when society pushed you to be like everyone else, as well as the sensibility to make others feel more hopeful when they were with you?

... Did you use the years of your life to grow in humility, gain in knowledge and learn to tread the planet more lightly than when you arrived?

... And did you learn to not take yourself too seriously, understanding that most of the troubles we worry about really don't ever happen, so it's best to remain joyful, grateful and relaxed?

These days I believe that pursuing a noteworthy legacy is the occupation of a screaming ego.

Being a courteous, masterful, steadfast and noble human being while your tender and brave heart still beats is the way of real heroism.

94.

A Hero Named Desmond Tutu

Desmond Tutu is one of the greatest leaders, humanitarians and change-makers of history.

Winner of the Nobel Peace Prize, he worked closely with Nelson Mandela for a free South Africa and the reconciliation of wounds caused by the injustices of apartheid.

I've learned so much from Desmond Tutu over the years.

… The importance of standing up for myself with unyielding courage under conditions where I've been mistreated, yet with a forgiving heart that still seeks out the good in all.

… The profound value and fundamental importance of every human being on the planet, regardless of the color of their skin, the nature of their gender, the nation of their citizenship or their station in life. Everyone matters, Desmond Tutu taught me. And must be treated with respect, understanding and love.

… The essentialness of each of us releasing the shackles of victimhood and doing what we must to exercise our human power in easy times and during trouble by turning uncertainty into creativity, bruises into bravery and any form of tragedy into victory. We must rebuild the relationship with our greatest selves.

When I met Desmond Tutu in a quiet room in Johannesburg, I was awed, moved (to tears) and entirely mesmerized by the grace of his presence. And by the gentleness with which this giant of leadership treated me.

With Desmond Tutu in South Africa

He once observed: "I am a leader by default. Because nature does not allow a vacuum."

Words of truth. Spoken by a legitimate hero.

As you advance toward your major cause and loftiest ambitions, please inscribe those words onto your spirit. Know that you can lead without a title, show inspiration without a position and exemplify virtuosity, civility and helpfulness to many without any formal authority. You have the agency to reclaim any of your native power given to circumstances you blame, and truly can make a mark by starting small and then remaining devoted to showing up at your leadership best, day after day. The way you become special and great is by practicing being special and great so often that all un-specialness and anti-greatness is cleansed out of you, like the sunshine of spring washes away all hints of a cold and cruel winter.

Genuine power can be revealed when a human simply remembers how to be fully human. Because nature does not allow a vacuum.

95.

The Life Regrets of People on Their Deathbeds

Care workers who help dying people to suffer less and end better have spoken of the most common regrets they have heard during their patients' last days.

I think it's worth paying attention to them. So we can avoid them.

Deathbed Regret #1: They Wish They Had Kept Greater Perspective

Human beings really do spend too much time worrying about things that will never happen.

And even when hardship appears, we forget that difficulties always end. Merry days eventually return.

To become wiser and more resilient is to maintain perspective no matter what unfolds, knowing that life's journey is really quite quick. Grace, maturity and strength require that we navigate our days in the spirit of thankfulness—never giving our burdens more energy than our blessings.

There's an old story that I shared in *Who Will Cry When You Die?* that I hope will remind you of the gifts that you've been given. And the value of staying optimistic.

One day a man with a serious illness was wheeled into a hospital room where another patient was resting on the bed next to the window.

As the two became friends, the one next to the window would look out of it and amuse his bedridden companion with vivid descriptions of the wonderful world outside.

Some days he would speak of the splendor of the trees in the park across from the hospital and how the leaves would sway softly in subtle breezes. On other days he would entertain his friend with step-by-step replays of the interesting and often odd behaviors of the people who walked by.

However, as time went on, the man in the other bed grew resentful at his inability to observe the wonders his companion described. Eventually, he grew to dislike him and then to hate him, for all the life that he could so easily see.

One night, during a particularly bad coughing fit, the patient next to the window stopped breathing. Rather than pressing the emergency button the other man chose to do nothing.

The next morning the patient who had given his friend so much happiness by telling him of the sights he had witnessed was pronounced dead.

As the body was wheeled out of the hospital room, the other man quickly asked the attending nurse if his bed could be placed next to the window, a request that was granted. But as the patient looked through the glass, he discovered something that made him shudder: the window faced a brick wall.

His former roommate had conjured up the fantastic stories that he had described purely from his imagination—as a loving gesture to make his moments a little better.

He'd acted out of love. And the decency that speaks to the finest of our shared humanity.

Deathbed Regret #2: They Wish They Hadn't Worried So Much about What Other People Think

Oscar Wilde said: "Be yourself. Everyone else is taken."

Oh, how many heartbeats we misspend in caring too much about how we look! We fail to take the chances that would materialize our primal genius because we don't wish to be rejected, dislike being embarrassed and desire to look cool. We've become a culture of attention seekers versus magic workers, donating our greatest days to the needless pursuit of approval. I gently urge you to keep in mind that in one hundred years *everyone* alive today will be gone. Why hold back on the realization of your promise and the following of your enthusiasms to be pleasers to people who won't be here in the future?

Your life will rise or fall depending on your willingness to appear foolish. And your interest in respecting your authenticity. By embracing the dreams that matter most to you. Even (especially) when no one else gets you.

Deathbed Regret #3: They Wish They Hadn't Wasted So Much Time

It's so very common to wish we had more time, yet completely squander the time that we have, isn't it? Seneca wrote, "In guarding their fortune, citizens are often closefisted. Yet, when it comes to the matter of wasting time, in the case of the one thing in which it is right to be miserly, they show themselves most extravagant."

Use your precious hours *responsibly*. Defend yourself against any occupation that is unworthy of your noble gifts and human talents. Chase not the petty interests that enchant the crowd. Your leadership, mastery, happiness and serenity cannot be found there. Ever.

In the era we currently inhabit it's common to overschedule our days with activities that make us feel we're being productive yet, in truth, have no value at all. We have become masters of minor things and experts of trivial pursuits. It makes no sense—and is an enormous misrepresentation of your highness—to succumb to the attractions and amusements being sold as important measures of success when our days are numbered. And an eventual death is in your cards. Yes—I am sorry to say it—but you will die one day. I will die one day. We all will be dead, sometime.

"How did it get so late so soon?" wondered Dr. Seuss.

Deathbed Regret #4: They Wish They Had Enjoyed the Pilgrimage of Life More

Having fun is highly productive. A positive mood is a great gateway into your masterwork and maximum impact. I know our society persuades you to think otherwise. That the journey must be hard and grueling. That life needs to be overly serious and immensely practical. But to suggest that working all the time is a more valuable activity than dinners with your family and friends, travels to interesting places and doing those things that make you happy is just a value judgment rather than a statement of truth.

Saying that we are living fully and completely only when we're busy is a story. And not every story you hear is true. Making time for instances of awe and beauty to unfold—and having a ton of fun while your heart is fully alive—is wisdom at its best.

So, of course, work hard. And yet also savor the fruits of your labor. So when you're near your finish line, you'll rest joyfully in the fact that you loved all that life so generously offered you.

Deathbed Regret #5: They Wish They Had Been More Kind and Loving

The final regret of those at their end is that they feel remorse over the harmful acts they did to others (it's interesting how common it is for people to mistreat the humans they most love, isn't it?). Failing to practice the virtue of kindness on a daily basis not only makes our world a darker, more miserable place, it corrodes your conscience—which destroys your happiness and tranquility.

360

We all, as human beings, have a native inclination to treat our brothers and sisters on the planet with reverence, compassion and love (yes, love). When we break from that drive in the unwise quest for more fame, fortune and applause (or simply because we haven't taken our personal growth and private healing seriously, so we behave as our worst versus best selves), we become filled with a regret that knows no limits. Because we are operating as people that we never wished to be. And betraying our heroic nature.

Don't hold back on being the most loving person you've ever met. It's a habit of the giants. And the truest luminaries of history. If you're good and people take advantage of you it's not because being good is bad. It's because you've allowed people to take advantage of you.

The one who loves the most wins. Or, as guitar maestro Jimi Hendrix observed: "When the power of love overcomes the love of power, the world will know peace."

96.

The Good You Do Lasts a Lifetime

It's so common to think that the good you do has no lasting value. That it doesn't really matter. That it likely doesn't count.

When I was a kid, my mom used to do something terrific for me. Once or twice a month, she'd make homemade french fries, drive the plate of food covered with foil wrap to my school and leave it at the front office for me, in a small box with a handwritten note on it that told me how much she loved me. She performed this exquisite act of goodness so I could enjoy her cooking. And have a hot meal. And feel her caring.

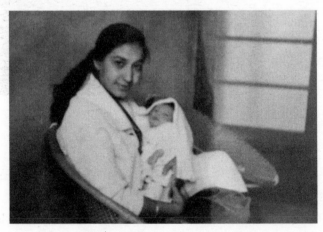

My mother and me, on my first day of life

Now, all these decades later, after all the colorful and wonderful experiences I've known, guess what still sticks with me as a favorite memory? Yes. My mother's magnificently simple yet wildly loving gesture of driving those golden and perfectly crispy French fries to my school. (And the faces of my friends who then began a negotiation process in the high hope of trading one of their tuna sandwiches, canned peaches and sliced carrots for even a single one of my price-less fries.)

While he was the center of the LA Lakers, basketball legend Pau Gasol attended one of my live events.

We got to know each other over the weekend and even better over a long and unforgettable dinner at my home, with my family.

At home with LA Laker Pau Gasol

After the conference had ended, I offered to drive Pau to the airport. Once there, I watched as fan after fan left the lines they had been waiting in to approach him for an autograph or a photo.

Though he had a flight to board, Pau would stop for each, smile his gentle smile, carefully sign the autograph—adding a few words of inspiration—and pose for the picture. (I recall meeting a guitar god in a local sushi restaurant who replied to my request for a photo with a curt "I don't like to have my picture taken," before walking past me.)

"Pau, you stopped for *every single person* who asked. You made time for each one of all those fans. You were gracious to everybody— never showed any tiredness or irritation at all," I observed as I walked him to his gate.

I'll never forget his reply. For it was so sage. And taught me so much.

"It takes so little to make someone happy, Robin."

He then reached down, gave me a hug, thanked me and went on his way.

97.

Be Happy to See Live People

I was in South Africa for a series of leadership presentations when I noticed that the gentleman who was driving me to the sessions was flooded with glee each time he saw another human being.

His eyes would sparkle. His smile would broaden. Each time he saw someone. It was astounding to see.

"You really seem to like people," I said.

"I've seen a lot of dead people," he replied softly. "So when I see a live person, it makes me very happy."

I remained silent. *Thunderstruck.*

Just imagine how our world would look if we adopted his philosophy. Putting down our devices, being less affected by selfishness and busyness and increasing our decency. By paying more attention to our collective humanity. And each person in front of us, friend or stranger.

Just imagine coming alive every time we spotted human life. Or any life, for that matter.

98.

Verses of the Everyday Hero Who Can't Be Defeated

Can you stand in your sorrow without needing to flee to the crushing demands of doing something?

Can you say what your wisdom knows needs to be said, even when you disappoint those who listen? And anger those who disagree?

Can you walk the hard path that few wish to walk and still know joy, serenity and freedom? Free of the hunger to fit in? And please the majority?

Can you risk being hated, to do what is right?

Can you be in the world yet not of it, able to savor the sweet pleasures of solitude, silence and stillness, remaining unlonely in your aloneness? Open to embracing the beauty of tiny graces and savoring the graces of the ordinary?

Can you reach for your higher visions, imagining what few dare to imagine and marching strongly in the direction of your most honest drives and still be peaceful, should you fail, welcoming all that destiny has written in your stars?

Can you love as only the fool loves, laugh like only the jester laughs and risk being labeled crazy for the supposed insanity of your dreams?

Can you push away the superficial to produce the monumental? And make a mark that ends up making you immortal? In your own natural and original way?

This is what I seek to know. Can you be true? To you?

99.

Windows of Opportunity and Your Second Chances

In *The Greatness Guide* I wrote about my "almost encounter" with Hollywood icon Harvey Keitel.

He was exceptional in so many movies and a goliath of his craft, sustaining his prowess over many decades. Making him both an A-Lister and Hall of Famer in his field.

I happened to be in a hotel lobby in my home city when I noticed him sitting alone in the lounge area. Just sitting there. Waiting, I guess.

"Wow! That's Harvey Keitel!" I was surprised to see him and awestruck that he was there.

My first instinct was to walk over, extend my hand and just have a chat.

Then, before I could be bold and strong, I was overtaken by my more primitive tendencies. Fear began to scream louder than truth. My hopes gave way to my insecurities. The threat of rejection told my optimism to take a break.

The internal rambling went something like this ...

... "He's probably waiting for a big-league producer and I'd better not disturb him."

... "What if he's unfriendly and mean to me?"

... "There are lots of people in this lobby and I'll look like a dork going over to meet this celebrity."

Oh, the windows of opportunity that a friendly universe sends us, only to be closed by our own cowardice, timidity and craving to look hip.

On our deathbeds it truly is what we *didn't do*—the people we didn't meet, the potential we didn't express, the projects we didn't finish, the enchantments we didn't chase and the love we failed to deliver—that floods us with regret ...

... *never* all the valiant acts we actually went ahead and did.

So what did I do, you wonder? Well, if you read the chapter in that book I wrote nearly two decades ago, you remember ...

... I did nothing. Zero. *Nada*.

I interrupted my enthusiasm to meet this cinematic hero with the decision to get back to my office. To go push some paper. To have a meeting or two. To check my messages. And so I left.

I thought about that experience a lot over the following months. I didn't feel good about my shyness—and weakness. I promised myself I would practice becoming more gutsy. And gallant.

As I wrote in that book, about that missed meeting:

If I see Harvey Keitel again, I promise you that I'll sprint toward him. He may think I'm a celebrity stalker until we start to chat. And then he'll discover the truth: I'm simply a man who seizes the gifts that life presents to him.

One of the gorgeous things about every life that I really, really, really wish for you to know, as we reach the end of our time together, is that *you really do get second chances.* You won't get a ton of them, unfortunately. But you will receive them.

And so ...

... I happened to be in Rome years later, working on a new book. After an early morning ride on my mountain bike in the splendor of Villa Borghese, the lovely park situated not far from the Spanish Steps, I went back to my room and placed myself in solitary confinement for the next five hours. Writing. Revising. Pretty much not moving.

After my intense work session, I decided to take my usual walk over to Piazza Navona, my favorite square in the world. This is my usual ritual in the Eternal City, after I write. I head out onto the ancient cobblestone streets to ground my energy after being up in the ether for so many hours, get some Roman sunshine and clear my head and heart with a fabulous walk.

As I neared the Pantheon and moved past the dense crowds in front of this fabled structure that the Roman Empire used as a palace of justice, I saw a lone man in dark sunglasses, standing off to the side. He was dressed casually and appeared to be very low-key. He was studying the building, taking in its splendor.

It was Harvey Keitel.

This time I behaved very differently. I acted precisely and swiftly, before my ego could slow me down. I walked straight to him, put my hand out and said, "Mr. Keitel, I'm a huge fan. It's great to meet you!"

He smiled. Placed the fullness of his presence onto me. Couldn't have been more friendly. "Thank you," he replied.

Emboldened, I continued.

"I loved you in *Reservoir Dogs*. Loved Tarantino's originality! Loved the fantastic dialogue. What a script! What a movie! Loved the names you all had for the heist. You were Mr. Pink! So good," I gushed.

He stared at me. For an eternity. "Mr. White," he muttered.

As I carefully extracted my foot from my mouth, I asked the legend if I could have a photo with him.

"Sure."

And here it is:

With film luminary Harvey Keitel at the Pantheon in Rome

"Well, I should be going," he said politely.

And off he went. Into the great crowd. Right by those soaring columns of the architectural jewel, into the hot sun of a perfect afternoon.

My prayer *for you*? Easy.

When a window of opportunity shows up, open the frame even more and jump right in, as quickly as you can, before the villains of your genius and the enemies of your greatness start telling you why you can't.

Reason destroys what could have been many life-changing experiences. Trust your heart. It really is so much wiser than your head.

But, if in your humanness you don't, breathe a deep breath and keep moving forward, a little clearer and more resolute on how you will show up with more daring next time. And a next time will come.

Because we all do get second chances. Like me and Harvey Keitel.

100.

Be Not a Dream Postponer

I was once stuck in traffic with a very old man in a convertible directly in front of me.

He was grinning. He had music playing. He seemed like he was *loving* life.

"TimeForFun" read his license plate.

Hmmm.

Too many wait until they are too old to do the things they've always longed to do.

... They take cruises when they can hardly walk.

... They set off on adventures that exhaust them quickly.

... They buy the things they've always wanted, yet can hardly enjoy them.

I'm in no way disrespecting older people. I respect all elders immensely.

And I absolutely agree that it's never too late to start anew. And be the resolute, powerful and inspirational everyday hero you were born to become.

I'm just making this point: *Don't put off your heart's most precious dreams*. Know that it's smarter to look foolish in the moment by doing what you know you need to do to have the life you seek rather than dishonor your urge by doing nothing. And ending up heartbroken on your last mile.

Who knows what tomorrow brings? Don't assume the future will be a place where everything you've put off because you're really busy right now can happen easily, effortlessly and excellently. Please.

Illness, accidents, wars, recessions, plagues, environmental disasters and attacks happen. More often than we are willing to admit.

Do you really want to postpone what you most want to do until a time when it may be too late to do it?

Life's meant to be lived right now. The future's just a sprinkling of fantasy. Isn't it? Let's not rely on it too much.

101.

A Philosophy for Returning to Human

Okay. Last chapter. And so I pray that you will …

… Go out into this beautiful and sometimes cruel world with a heart full of heroism and eyes set to embrace the glory of your fullest powers.

Yes, some seasons will bring misfortune and some times will be difficult.

Yet there is much good in daily life. Neighbors who appreciate you, friends who enliven you and family that adores you.

When it comes to those who wish less than your lofty visions for you, know they know not what they do. Send them the good wishes that reflect your patience. And the kind understanding that displays your sincere forgiveness. It is a grand act of honor and strength to keep pleasant feelings toward all others within you.

Work richly and with dignity, giving more than you receive, and produce the magic that salutes your maker. And respects your exceptionalism.

Keep your life simple, as an addiction to acquisition and deep craving for more can stifle your spirit and hurt your good heart.

Give more than you take. Be more helpful than is necessary. And treat each person you meet with dignity. This is a route to sustained spiritual liberty and enduring outer success.

Enjoy the company of wise people, the companionship of inspiring books and a healthy relationship with your sovereign self.

When the crowd seeks to make you like them, stay true to your path—leading by your virtues and the values that feel most real to you.

Remain bold, knowing that the meek and timid do not know the soaring flights that come by leaning into your fears. To postpone the life of your ideals is to invite resentment into your days.

Remember that terror is closer to triumph than complacency is. And that fear becomes faith when you walk into it.

Enjoy the rewards of your labor and the dividends of your masterwork.

Love compassionately, respecting all around you and the Earth that nourishes you.

Do all this to unite with the highness within you to fully materialize the everyday hero that you are.

What's Next on
Your Heroic Adventure?

The end of this book is the beginning of your own journey into everyday heroism. To help you integrate and then sustain the philosophy and methodology you've just learned, Robin Sharma has created the following growth tools for you, all being made available absolutely free:

The Everyday Hero Masterclass
An innovative digital transformation program that will cause you to multiply your positivity and productivity, accelerate your happiness and magnify your impact, while you lead your field.

The Everyday Hero Challenge
You'll receive a stream of content-rich and enormously practical coaching videos, mentoring modules and world-class inspiration from Robin Sharma so you stay with your commitment to operating at the peak of your abilities. And maximize your victories as someone who displays ever-increasing genius while exemplifying the elements of daily human greatness.

The Everyday Hero Mastery Meditations

To help you experience deep focus, upgraded creativity, advanced performance and profound peacefulness all day, Robin Sharma has carefully created and meticulously calibrated a series of unique guided morning meditations that will cause you to rise to your finest, as a leader, producer and person. You will love them.

The Everyday Hero Manifesto Lost Chapters

Get full access to the chapters Robin Sharma kept out of this book. Discover highly original insights, learning models and systems to realize your talents, increase your artistry, grow a world-class company and lead a marvelous personal life.

To get full access to all of these valuable resources being made available to you at zero cost, go to:

TheEverydayHeroManifesto.com

The author loves connecting with his readers on Instagram. Subscribe to his feed @robinsharma and be sure to tag him with a photo of you holding this book. He'll post the most interesting ones.

Fuel Your Rise by Reading All of Robin Sharma's Worldwide Bestsellers

Whether you're at your mountaintop of world-class or just starting your climb, reading is one of the master habits of The Great Ones.

So here's a complete list of the author's internationally acclaimed books to support your ascent into exponential productivity, total craft mastery and living beautifully—while you make your mark on history.

[ ] *The 5AM Club*
[ ] *The Monk Who Sold His Ferrari*
[ ] *The Greatness Guide*
[ ] *The Greatness Guide Book 2*
[ ] *The Leader Who Had No Title*
[ ] *Who Will Cry When You Die?*
[ ] *Leadership Wisdom from The Monk Who Sold His Ferrari*
[ ] *Family Wisdom from The Monk Who Sold His Ferrari*
[ ] *Discover Your Destiny with The Monk Who Sold His Ferrari*
[ ] *The Secret Letters of The Monk Who Sold His Ferrari*
[ ] *The Mastery Manual*
[ ] *The Little Black Book for Stunning Success*
[ ] *The Saint, the Surfer, and the CEO*

My 25 Books to Read Before You Die List

"If we encounter a person of rare intellect, we should ask what books they read." —RALPH WALDO EMERSON

Anthem, Ayn Rand

As You Think, James Allen

Bring Out the Magic in Your Mind, Al Koran

Fahrenheit 451, Ray Bradbury

Hope for the Flowers, Trina Paulus

How to Win Friends and Influence People, Dale Carnegie

Jonathan Livingston Seagull, Richard Bach

Long Walk to Freedom, Nelson Mandela

Man's Search for Meaning, Viktor E. Frankl

Mandela's Way, Richard Stengel

Meditations, Marcus Aurelius

My Experiments with Truth, Mahatma Gandhi

Steve Jobs, Walter Isaacson

The Alchemist, Paulo Coelho

The Autobiography of Benjamin Franklin

The Catcher in the Rye, J. D. Salinger

The Diving Bell and the Butterfly, Jean-Dominique Bauby

The Giving Tree, Shel Silverstein
The Go-Getter, Peter B. Kyne
The Gospel of Wealth, Andrew Carnegie
The Little Prince, Antoine de Saint-Exupéry
The Power of Positive Thinking, Norman Vincent Peale
The Prophet, Kahlil Gibran
The Seven Spiritual Laws of Success, Deepak Chopra
Think and Grow Rich, Napoleon Hill

My 25 Favorite Films

Here's a list of my favorite films. Some have shaped my philosophy. Some have influenced my creativity. And a number of them have simply entertained me. Enjoy them all.

At Eternity's Gate	*Joker*	*The King's Speech*
Burnt	*Life Is Beautiful*	*The Lunchbox*
Darkest Hour	*Maudie*	*The Matrix*
Dogman	*Midnight Express*	*The Wrestler*
Fight Club	*Million Dollar Baby*	*Thunder Road*
Harry Brown	*Queen & Slim*	*Wall Street*
Heat	*The Florida Project*	*Whiplash*
Hell or High Water	*The Gladiator*	
Into the Wild	*The Hurt Locker*	

My 25 Favorite Documentaries

I adore documentaries. They fuel my inspiration, offer life wisdom and provide private glimpses into the lives of fascinating people. Below is a list of twenty-five superb ones.

Amy: The Girl Behind the Name
Crossfire Hurricane
Good Fortune
Hal
I'll Sleep When I'm Dead
Iverson
Jason Becker: Not Dead Yet
Jiro Dreams of Sushi
Man on Wire
McConkey
McQueen
Metallica: Some Kind of Monster
Miles Davis: Birth of the Cool
Mr. Dynamite: The Rise of James Brown
Pavarotti
Quincy
Runnin' Down a Dream: Tom Petty and the Heartbreakers

Searching for Sugar Man
Senna
Sunshine Superman
The Last Dance
The September Issue: Anna Wintour & the Making of Vogue
Williams
Wingman
Won't You Be My Neighbor?

ABOUT THE AUTHOR

Robin Sharma is a globally respected humanitarian and the founder of a not-for-profit venture the helps children in need lead better lives. He has a particularly strong focus in ensuring kids suffering from leprosy rise.

Widely considered one of the world's top leadership experts as well as an icon in the field of personal mastery, this pathblazer's clients include many Fortune 100 companies, famed billionaires, professional sports superstars, music luminaries and members of royalty.

Organizations that have engaged Robin Sharma as a keynote speaker to help them build employees who lead without a title, produce exceptional work and master change in these complex times include Microsoft, Nike, Unilever, GE, FedEx, HP, Starbucks, Oracle, Yale University, PwC, IBM Watson and the Young Presidents' Organization.

To inquire about his availability for your next conference, visit robinsharma.com/speaking

The author's #1 bestsellers, such as *The 5 AM Club*, *The Monk Who Sold His Ferrari*, *The Greatness Guide* and *The Leader Who Had No Title*, have sold millions of copies in more than 92 languages and dialects, making him one of the most influential writers alive today.